ONE  MAN GRAND BAND

THE LYRICAL LIFE OF

RON HYNES

HARVEY SAWLER

BREAKWATER

P.O. Box 2188, St. John's, NL, Canada, A1C 6E6
WWW.BREAKWATERBOOKS.COM

LIBRARY AND ARCHIVES CANADA CATALOGUING IN PUBLICATION

Sawler, Harvey, 1954-, author
One man grand band : the lyrical life of Ron Hynes / Harvey Sawler.
ISBN 978-1-55081-631-0 (paperback)
1. Hynes, Ron. 2. Composers--Canada--Biography.
3. Singers--Canada--Biography. I. Title.
ML410.H997S27 2016   782.42164092   C2016-900763-4

We acknowledge the support of the Canada Council for the Arts, which last year invested $153 million to bring the arts to Canadians throughout the country. We acknowledge the financial support of the Government of Canada and the Government of Newfoundland and Labrador through the Department of Tourism, Culture and Recreation for our publishing activities.
PRINTED AND BOUND IN CANADA.

Canada Council
for the Arts

Conseil des Arts
du Canada

Canadä

Newfoundland
Labrador

Breakwater Books is committed to choosing papers and materials for our books that help to protect our environment. To this end, this book is printed on a recycled paper that is certified by the Forest Stewardship Council®.

FOR CHARLOTTE STEWART

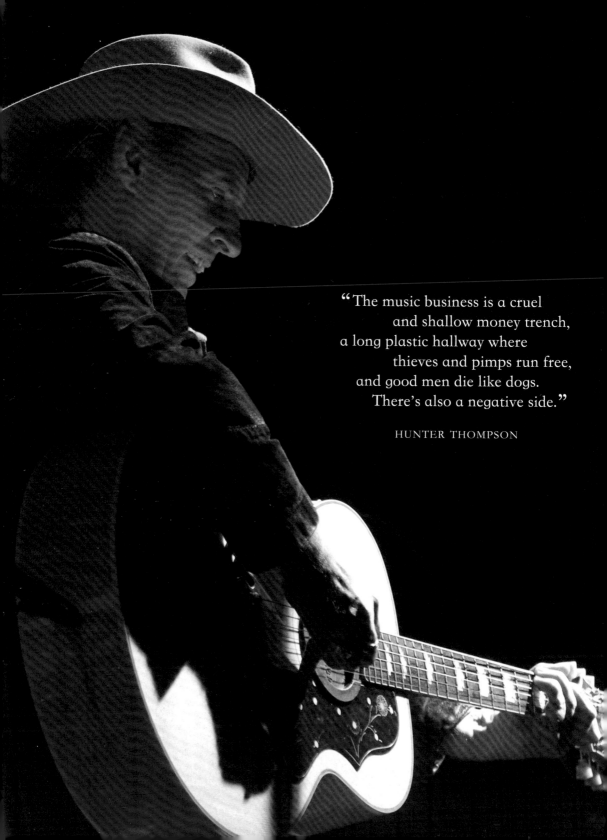

"The music business is a cruel
and shallow money trench,
a long plastic hallway where
thieves and pimps run free,
and good men die like dogs.
There's also a negative side."

HUNTER THOMPSON

CONTENTS

"It is those we live with and should know who elude us, but we can still love them. We can love completely without complete understanding."

NORMAN MCLEAN
(the signature line at the end of Ron's e-mails throughout 2015)

IF THERE IS ANYTHING I LEARNED through my time with Ron Hynes, it was this: expect the unexpected.

Like the odd fact that he was a student at the Arthur Murray School of Dance in Victoria, British Columbia, when he was twenty-three and, according to Ron, that actor and fellow Newfoundlander Gordon Pinsent did the very same thing, but in Montreal. Or that he absolutely loved shopping for hats and boots and scarves and jackets. Or that his girlfriend was a doctor in far flung Toronto. Or that he loved old westerns. Or that he wore salon-applied acrylic fingernails in order to play guitar. Or that he relished the idea, like American country legend Hank Williams, of having an alter ego. Or that he handed around his prized instruments with great regularity and then usually regretted doing so. Or that during his worst infestations involving crack cocaine, he could seem like Jack Nicholson's horrifying character, Jack Torrance, in *The Shining*. Or that, like great photographers who see images the rest of us don't see, Ron could find the value and romance and tragedy and beauty of stories where most of us might see no story whatsoever—stories which he translated into lyrics and melody.

Or how about the crazy fact that on the verge of dying, on November 12, 2015, he asked me to join him on LinkedIn. Six days later, on November 19, he died at around 6 p.m.

With so many dimensions, it was easy in the beginning to become hooked on the narcotic of Ron Hynes. Then at other moments, it became just as easy to consider abandoning this biography project altogether. Until his closing months in 2015, as he became more and more responsive to my questions and absorbed in the fact the biography was happening, I never really knew whether Ron might simply walk away from the project himself.

In his final days, his sense of humour remained intact. On November 6, he e-mailed to see how the book was coming along.

> Winter slowly creeping in here. Any news from your way re a first
> draft of a finish of the Ron saga? Wouldn't have your life for love or
> money putting word to paper concerning a ragged assed contender
> like me.

Although I knew through the grapevine what state he was in, that he was basically on his last legs, I laughed out loud when I read the note. And more so when he wrote later that day to say his next album would be titled *The Ragged Ass Contender*.

Earlier, on November 4, after Ron had gone public through Newfoundland mainstream and all forms of social media about his cancer having reappeared, he wrote to me in the middle of the night.

INTRODUCTION

> The Facebook post I wrote yesterday afternoon now has a
> response close to 500 and counting. It's close to three a.m. and
> I'm wide awake with gut wrenching pain. For someone
> who's attempting to alleviate the anxiety of his audience, this
> isn't the way I should be feeling.

After a long and winding road, involved as I was on the fringe of his life, I suddenly felt very close to him.

The initial idea to write Ron's biography sprang from a discussion with his agent and manager, Charles MacPhail, a central Canadian having absolutely no real connection to Newfoundland other than his coincidental relationship with Ron. Commissioned in 2013 to write a fiftieth anniversary book for the Confederation Centre of the Arts in Charlottetown, Prince Edward Island, I met MacPhail during a phone call while seeking Ron's inclusion in a section of that book which was themed to focus on fifty remarkable or well-known Canadians who'd had a connection to the Centre. Ron, of course, was one of these individuals and he does appear in that book alongside forty-nine other artists: singers, dancers, comedians, actors, authors, and visual artists.

MacPhail, a bearded, balding, gray-haired guy who loved Ron, cursed and complained incessantly about trying to manage Ron's music career and his personal life and finances. He grumbled and groaned to me more than just a few times that he really didn't need the endless complications associated with Ron Hynes in his life. He'd rather just maneuver his ride-on lawn mower and grow hostas in his Perth, Ontario, backyard. But MacPhail's problem was he loved Ron Hynes. He really had no choice. He could not abstain from Ron Hynes. As it became for me, Ron was MacPhail's DOC or drug of choice. And we both knew there was no twelve-step program for our uncontrollable compulsion.

Ron was a remarkable Canadian for all kinds of reasons—some personal, but most having to do with his very public success in the music business; some highly appealing and some not so appealing. He was, after all, a six-time East Coast Music Award winner, a Genie Award winner, and a past JUNO, Canadian County Music Association, and Canadian Folk Music Awards nominee. He was recipient of the 2008 SOCAN National Achievement Award for songwriting career success, and holds an honorary PhD from Memorial University for his contributions to the cultural life of his beloved Newfoundland and Labrador. He has also been a recipient of both Artist of The Year and the prestigious Arts Achievement Award from the Newfoundland & Labrador Arts Council, as well as a Lifetime Achievement Award from the St. John's Folk Arts Council. From 1974 to 1976, Ron was the in-house composer for the Mummers Troupe—it was while touring with the Mummers in 1976 that he imagined and composed his signature song, "Sonny's Dream," an inspiration from God, he felt, that happened in just ten minutes with a pencil and scribbler in hand on a highway in Saskatchewan. He'd spent an interminable amount of hours worried that he'd heard the tune someplace before, the way Paul McCartney is said to have agonized over whether the song "Yesterday" had come from some place other than his own ingenious mind.

Ron also composed music and lyrics for *East End Story*, *Dying Hard*, *The IWA Show*, and *The Price of Fish*. His songs have been recorded by artists world-wide, including Emmylou Harris, Mary Black, Christy Moore, Denny Doherty, Murray McLauchlan, John McDermott, Prairie Oyster, The Cottars, Hayley Westenra, and many more. He was, irrefutably, a remarkable Canadian.

One discussion led to another with MacPhail and it suddenly occurred to me (and MacPhail confirmed) that no one had taken a serious cut at writing Ron's biography. There'd been a feature-length documentary film with Ron as the subject, Bill MacGillivray's *The Man of a Thousand Songs*, but oddly, no book. A couple of writers had apparently begun discussions at different intervals, but nothing concrete ever materialized.

MacPhail was keen, so I pursued and landed a publisher and we then set about to convince Ron that his biography would be a good thing. He didn't know me from Adam, a writer from another Atlantic island, Prince Edward Island. Admittedly, it was a long, slow crawl before I felt confident that I could count on him to cooperate in seeing the book through. The perilous thing about biographies—and I've worked on several—is that an authorized work normally demands the complete cooperation of the subject. There is also always the risk of pouring a ton of work into a biography only to have the subject change his or her mind and go south on the idea. Writing Ron's biography was extremely shaky and off-putting at the outset, nerve-wracking at the mid-point, and finally, highly collaborative and gratifying in the final going.

I'd seen Ron perform at the Zion Presbyterian Church in Charlottetown, PEI, on January 16, 2012, in a CBC television-produced tribute to the late PEI singer-songwriter Gene MacLellan, as part of the province's annual Music Week. I had no idea at the time that two years later I'd be engulfed in his biography. He was one in a string of performers booked for a CBC made-for-television tribute to MacLellan. Called *Just Biding My Time* (the title of one of MacLellan's best-loved tunes), it was aired on radio for CBC's *Atlantic Airwaves* show and broadcast in June of that year on the full CBC television network. The cast featured PEI's Lennie Gallant and MacLellan's daughter, Catherine (a songwriter and performer in her own right).

Hynes revered MacLellan and had written the beautiful and stirring "Godspeed" in his honour, so it was a no-brainer for the show's producers to have him on the bill. It was a lovely but, for two of the performers, torturous event, thanks to a succession of technical glitches. Ron and Lennie Gallant were forced to repeat their performances three times over before the show's producers were sure they'd captured what they needed. Remarkably, Ron reached deep down and found the same level of emotion in take three as he'd offered up in the original. When the show aired six months later, the television audience would never know the difference.

Doing so took grace, patience, and professionalism. These moments shaped my first impressions of Ron. He not only managed to pull off the songs with genuineness, but in doing so, he made the audience grow increasingly sympathetic. Rolling his eyes in typical Ron fashion and expressing his disbelief at the producers, "You've got to be kidding," he pulled the audience closer to him.

I didn't realize it at the time, but the rolling of the eyes and his exasperation were part of the minute-to-minute theatre of Ron Hynes, the skill which his nephew Joel Hynes talks about when he says, "It's as if the camera is always on…and it doesn't matter if there is a camera around or not. There is always an element of the performance barrier up. You never know which side of him you're gonna talk to."

Nothing, it seems, could be more true.

My next exposure to Ron was in 2014 at the Trailside Café in Mount Stewart, PEI. The first thing he said from the stage was, "Hi Mac," in recognition of the CBC broadcaster and East Coast Music Awards enthusiast Mac Campbell, who was seated at the edge of the stage with his wife, Edwina, and another couple. After acknowledging Campbell, he turned to the audience and subtly joked, feigning conceit, "I know people." Before the year was out, Ron would make a highly personal pilgrimage to Campbell's PEI home to perform a private concert just days before Campbell's death from cancer at age sixty-nine. Before another year was out, Ron too was gone.

Ron and I spoke that night at the Trailside as I introduced myself at a distance of five or six feet between his first and second sets. I was suffering from a terrific cold and he was just coming off one. On explaining why I could not shake his hand, he waved me off with a look of horror on his face, not wanting a relapse of the bug which had aggravated his healing process from throat cancer, diagnosed and treated in 2012, and which had pretty well ruined his ability to perform all that Spring.

I was introducing myself and still in the pitch stage regarding his biography. Funnily, at the outset, I didn't know whether to call him Ron or Mr. Hynes or Hynes. One is too familiar, another too formal, and the other too distant. A small part of me wanted to immediately get on his good side, vaunting him up by addressing him as Dr. Hynes, because he is one, thanks to his honourary doctorate from Memorial University of Newfoundland.

Even though Charles MacPhail was keener than hell, Ron seemed very much on the fence about it all. Over the coming weeks and months, I was never sure whether the biography was truly authorized or not. It would take months for me to feel the assurance that Ron was really on board. In hindsight, I slowly learned that this confusion over Ron's being on board or not was directly linked to his substance abuse. It took getting to know the real Ron Hynes before I could comfortably develop the narrative and believe the book would come to be. That is, if anyone can really get to know the real Ron Hynes. He is easily the most complex person I have ever written about.

Readers may recognize that this book was re-written following Ron's death; therefore, the verb tense has been changed to the past—a particularly arduous and heart-breaking process. However, in being true to the voices of the people I interviewed, their words remain in the present tense and in the context of when Ron was alive.

> " He's ours
> and we've got to take
> care of him. "
>
> RIK BARRON
> (Newfoundland singer, musician, and raconteur)

PART I

THE INNOCENCE

CHARLIE FREEBURN'S MEADOW

RON HYNES WAS BROUGHT UP IN the Roman Catholic school system in Ferryland, Newfoundland, where he was taught by convent nuns who lectured all the little children that a priest was greater than an angel because he represented God on earth and that it was a mortal sin to pass a church and not make a visit. In the world of Roman Catholicism, circa early-1960s, that was just the tip of the iceberg. There were also teachings about venial sin, mortal sin, the darkening of your soul, and the ultimate turpitude: because Ron and his classmates were all descendants of Adam and Eve, they shared a blight known as Original Sin, which only the sacrament of Baptism can erase.

Ferryland is a town on the south end of Newfoundland's Avalon Peninsula, a place originally established as a station for migratory fishermen in the late sixteenth century but which had earlier been used by the French, Spanish, and Portuguese. By the 1590s, it was one of the most popular fishing harbours in Newfoundland, a place noted, for example, by Sir Walter Raleigh. The town looks over the rough and raw Atlantic, noted for its long, high cape of rock and grass, for its lighthouse and lighthouse picnics and as the town's website oddly proclaims, as "The birthplace of religious tolerance and freedom of worship in the New World." (It was the first place in British North America where an English-speaking Roman Catholic priest said mass.)

When you say "Ferryland" to most people, they think you're saying "Fairyland," like it's a place Disney built. The name is actually the blended Anglicization of *Farilham*, derived from the Portuguese fishermen, and *Forillon* by the French. The lands where Ferryland is today were granted by charter to the London and Bristol Company in the 1610s, and the vicinity became one of a number of short-lived English colonies. In 1620 the territory was granted to George Calvert, 1st Baron Baltimore (Lord Baltimore) whose namesake is Baltimore, Maryland. Lord Baltimore oversaw the establishment of the colony at Ferryland, which today remains a strong point of curiosity for archeologists. But there came a point at which Lord Baltimore simply found the weather exceedingly harsh and decided to move his family to the significantly fairer climate of Maryland. His parting words reportedly were, "I commit this place to the fishermen that are better able to encounter storms and hard weather." Virtually forgotten for centuries, excavations of the original settlement began in the mid-twentieth century and were renewed in earnest, under the auspices of Memorial University, in the late 1980s, and continue to this day.

It is against this significant historical and noteworthy religious backdrop, all of it emphatically punctuated by the powerful presence of the sea, that Ron Hynes grew up and returned to in his final years.

One day, nine-year-old Ron was on his way home from school for lunch, passing Holy Trinity Church as he did every day. Something made him remember the teaching that a good Catholic should never pass by a church without paying a visit to God. Failure to do so was considered a sin, probably venial in nature, but still, a sin nevertheless. Whether venial or mortal in nature, Ron had been taught that any sin is certain to blacken one's soul like something charred on a barbecue.

Once inside, Ron approached the altar, then turned his attention to the cascading bank of unlit vigil candles where parishioners would light, kneel, and pray before a statue of either Jesus or the Virgin Mary. The practice of lighting candles in order to obtain some favour probably originated in the custom of burning lights at the tombs of the martyrs in the catacombs. Ron decided to light a candle with one of the wooden stick matches that were always provided there. Lighting just one candle did not feel to be a sufficient degree of adoration to Ron, so he proceeded to light the works, bathing the interior of the church in candlelight. He lingered for a bit, but suddenly remembered that lunch awaited him at home. Before leaving, he snatched a handful of the wooden matchsticks.

As Ron left the glowing church, he decided to take the "above the road" route, as it was known in Ferryland, all the while playing with the matches.

"I'm playing that game where you balance the match on the brimstone with your index finger and snap it through the air, creating a flying-match-on-fire effect," Ron recalled. "As I climbed the fence of Charlie Freeburn's meadow, I snap a match which hurls its fiery way toward the tall, dry grass. The match lands and ignites the grass and sparks are jumping and starting tiny fires everywhere. I try to stamp them out, but they keep sparking and finally there are too many and I'm burning holes in my running shoes."

So Ron panicked, jumped the fence and ran for home.

"On a tiny hill above our house, I turn like Lot's wife and the entire harbour is obliterated with black smoke."

Ron arrived home, acting as though nothing had happened, and sat and picked at his lunch in silence. On the way back to school, he encountered Charlie Freeburn furiously trying to rake out the flames. The entire field had burned to black, smoke rising everywhere.

"It's a wonder his house survived but it had a rock and concrete foundation so there were no problems there, thank God. I decided I'd better throw him off the scent, so I approach the fence and say, 'Hey Mr. Charlie, what are ya doin', burnin' your grass are ya?'"

"You did this Hynes," said Mr. Freeburn. "I saw you jump the fence and run."

"Go away, b'y," said little Ronnie. "You're crazy."

Knowing Charlie Freeburn was on to what he'd done, Ron tore off lickety-split and headed straight back to school.

"I'm sitting in the last row writing note after note along the lines of 'Dear Mr. Charlie, I knows you t'inks I burned down your meadow, but I didn't.' But it was hopeless. I was in hell."

Walking home from school later that afternoon, he ran into young Calvin Johnson, who said, "Did you hear someone burned poor Mr. Charlie's meadow. He sells that grass every year to make some money. What a cunt to do that."

"Yeah, what a cunt," Ron replied.

The plot was thickening.

The next day was a Saturday.

"Mom gives me five cents, so off I go to the store just up the road from the house and buy five Bazooka bubble gums. I know if I go home with them she'll make me give one to each of my brothers and my sister, so I stuff all five in my mouth.

"I'm leaving the store with a mouth filled with Bazooka bubble gum and there's the RCMP cruiser waiting outside. The cop gestures with his finger and I climb in the car and start to cry."

"Where do you live?" Constable Frazer asks Ron.

"'Right there,' I say, crying with a mouth full of gum. He drives the few feet down the road and as we exit the cruiser, Calvin Johnson and a few other kids go by. They know. The whole town knows for Christ's sake."

"Well Mrs. Hynes," says the constable, "do you know what your son's gone and done?"

As Constable Frazer relates the entire crime to Ron's mother, he asks, "What should we do, Mrs. Hynes? Perhaps a few days in jail on bread and water would do the trick."

"My mother agrees of course. She just wants to get him out of the house and deal with it herself."

Constable Frazer decides to leave matters in Mrs. Hynes' hands and takes his leave.

A short spell went by.

"I'm sitting on the daybed in the kitchen, I've stopped crying, and I'm enjoying my Bazooka bubble gum."

Mrs. Hynes busies herself, doing the dishes and sweeping the floor. The longer she labours, the more Ron convinces himself he's out of the woods, that he's in the clear. Never formally charged but acquitted nevertheless. He's a free man. No jail cell with bread and water for him.

"But as she passes me on the daybed," he recalls with perfect clarity, "she slaps me so hard across the face that it hurts to this very day."

Ron was completely ostracized from the entire community for about a year. When his father came home from being at sea, he paid a visit to Mr. Freeburn and compensated him for his losses.

"I remember attending his funeral when he passed," said Ron, "and thanking God that he hadn't burned to death in his house."

FERRYLAND

AS IN DOZENS OF OTHER NEWFOUNDLAND and Labrador communities, the lighthouse at Ferryland, about an hour south of the capital city of St. John's, is a dominant icon. Brighter than the vigil candles at Trinity Catholic Church, the lighthouse at Ferryland Head has long stood as a beacon to passing ships, a stark warning of the dangerous jagged shores, yet a comforting reminder to sailors that they were not alone in the pitch-black night. The lighthouse is still operational; however, it has been automated since 1970. For the 100 years previous, the lighthouse was staffed by families who lived in the two-family dwelling. Today it's famous for its popular Lighthouse Picnics, the brainchild of two women who've turned the place into a destination and part of the Canadian Tourism Commission's Signature Experience Collection.

The first light-keeper was the famous Newfoundland ship builder Michael Kearney, and the first assistant keeper was William Costello. Over the next 100 years, the Costello family would be the primary keepers of the light at Ferryland Head right up until 1970, when Billy and Kathleen Costello were the last family of lighthouse keepers. Newfoundland's renowned artist, the late Gerald Squires, and his family lived in the lighthouse dwelling during the 1970s, and it is here that Squires completed some of his finest work, including what is referred to as *The Ferryland Downs* series. Squires was Ron's favourite artist.

Squires died just a few weeks before Ron, on October 3, 2015, and was best known as a landscape painter, though he also worked as a sculptor, a print maker, and a newspaper artist. Born in Change Islands, Squires moved to Toronto in 1949, where he lived (mostly) until he returned to Newfoundland. He was made a member of the Order of Canada in 1999 and shared with Ron the honour of a doctorate from Memorial University. They also shared the small but important connection that Squires painted an image of the Ferryland lighthouse on the resonator of a banjo Ron had at one time.

"It's one of a number of instruments that escaped my hands over the years," said Ron. "I'd love to have it back and will someday, God willing."

ONE MAN GRAND BAND

Ferryland was at the core of Ron's life, whether as an unwitting nine-year-old pyro-maniac, or during his final years as one of Canada's most prolific and admired songwriters. This is the place of his true roots, even though of the thirty-two people listed as settled at Ferryland in 1622, there wasn't a Hynes amongst them.

More than a million artifacts have been unearthed as the result of archeological digs at Ferryland over the years, carried out in phases since the 1930s by a Dr. Brooks, an entomologist from the Carnegie Institute in Pittsburgh. He concluded that Avalon was at the western end of a tombolo beach that connects the mainland with the Ferryland Downs and that this was the Colony of Avalon established by George Calvert (1579-1632) the first Lord (or Baron) Baltimore, a man who took an interest in the British colonization of the Americas, at first for commercial reasons and later to create a refuge for English Catholics. He became the proprietor of Avalon, the first sustained English settlement on the south-eastern peninsula of Newfoundland. But with the winter temperatures, prevailing winds, and constant struggles of settlers, Sir George looked south to warmer climes and pursued a new royal charter to settle the region we now know as the state of Maryland.

The digs renewed in the late 1950s when a man named Russell Harper carried out test excavations on land adjacent to the south shore of The Pool, as the sheltered inner harbour has been known since at least the 17th century. Harper recovered ceramics, iron nails, bottle glass, and other artifacts. You can still see the archeological dig in progress today, halted seasonally of course as the winters can be brutal here. And you can visit the large, modern interpretive centre to view a mere fractional sampling of the countless artifacts unearthed, cleaned, catalogued, and stored away over the decades.

But the most famous artifact linked to Ferryland is Ron Hynes himself. Most of what usually comes out of the ground is splintered, scarred, or cracked, not unlike Ron in his final years, a mere shard of his previous sparkling self as entertainer, physical penance to his serious substance abuse. Apart from Lord Baltimore, Ron is the most famous favourite son of Ferryland, the once-youthful composer and performer, comedic straight man, and one of the few performers around who has a slogan synonymous with his name in the manner of Frank Sinatra or James Brown (The Chairman of the Board and Godfather of Soul, respectively). Ron is widely referred to and known as The Man of a Thousand Songs.

The story behind that moniker has been told by Ron on stage and off a thousand times. One version is that when his agent at the time was trying to book him in Ireland, and the agent was asked questions like, "How many songs does he know?" or "What kind of songs does he play?" or "Does he want a set list?" Ron said, "Just tell them he knows a thousand songs." In true Ron fashion, the next time he tells this story, it had nothing to do with Ireland whatsoever. In that version, his agent had been speaking to a guy booking Ron for the Holiday Inn in Dartmouth, Nova Scotia.

Except when touring or in Toronto visiting his girlfriend, Dr. Susan Brunt (sister of Canadian celebrity sports writer and broadcaster Stephen Brunt), or in his final days staying with a friend in St. John's, Ron returned to the family home, a three-storey building vaulted up over the winding secondary highway also known as The Irish Loop, which links St. John's to the southern tip of the Avalon Peninsula at Trepassey. Before his father died, Ron and his siblings were asked about their interests in it once their mother would be gone. Ron was the only one who responded, so he inherited the one thing in his life that resembled normalcy: the family home. Everything else in his life was momentary and transient.

RONALD 'ST. JOSEPH' HYNES

Dateline Annapolis, Maryland, September 19, 1967–Governor Spiro T. Agnew today issued a proclamation declaring September 20, 1967 as 'Maryland-Ferryland Day' in a reciprocal gesture to the government and the people of Canada and to the citizens of Ferryland, Newfoundland.

The proclamation called upon all citizens of Maryland "to observe this day, with the citizens of Canada, by honoring George Calvert, the first Lord Baltimore, whose courage, wisdom and foresightedness are manifest in his performance as a principal settler of Newfoundland and as and as the founder of the State of Maryland."

IN RECIPROCAL RESPONSE TO GOVERNOR AGNEW'S proclamation, the people of Canada and Ferryland, in turn, paid homage to Lord Baltimore.

Back home in Ferryland, a dais was set and an event held with several hundred people present, presided over by Newfoundland's founding Premier Joey Smallwood, the local federal Member of Parliament Richard Cashin, a host of other dignitaries, and seventeen-year-old Ron Hynes. The school hosting the event was named St. Joseph's Central High. When Ron had been in grade school at Ferryland's Holy Trinity Church, the parish priest, Father John Cotter, came to announce that construction was to begin on a new high school and he that he was soliciting students for a name for the school.

"I suggested St. Joseph's because he was my patron saint and my baptismal name," says Ron. "Who knew?" Ron mused.

Schools were closed for the day from Ferryland all the way to Trepassey; instead of being in their classrooms, students were bussed in for the ceremony. A dance and celebration held that night in the community rounded out the commemoration.

When he originally told me the story, Ron's memory convinced him that Agnew had actually been in attendance in Ferryland that day. But the record from the Maryland state archives showed differently. While Agnew agreed to have the proclamation released, and he actually did read it aloud in Baltimore, it was Cashin who read the reciprocal version from the dais in Ferryland. But not before being introduced by the upstanding seventeen-year-old local student who, when he was finished, was congratulated at the mic by either Smallwood or Cashin for his effort (Ron couldn't recall which). Whichever of the two politicians it was, he playfully remarked that young Ron would no doubt have a good future in politics, in deference to the succinct and orderly manner in which he had delivered his introductions. In literal terms, the politician's playful comment could not have been more far off. But in other terms—in cultural-political terms—young Ron Hynes would go on to establish a name, create a persona, and make a statement on behalf of Newfoundland that would outweigh the value and impact of anyone else on the dais that day with the exception of Joey himself, the man who controversially brought New-foundland into the Canadian Confederation in 1949; Joey, the proverbial god of what's become known as The Rock.

Juxtapose that well-spoken student—the supposed politician in the making—against the life of the hard-living, troubadour musical phenomenon that Ron became.

MISTAKEN POINT

EVEN BY NEWFOUNDLAND STANDARDS, MISTAKEN POINT is a remarkably barren, rocky seaside landscape. Looking at the map of North America, the point hangs out there in the northwest Atlantic Ocean with its nearby Cape Race Light Station serving as a beacon to Europe and Africa. The station has been operating as a warning site to mariners since 1856. The most recent tower, erected in 1907, employs a giant hyper-radial Fresnel lens, one of the most powerful found anywhere in the world. Here is also where the Myrick Wireless Centre interprets the earliest wireless days of telegraphy in Newfoundland when Cape Race was one of the busiest Marconi stations in North America, including the fact that the distress call from the Titanic was first heard and answered here.

Mistaken Point is literally at the end of the road, on a truly continental scale, situated on the extreme margins of the Avalon Peninsula, hopelessly exposed to the whims and perils of the ocean and an extreme harshness of climate. Mistaken Point is said by some to be the fog and rain capital of Newfoundland, a province already well known for its fog and rain. Blanketed in fog for many months at a time, the fog horn at nearby Cape Race gets a continuous workout. For anyone who would care to reside here, there are copious amounts of time for reflection.

The site is two or more hours from St. John's and about an hour south of Ferryland; accessed through the community of Portugal Cove South (Portugal Cove North is far away at an area north of St. John's) and continuing along a rugged journey over a gravel road fraught with dips and boulders suitable only for a four-wheel-drive or a lunar rover.

If places had feelings or a conscience, Mistaken Point would surely feel sorrowful and ashamed. Because make no mistake, the point came by its shame honestly, taking its name from the deadly results of being mistaken for Cape Race in the area's perpetually foggy weather. Sailors who made this mistake were fooled into turning north, thinking they had reached Cape Race Harbour, but instead would immediately run into the point's treacherous rocks.

MISTAKEN POINT

Those same rocks are now into payback. Because the site is home to some of the oldest fossils on earth, scientists and bureaucrats in bow ties and studious glasses from the United Nations Education and Scientific Organization (UNESCO) in Paris are deliberating over whether or not Mistaken Point should be declared a World Heritage Site. Pre-Cambrian in age, the geology holds the oldest known fossils of complex organisms, some 560-575 million years old, from a time when life only existed in the sea. A team of experts visited the site in 2015 as part of the World Heritage Site evaluation process, with their decision expected in 2016.

I am on a Mistaken Point mission, seeking out a place named Long Beach, which I know is in the vicinity. Unwisely, I risk the underbelly of a rented Chev Impala by churning its wheels over a rocky road completely ill-suited to anything but a raised four-wheel drive. As I pass the Edge of Avalon Interpretive Centre en route to the Mistaken Point Ecological Reserve, it becomes clearer with every passing metre why there are warnings on the centre's door that it is off limits except by escorted guides and properly designed vehicles. Notwithstanding the perils of the road, local officials don't want people monkeying around with the volcanic-ash-embedded fossil finds and other environmentally sensitive things. While there, for the record, I never touched a thing.

Driven by my curiosity and throwing caution to the wind, I plowed through the rock beds and maneuvered around imposing boulders. Along the way, I encountered a succession of uniform signs (designed and posted by the Edge of Avalon organization) which identify the following intriguing, locally derived place names: Drook, Rookery, Freshwater, Bob's Cove, Bristol Cove, Mistaken Point itself, and ultimately, Long Beach. Along the way, there is something about their charcoal colour and the way they are etched into the land and seascape, which makes you appreciate that these really are, really old rocks.

A couple of kilometres on, there is a handful of tiny makeshift cabins by the side of this rarely traversed road, places used as modest summer retreats by locals. The foundations where there were a number of two-storey homes, are also in evidence. One of these belonged to the O'Neils.

Long Beach and the O'Neil home were the beginning of the road for Ron Hynes and his musicality, for this is where he met his uncle on his mother's side, Thomas O'Neil. Most people call him Sonny—Sonny in Irish vernacular what Junior or Jr. is elsewhere. So it goes without saying that Sonny's father's name was also Thomas.

Long Beach was an important place in Ron's life because it is where Thomas 'Sonny' O'Neil introduced him to both the guitar and the button accordion and the songs of such iconic, old-style country music stars as Ray Price, Johnny Cash, and Marty Robbins.

During his early teens, Ron would visit the O'Neils during the summer and hang out with Sonny, making for some of the most joyful and carefree moments of his life. That there were twelve years between the two, Sonny being the elder, didn't seem to matter. In this remote and isolated place, there was nothing for Ron to do but spend endless hours of his adolescence free to roam and play and absorb Sonny's love of music. The only distractions were the magnificence of the sea and the rocks.

There is innocence in the sense of Ron not knowing, spending these simple times with his uncle, that he was sowing the seeds for God's ultimate gift to him, the internationally loved song, "Sonny's Dream."

Sonny, the real McCoy, is like all of the others who once lived at Long Beach—long gone from that place of isolation, contemplation, and freedom. He lives today in a meticulously kept condo in a quiet semi-residential/semi-commercial area of St. John's. He's a serene, completely unassuming man in his late seventies, living alone amid older but well-maintained furnishings and knick-knacks. Apparently Sonny was never married, never had children, and had fairly ordinary jobs throughout his life. One career effort at being a signalman didn't work out because he has weak eyesight. Music is a part of Sonny's past and not his present.

Sonny hasn't got much to say about his *fame*, as it were, about the fact that his name has been sung about countless times around the world. And as characterized in the song, he no longer sits watching the sea from the stairs, town is no longer a hundred miles away, and his dream is far simpler than what Ron portrayed in "Sonny's Dream." More to the point, the dream was not Sonny O'Neil's dream at all. The dream was all Ron's. It was about his life. "Sonny's Dream" is, we discover, Ron's autobiography.

" He went to St. John's and
the musical world of Canada.
That was his dream. "

GREG MALONE
(Wonderful Grand Band alumnus)

PART II

THE MUSIC

DEL SHANNON

NOT TOO LONG AFTER BURNING DOWN Charlie Freeburn's meadow and parts of summers spent at Mistaken Point with his Uncle Sonny and family, Ron began to develop his own music sensibility beyond the stylings of Sonny's favourites—Ray Price, Johnny Cash, and Marty Robbins—and the few figures in Newfoundland who were known for making music, including Harry Hibbs. Following Ron's introduction to the instrument, Hibbs would be loosely tied to his early attachment to the button accordion.

"There was one in the house at Long Beach, at my grandmother's place. I remember trying to get something out of it."

But the accordion quickly fell by the wayside when his father brought home his first guitar, what would now be a vintage SS Stewart six-string, which Ron described as an archtop, orchestra-style guitar, hand-made in the style of a fine cello with a natural varnish finish, tortoise shell trim, and real mother of pearl fret inlays. Thomas had picked it up in Frobisher Bay, of all places, and had written to Ron's mother, Mary, to say he was bringing it home. Ron said he could hardly wait over the days and weeks to see the taxi pull up into the yard with his father and the guitar in tow. He remembers his father's taxi driver being a Delahunty man from Calvert who came into the house and tuned it for Ron.

"It laid around for a year," said Ron, "till I finally delved into it and just fell in love."

It took, and for "days and days and days," Ron applied himself and learned the Harry Hibbs song, "Roses Are Blooming," even though he would have heard Hibbs performing the tune while accompanying himself on the accordion, not the guitar.

> Roses are blooming, come back to me darling,
> Come back to me darling and never more roam;
> Robins are singing, church bells are ringing,
> Roses are blooming, so come back my own.

The days have been long dear, the nights have been dreary,
I missed you my darling since you went away;
But still I kept hoping that you would remember,
That you would remember and come back some day.

Roses are blooming, come back to me darling,
Come back to me darling and never more roam;
Robins are singing, church bells are ringing,
Roses are blooming, so come back my own.

On another trip, Ron's father bought him a grey fedora, which of course became the signature part of his look. So between the guitar and the fedora, Ron says his father invented Ron Hynes, that he started his career for him without ever knowing it.

"If only he'd known what he was doing," said Ron.

From then on, Ron was naked without a guitar draped around his neck. But his talent for playing instruments was vastly more versatile. He quoted a line to me from John Lennon, where Lennon says, "I'm an artist. Give me a tuba and I'll get you something out of it." That line comes from the extensive, two-part 1971 *Rolling Stone* magazine John Lennon interview, part one of which was titled, "The Working Class Hero."

"Dylan introduced us all to the harp rack as accompaniment to the guitar," said Ron, an accompaniment frequently associated with Lennon as well. "So I did that a lot in the early coffeehouse days, and when the Grand Band started up, everyone had a guitar, so I opted for banjo and mandolin. In high school I studied piano and at one point played for an entire school concert. I'm fascinated by the dobro and saxophone, though I've never played either. Well, life is long," he added, suggesting he just might yet, but unfortunately, he never got the chance.

Ron's early curious music sensibility went far beyond Uncle Sonny's favourite country artists and the Newfoundland-ness of Harry Hibbs, toward the discovery of his very own musical heroes. Ron abandoned piano to try and learn Buddy Holly's hit "Rave On," but no one was more important or formative to Ron than the 1950-60s teen idol, Del Shannon.

DEL SHANNON

Shannon was a key figure in rock and roll's transition from the 1950s to the 60s, one of those artists who served as a link between the peak of Chuck Berry, Buddy Holly, Elvis Presley and that next big thing—The Beatles and the British Invasion. He was among the relatively few self-reliant rock and rollers of the teen-idol era. He wrote his own material, played guitar, sang, and did not project a manufactured image. Shannon turned out a solid run of hits during the first half of the Sixties, including one bona-fide classic, "Runaway," and seven more top forty singles. He also influenced up-and-coming bands of that runaway British Invasion, including The Beatles.

Born Charles Westover in Coopersville, Michigan, Shannon was an early fan of Hank Snow, Lefty Frizzell, and like Ron, of the legendary American country music legend, Hank Williams. Shannon picked up the guitar in his pre-teen years and by the time he was fourteen, was playing at school shows. The guitar was his constant companion, playing it everywhere he went, at high-school football games, in the school hallways, at noon hour—everywhere. Shannon's obsession with the guitar as constant companion, widely attested to, is a comparable characterization of Ron.

But what had really caught Ron's ear about Shannon, what completely hooked him, was Shannon's rough falsetto vocal style, so predominant in hits like "Runaway," "Hats Off to Larry," "Handyman," and "Little Town Flirt." Technically speaking, the term falsetto describes a form of vocal pronunciation that enables singers to deliver notes beyond the vocal range of their normal or what is called their modal voice. Although he really didn't consider himself very good at it, Ron loved to end certain songs with a bit of a falsetto treatment.

"I was always a big fan of the early falsetto singers, guys like Brian Wilson, Roy Orbison, Frankie Valli, and Del Shannon especially."

Speaking of Orbison, Ron wrote the song "Roy Orbison Came On" while travelling on Circular Road in St. John's in the early 1990s.

"I had started writing about Del," explained Ron, "but the name didn't play well with the rhythm so it got switched to Roy. It's a great song to play live with my band; a Fat Cat [a bar on infamous George Street in St. John's] favourite."

Ron says he used to cover a song of Shannon's called "Hound Dog Man," which was written about Elvis Presley.

"I may resurrect it one of these days," said Ron, one of numerous references he made to the future which he never lived out.

"Those guys were truly an inspiration, with voices that sounded like they'd just dropped in from another planet. You have to stay clean and disciplined to retain that style of voice. It always sounds so otherworldly."

Ron was always more than aware of what it takes for a singer to keep his voice conditioned. He talked about how even coffee could flatten your voice out, which led him to sometimes have green tea instead before a performance. He would often say to avoid coffee and beer and cocaine at all costs, but to instead have a six-pack of nurses. Other times he would quote the late comedian Tommy Sexton about the benefits of drinking water and tea while touring in order to sustain one's self. Ron said he agreed with Sexton, but also to combine the formula with late-night pizza and beer and lots of pretty nurses.

Inspired or not, one of the most telling things about Ron Hynes is that when it came to staying clean, in his later years, he had more downs than ups, and it would ultimately prove to be his undoing.

He went on to write about Shannon, and others of his falsetto ilk, in the song "1962 (The Once)." Whenever he performed it, Ron reached for *his* falsetto voice, tailing off the closing lyric with the line, "That's all gone, it won't come back again."

"That song is the closest I ever came to something about my early teen years in Ferryland; wiener roasts on the beach below Keough's jukebox and pool joint. It's my clumsy attempt at a Brian Wilson, Frankie Valli, Del Shannon, Roy Orbison impersonation," joked Ron. "Sometimes it works, sometimes it don't," and far less so after he experienced his traumatic bout with throat cancer beginning in 2012.

1962 (The Once)

I dreamed it was 1962.
I dropped a quarter in a juke box,
And played a song for you;
Kissed you by the Pinball King,
Listenin' to Del Shannon sing;
And I had all his records,
He was my favourite then.

But that's all gone,
It won't come back again;
That's all gone,
It won't come back again.

I woke up, I put on my father's shoes,
Sittin' on the front porch
just like he used to do;
Stepped across the mornin' sand,
The skyline only showed a sign of rain,
And mine would be the only
footprints that remain.

But that's all gone,
It won't come back again;
That's all gone,
It won't come back again.

There was something that
I meant to say,
Yeah, yeah;
Too many words got in the way,
Yeah, yeah.

And I dreamed it was 1962.
I lit a fire on the beach,
And lay in the sand with you;
Sang songs until the rain would come,
Straight across the fields we'd run;
You wrapped your sweater
round my first guitar,
I walked you home.

But that's all gone,
It won't come back again;
But that's all gone,
It won't come back again.

There was something that I meant to say,
Yeah, yeah;
But too many words got in the way,
Yeah, yeah.
Yeah, yeah.

And I dreamed it was 1962.
I dropped a quarter in the jukebox,
Played a song for you;
Kissed you by the Pinball King,
Listenin' to Del Shannon sing;
And I had all his records,
He was my favourite then –
Him and Brian Wilson.

But that's all gone,
It won't come back again;
But that's all gone,
It won't come back again.

OBSESSION

BRIAN BOURNE CHERISHES THE FACT THAT he accompanied Ron musically, off and on, since 1976 or 1977, when they first crossed paths in Ottawa while doing gigs at the Red Rock Hotel. Scroll ahead to 2014, when Bourne was backing Ron in performance venues across the Maritime Provinces, including places like the Chester Playhouse in Chester and the Carleton in Halifax, Nova Scotia, the Victoria Playhouse and Trailside Café on Prince Edward Island, and Rita MacNeil's Tea Room on Cape Breton Island.

Bourne is a sixty-two-year-old, Quebec-born, Nova Scotia-based musician who couldn't possibly look more the part of a musician, with his beard, dark glasses, button-down cap, and cool, laid-back demeanour. He has played mostly bass guitar in a wide range of bands in the Maritimes and in Ontario since the 1970s and has backed an extensive list of truly international-level performers, but along the way has also played a lot of the Chapman Stick over the past twenty-nine years. Self-taught on the instrument, he searched for and bought one after reading about it in *Guitar Player* magazine. He learned how to finesse the Stick while sitting in his basement playing along with old records.

The Chapman Stick was invented in 1969 by Los Angeles-based American Emmett Chapman in 1969, a guy who'd seen guitar players over the years with their right hand strumming or picking or plucking and their left hand fretting. Chapman examined how a player's right hand would sometimes sneak up and tap some notes on the fret board, and then have both hands tapping on the fret board. As a result, he came up with a stereo-rigged instrument which looks like a 2 x 6-inch piece of wood with strings. Instead of looking like a traditionally stringed instrument, the Stick has eight, ten, or twelve individually tuned strings and has been used on music recordings to play bass lines, melody lines, chords, or textures. Designed as a fully polyphonic chordal instrument, it can also cover several of these musical parts simultaneously. Bourne's Stick has a set of five bass strings and a set of seven guitar strings, each set having its own pickup.

"It is sending two signals out, one goes to the bass end, and the other goes to the guitar end," says Bourne. "But you strike the strings with the ends of your fingers. You're playing like a piano. You've got the dexterity of the piano with the expression of a guitar. This guy Chapman came up with something new, a whole new language for fingers and strings. Even as an experienced musician, it was certainly like going back to square one when I first picked it up. Each side tunes differently: fourths and fifths. So, the thing that is common about both sides is you are going from the center of the neck outwards to go up in pitch. So, you kind of play it like a piano but you can do all the bends, trills, and guitar tricks."

Four years after the invention, Chapman went into mass production, but while the instrument's been in the marketplace for more than four decades and has seen all sorts of variations, it's still very much under the radar. You don't see a lot of guys playing Chapman Sticks sitting around the campfire.

The Chapman Stick is important to spend so much time talking about because it is as unusual on stage as Ron could sometimes be. Most audiences have no idea what the instrument is, although they all love the sound, and so did Ron. With its warm, sultry tones, it is a near-perfect accompanying instrument for Ron's style of music.

Bourne and Ron had a muted but definite chemistry on stage, even though it was always clear to audiences whose show it was. Ron could be demanding on stage and would not hesitate at times to exhibit who was in charge. Bourne says the key was to know the songs, which was not so easy all the time because Ron was always generating new material. Bourne recalls having to be coached by Ron on a new song over the phone one night.

"The fact that we go back since the frigging Ming Dynasty probably helps. It relaxes. The familiar things are always good. You're comfortable with somebody and stuff. But back then, and still today, I look up to him as the best in the country for sure. You know, up with all the best. And so, it is a class gig."

Bourne says Ron didn't usually do a set list, but because they'd performed together so much, he would sometimes afford Bourne that luxury, for which he was appreciative. Ron certainly enjoyed the pleasure of calling the shots, of calling the set list.

"I can't remember any songs now," says Bourne. "It's all on sheets. It's all charts.

Whenever we play a few gigs in a row I'm more able to throw away a few of the papers."

When they'd met back in those Ottawa days, Bourne was with a country-rock band and Ron was performing solo but was also touring with a group called the White River Bluegrass Band. They all hung out at the same band house provided by the host bar. What Bourne remembers the most about that time is that "Ron wore his guitar like a shirt. He wore it all the time. He woke up, it was on." At the band house or at the place he was staying, "he walked around the apartment with that frigging guitar on."

"He was totally consumed with this work of the songwriter," Bourne says, "and making it better and tweaking it, and tweaking it, and just making it better and writing a better song. Just getting better. Always. Always. He always had the guitar on, literally, all the time. That's how deep he's into it, and that's why he's so good. And listen, he was the first Newfoundlander to release an all-original record. I mean, all the other boys, great stuff, it's all beautiful, but as far as original stuff on recording, Ron was the first."

"I just wanted it," said Ron, referring to his love for music and songwriting. "I wanted it so much. I wanted it so much I thought I was going to die, you know. And at the same time, you're in there pretending to be doing your homework and hoping against hope that your mom does not come through the door and catch you listening to Del Shannon singing 'Runaway,' or listening to whoever was on the VOC top ten."

The guitar truly was a stringed appendage of Ron's body. The guitar defined him as an artist far more than most. But even his ardent fans usually don't stop to think about it. Of course there are exceptions, such as people who've studied Ron.

"I think his guitar playing has been overlooked," says filmmaker Bill MacGillivray, who produced and directed the documentary *The Man of a Thousand Songs*. "It is often simple but always extremely tasteful and perfectly true."

Bourne says Ron's obsession with and focus on music often painted a picture of him to strangers as being aloof or arrogant, but rather, he was just so absorbed with his music. Like he was lost in it. Bourne adds that Ron was so focused on his art that it was partly to the detriment of his social life. Sometimes he could make people feel like, "Well, geez, he doesn't want to talk to me."

"He was always busy musically. He was working twenty-four hours a day in his head."

THE WGB

WHILE IT'S TRUE THAT RON WAS working all the time creating music, he really had no idea where it was he was going. Only coincidence, circumstance, chance introductions, and fate would determine that. Coincidence, circumstance, chance introductions, and fate led the way and collided at once with the accidental advent of Newfoundland's Wonderful Grand Band—the WGB.

The WGB was Newfoundland's incredibly popular trad-rock band from 1978 to 1983, co-founded by Ron with several performers who were associated with some members of the original CODCO comedy troupe and a group of Newfoundland musicians. Altogether, the band did six years combining stints on television, radio, touring, and two albums: *The Wonderful Grand Band* and *Living in a Fog*.

A momentous evolution of happenstance creativity led to the invention, evolution, and popularity of the WGB. Nothing else quite like it was going on anyplace else in Canada. In fact, more than thirty years later, some of the best comedy and entertainment in the country remains loosely linked to both *CODCO* and the WGB through programming such as CBC's *This Hour Has 22 Minutes*. Even CBC's highly popular satirical show, *The Rick Mercer Report*, echoes this era.

Many other linkages and chance circumstances were to follow, but the true ground zero for the WGB phenomenon began in 1973 when comedian Tommy Sexton and Diane Olsen wrote a comedic show about Canadian stereotypes of Newfoundlanders called *Cod on a Stick*. The original cast consisted of Sexton, Olsen, Greg Malone, Cathy Jones, Mary Walsh, and Paul Sametz. The show ran in St. John's, with Scott Strong replacing Sametz, and then toured the province with Robert Joy replacing Strong. When the show was taped by the National Film Board in 1974, Andy Jones appeared in the cast as well. Versions of this troupe took to stages over the years which followed, but the CODCO concept remained loose until the show took to the CBC airwaves in 1987. So it was really the comedic formula associated with *Cod on a Stick* and early iterations of CODCO which set the stage for something even bigger, combining both comedy and music, which preceded the national television comedy sensation *CODCO*.

Enter the music part of the WGB formula. With his hair still long, as though he's stuck in the 60s or 70s, Sandy Morris looks every bit the rock-n-roll guitar playing stereotype. Exactly when he met Ron is a little bit grainy for him, but Morris does remember pretty much everything else worth remembering about the birth and lifespan of the WGB. He seems more organized than most others from the WGB era, still maintaining a collection of WGB memorabilia, including a wealth of photos and clippings and, most surprisingly, a couple of original hand-scrawled set lists which the band used from around 1975 or 1976. Those set lists were created by both Ron and Morris.

"I don't exactly remember when I met Ron, but vaguely, I was in England in 1971, and when I came back in October or November of '71, I started just playing locally again, getting involved with all local people. And during that timeframe, I'd say '72/'73, Ron was in from Ferryland doing kind of a folk circuit. There was a place called the Tudor Inn where folk musicians used to play.

"It was a bar, but it featured kind of folk and jazz, as opposed to dance bars around. It was a small underground kind of stone room, and really all the folk singers loved playing in there. There were a few coffee house type situations too where Ron would have played. And I was already into that circuit playing with other singers. And I would have met him around there.

"It turns out after I had met Ron and got to know him for a while, we discovered that every summer he would come in from Ferryland and stay directly around the corner from where I grew up. I was on Henry Street, and he was Dick Square and they are like just right here in town, right around the corner from one another. But in the summertime, I would go out to the country for the summer, and Ron came from the country into town, so we missed each other growing up, but otherwise we would have been hanging out on the same street corner together. I'm talking about when we were kids. Because when we actually met we were probably eighteen, nineteen, or twenty, around that age."

Here's the thing that impressed Morris and everyone else about Ron. Everyone back then was trying to write songs. The Beatles happened and the Rolling Stones, and they realized that if people could write their own music, they made more money. Like Simon and Garfunkel.

The Wonderful Grand Band: (clockwise) Tommy Sexton,
Greg Malone, Rocky Wiseman, Glenn Simmons, Jamie Snider,
Ian Perry, Ron Hynes, and Sandy Morris.

The WGB, circa 1977: (left to right) Sandy Morris, Kelly Russell, Bryan Hennessey, Rocky Wiseman, Bawnie Oulton, Ron Hynes.

"We were all writing songs together and alone and trying to come up with tunes," says Morris. "But Ron came along and he was a songwriter. He wasn't *trying* to write songs. He *was* a songwriter. And there was just a big difference. Like he was a songwriter, and there was no two ways about it. He wasn't just a singer; he was a songwriter. You knew it right away."

Morris met Ron after his first album, *Discovery*, came out. It wasn't just Ron's first album; it was the first album of original tunes, apart from traditional music, in Newfoundland. Ron had written an album's worth of songs on his own that he was able to get out and have. That is the genus of when his song writing became his signature calling card.

Ron and Morris started doing duos together around then during the bar era when bands played five or six nights a week and there were loads of places to play and the money was decent.

"It was just the two of us most of the time. We did that for years and years, and around '76/'77, we started doing gigs with a few extra guys. In my head I kept hearing Ron's songs with drums and bass and harmonies and stuff, right. I just wanted to fill it out. I really wanted it to have harmony, and I wanted it to have parts. I wanted this, but Ron never thought at that time on that level. Ron was just thinking about the next gig and the next whatever he was going to. So, we started doing some gigs, of which I've got some pictures."

Morris was working a lot on TV back then. There was a whole local TV industry primarily because of the CBC's building presence in St. John's.

"I would do two or three shows a day because there would be coffee shows and you would go on and do a little performance in the afternoon. There was a series here that lasted for years called *All Around the Circle* and I ended up being a regular in the band. And I managed to get Ron on that show and the producers were impressed. Well, Ron was the only guy coming on the show writing his own tunes, and they were accessible to us. It wasn't like some weird stuff. The comment was always, 'Oh my God, he is playing one of his own made up tunes, oh no, right?' But you know, with Ron, people liked the tunes he was writing because they related to people."

People, says Morris, could tell it was different.

"We ended up doing a whole bunch of television together," says Morris, filling in some of the details about the evolution of the WGB from both CODCO, the comedy troupe, and what evolved to become a local television series called *The Root Seller*. "And around 1976/77, we started doing gigs, with like, you know, with sort of a slightly bigger group with musicians, drums, bass and fiddle and various things, and kind of flesh out the sound a little bit. We did some concerts, and played a few gigs. And then one of the producers came to me and said, 'You know, we've been trying to get a show as popular as *All Around the Circle*, and ever since it closed, we tried country music, and we've tried Irish music, and we've tried everything, and none of it is working. And you are out there in the community working with all these people, so come up with an idea for a show.'"

From Sexton's and Olsen's ground zero in 1973, four years later *The Root Seller* became that next rung on the ladder, that next idea which helped the WGB come to be. It was a six-part mini-series written by Greg Malone, Mary Walsh, and Mary White and hosted by comedians Greg Malone and Mary Walsh in character as Mr. and Mrs. Budgell, the outrageously dysfunctional couple who run a St. John's boarding house as the backdrop for a comedic soap opera. The Budgells were one in a series of situation skits which had originated with the CODCO comedy troupe.

The Root Seller had special weekly guests, including artists such as Emile Benoit, Rufus Guinchard, Minnie White, Cathy Jones, and Jimmy Oulton. It was an instant local favourite, but unbelievably, only two of these shows, with special guests Minnie White and Emile Benoit, have actually survived within the CBC archives. The rest were lost or destroyed. The musicians on *The Root Seller* were Kelly Russell, Sandy Morris, Ron Hynes, Glenn Simmons, Rocky Wiseman, Bryan Hennessey, and Bawnie Oulton.

All these years later, Greg Malone isn't Mr. Budgell any longer, or at least not for the time being. He's too busy being married to Mary White and doing myriad other things both politically and artistically.

Mary White is Malone's better half and the original producer and manager for the WGB. During our interview, Malone warns me not to call her Mary but to strictly call her White or Whitey. This makes her sound as tough as an American gangster, which is appropriate because she nearly is. So unlike everyone else involved in this book, I'm intimidated before I get to meet her. She is The Great Whitey, as Malone calls her.

"Whitey was the general manager for the band," says her husband. "She cut all the contracts and organized the tours. Towards the end, someone else took over for the last two years, but you know, she got the show to the CBC and all that stuff up and running. Then she was general manager for *CODCO*, cut all the deals for *CODCO*. All the CBC contracts for *CODCO* which were Cadillac contracts, the best yet. She was ahead of her time and she cut them all."

These were contracts for shows in St. John's and in Toronto and in Halifax. *CODCO* was done in Halifax, the Wonderful Grand Band in St. John's, and they did shows in Toronto too. The CBC, both in St. John's and in Toronto, were happy dealing with White because she was straight up.

"And she always came on the road," says Malone. "She was the nurse. She ran the light board if she had to. She got the money. She called the shots."

"When he had his cancer," says Malone, "Ron depended largely on White then, as he had before, and apparently does now, for spiritual advice.

"Everyone does," according to Malone. "Everyone goes to her. Cathy [Jones] still goes to her now for all advice. She calls her at least once a day."

Malone is not shy in boasting about his wife.

"She is an extraordinary person in that she has no personal ambition, and no personal agenda. She really doesn't, and so you know when you are talking to her she is only thinking of you. Ron found that out over the years."

White confesses that she is, essentially, a born manager. It isn't just in her DNA. It is her DNA. She's also performed, but performing just wasn't her thing. Managing, she says, interestingly, is all about being confident. She credits that sense of confidence by being fourth in a house with twelve kids growing up in Perry's Cove, Newfoundland, near Carbonear. Everybody in her family, she says, is confident.

As it was for Morris, White's introduction to Ron is kind of blurred. There were always so many people around the arts and music scene in St. John's, crowds and crowds of faces. She suspects it was through Morris, who was with the Philadelphia Cream Cheese Band at Memorial University, and other guys like Brian Hennessey, and the artistically and influentially towering Noel Dinn, who was the founding member of the popular Newfoundland band Figgy Duff. White does, however, have a faint recollection of going to see *The Exorcist* at a theatre in Toronto, with a bunch of Newfoundlanders, and Ron being in the group.

Malone talks about the closeness both he and White had to Morris near the beginning of their success.

"So myself and Whitey, who is my partner through it. Me and Whitey and Sandy lived together for a long time and during the Wonderful Grand Band and were a ménage à trois through all that time," he joked, speaking figuratively. "It was Greg, White, and Sandy throughout."

But at some point, Ron entered the scene.

"Ron just came into our life by osmosis like any other musician or artist at the time. It's a fairly small community here in St. John's. It's very concentrated so you more or less get to meet everybody eventually in your milieu."

White worked with CODCO back in the comedy troupe's heyday, in the mid-70s.

She was part of the fabric of what was happening around the local CBC in those days, a time during which the network was producing lots of musical variety shows like *All Around the Circle*, the tapes for which, as stated previously, have unbelievably been erased.

According to both she and Malone, the CBC was erasing history for the cost of a tape: forty-five bucks a tape maybe. Malone got in trouble at the time with the St. John's CBC brass for complaining about the ridiculous practice, but at least he eventually stopped them from erasing any more of the material.

"Foolishness!" says Malone about the practice. Which it was.

The musical and comedy variety shows were a reflection of the talent stomping around St. John's at the time and the fact that Newfoundland viewers were not content to simply have the local news. There was more local variety production on the Rock than probably anywhere else in the CBC system. CBC Nova Scotia was into it to a degree with *Singalong Jubilee* and such, but in St. John's it was even more constant.

"There was always a local show on the go," according to White.

One would think local programming of that type would require earmarked funding.

"There was no money for programming," says White. "There was only money for the station, and for news, and stuff like that, but I guess, what do you call them, the executive directors, the producers, whatever, at CBC, they pooled the money and made enough to do some shows out of it, right? Very cheap little entertaining shows. So, Sandy [Morris] had done three or four of those, and they were running out of ideas, and the producer at the time or the director, I suppose he was the director, Kevin O'Connell, said to Sandy, 'Why don't you put together a band and do a show.' And Sandy said no, he wasn't interested because he was sort of fed up with that kind of stuff. I don't know why, but he said he wasn't interested." White was upset about it because she really wanted to get a good show underway.

According to Malone, while the CBC was keen to produce something with music involved, no one, not Sandy Morris nor anyone else, was really moving on the opportunity. Morris for example said he didn't know what to do or where to start. Finally, White reacted and said, "What do you mean you don't know what to do. This is a chance to do a show, you idiot!"

It turned out that the crux of the matter was that Morris was interested in a show, but he wanted a show with Ron Hynes in it.

"So I said, 'Well, ask Ron,'" says White.

"So, between Greg, White, and myself, we came up with the idea for the Wonderful Grand Band show," says Morris. "And I think Ron was still in Ontario at the time because I think I phoned him up and said, 'Ron, you want to come back and do a television series?'"

Morris says that was probably around the end of 1979 through early 1980, and then CBC came back after having dropped *The Root Seller* series.

Morris also wanted to work with Glenn Simmons and Boomer Stamp at the time. He was really into that. And he also wanted to work with Kelly Russell who was doing a string of conventional type things to Newfoundland songs, following in the tradition of Noel Dinn and Figgy Duff.

So in a sense, the WGB was a derivative of Dinn and the Figgy Duff phenomenon, with whom Morris had played, with the difference being a healthy dose of original Ron Hynes songs and Ron Hynes himself.

"So, we did, we pitched that show to CBC," says White.

"That show" was, to retrace the chronology, *The Root Seller*. The network only produced six episodes, but they were huge in terms of where it took the lives of Ron and White and Malone and Morris and everyone else in their midst.

"It was mostly me who did the pitching," says White. "Sandy was like the in-the-door guy, for sure, because he'd already been in there and had a working relationship with Kevin O'Connell and everyone. The show would turn out to be Mr. and Mrs. Budgell from CODCO comedy troupe fame, and a band, the Wonderful Grand Band. That's what we did. We did six episodes."

It was Morris who White credits with naming the band for *The Root Seller*.

"Sandy said at one point, 'It is a wonderful grand band,' and Kelly's [Russell] mother said, 'Well, it must be a wonderful grand band because I never hear you complaining about it. I never hear any fighting about it,'" which is what band members inherently do. "So, the name stuck and we went with that," says White.

With her managing and producing, and Malone and Mary Walsh in with White on the writing, the Wonderful Grand Band was born. According to Malone, White created the idea of the Wonderful Grand Band. It was her idea. She put it together and made Sandy Morris pull the talent together.

When the six episodes of *The Root Seller* were over, the band wanted to keep going because they were having such a good time, and they were popular, so they did a few gigs, including what would be a momentous and direction-setting series of live stage shows at Toronto Caravan, that city's longstanding multicultural festival which was held every summer. Caravan was the brainchild of Torontonians Leon Kossar and his wife, Zena, who in 1969 brought the idea of putting Toronto's multicultural communities on stage to fruition; an idea that former mayor David Crombie says changed the way Torontonians viewed each other. The Kossars had earlier produced the colourful *Nationbuilders Show* at the Canadian National Exhibition from 1963 to 1970, a series of events, amongst others, which gave the participating community organizations a new image of professionalism.

"So they would have a Caribbean pavilion and a Russian pavilion," says Sandy Morris, "and Newfoundland was the only province from within Canada that had its own pavilion. The year we were invited up to play it was for three weeks at the Masonic Temple there on Yonge Street, where Hendricks had played. We were delighted just to be in the same room."

Nothing could have been less predictable—a bunch of Newfoundlanders gathering together in a far-flung and ridiculous enough place so far off the Newfoundland radar that the idea could have become fodder for a later WGB comical skit: namely Toronto.

The gig came together when White booked the band with Newfoundlander Bob O'Brien, a Toronto-based publicist who was involved with Caravan. The Masonic Hall production was something they all cobbled together, with White handling lights and sound at the back of the room and her husband Malone agreeing to appear, albeit reticently.

"I had to talk Greg into it because he didn't want to do it," says White, "and the CODCO people had just gone on a show across Canada and they didn't invite him in," a nasty topic she wasn't much prepared to discuss, but which sounded of infighting amongst the performers.

It was a tough sell for White on Malone because he was all about comedy, and Morris and Ron and company were all about music. However, White, being White, she won the day and Malone agreed to the gig.

"She blackmailed me into doing it," says Malone. "I was the theatre guy; I had nothing to do with that. I didn't really want to, but I did it anyway. So that was the beginning of the Wonderful Grand Band."

Once underway, the band started to play—White believes the tune was "Joe Smallwood's Reel"—when all of a sudden, Malone appeared as Mr. Budgell, jumping over the amps, landing on the stage and dancing. In that instant, the room erupted.

"Everybody in the room raised off the floor," according to White. From her vantage point at the back of the room running the lights and the sound, she suddenly couldn't see the stage. The result, according to White, was "explosive."

"It was just a very spontaneous thing that became a regular feature, really fast. It was super. It was super that, like you know, we blew Toronto away."

Mr. Budgell didn't just land on both feet on that Masonic Temple stage. He landed both feet squarely on the Canadian entertainment scene. It was a precurser of what was to become a truly Newfoundland and Canadian cultural phenomenon; an unscripted marvel which Canadians grew to love and cherish.

Morris's characterization of the reaction to the Toronto Caravan gigs matches that of White.

"We ended up blowing the roof off the place. It was the most popular pavilion in the whole Caravan that year. Every show, we did three shows a night, half-hour shows, they weren't very long. Every show would just fill the place. The place would be packed to the rafters and people went crazy for it."

The show was the first time anyone in Canada had actually incorporated comedy with a band in a live performance.

"It took off so big," says Morris, "it was such a huge thing, that as soon as we came back to the island, we said, we've got to do it here. If it's that big a hit in Toronto, people will love it here too."

It was like a pilot for the Newfoundland television show which had amazingly begun with a Toronto audience. It *was* a Toronto audience and with a large Newfoundland contingent, but even the pure Torontonians loved the Newfoundland humour.

History had actually repeated itself when the WGB found its form in Toronto. The same thing had happened with the CODCO comedy troupe as everyone from St. John's had gone to Cabbagetown to try and make their fortune. It was like the 1970 Canadian feature film *Goin' Down the Road*, except that Tommy Sexton, Diane Olsen, Cathy Jones, and Mary Walsh were attending Ryerson rather than seeking work like the two footloose characters, Pete and Joey, in *Goin' Down the Road*, characters who drive their old Chev from Cape Breton Island to Toronto with the hope of finding jobs, but instead become adrift in the big city.

As Morris says, the Caravan incarnation proved to be wildly successful, and in 1979 Tommy Sexton joined Malone to complete the team. According to Morris, Tommy Sexton was so jealous of Greg that he had to get involved because he just said, "'You're not doing this with the band without me,'" so he came and the two of them had their characters.

"It just went nuts," says Morris.

Of course, the comedic team of Malone and Sexton fronted the comedy for the WGB television productions until the group finally split in 1983. But lots of music and comedy history was to be made before the WGB's final curtain.

"The WGB turned out to be the most viewed show on Newfoundland television back in the day. There were only two channels, but, according to Morris, "We had something like 90%, or 85%, or 89% of the audience that was watching TV.

"The money was good. For the time it was great, and to have a TV series, and then we had live gigs of course, there was still the bar scene. So you were working seven nights a week in bars. We ended up, by '84 when we broke up, making $10K a week in a bar, right? Which back then was unheard of, you know. Only a few bands were able to do that. I think we were getting that per episode of TV as well, so you know, money was rolling in. And we were doing well off the island in Halifax, Toronto, even BC. We got out there a couple of times. We even did well with audiences out there."

The WGB was born in Toronto, but was popularized at home on CBC television, with some forty half-hour episodes being produced and aired between 1980 and 1983. In 2009, two volumes of the original WGB TV series were released on DVD after years of consultation and planning between the band (White) and the CBC. The DVDs, *The Best of WGB* Volume 1 and 2, were a sensation, bringing to life once again some all-time favourite characters like Mr. Budgell, Nanny Hynes, Dickie, Mavis, and Carmel Ann, and including many of the group's classic hit songs like "Sonny's Dream," "Living in A Fog," "Go For Love," "UIC," and "Babylon Mall," which featured Tommy Sexton. The DVD release and tour were undertaken, in part, as a tribute to Sexton, who died in 1993 of complications from AIDS.

Eventually, Ron undertook his first solo album back around '93 and the band broke up unceremoniously. "It was just a bad scene," says Morris. It had all just become too much.

This outcome coincided with the winding down of the bar scene when bands of the WGB's calibre had full-week bookings and were making good money. By the time the Grand Band got to its final version, there were ten people on stage, so touring was fourteen people. It was really expensive. This is Mary Walsh and Cathy Jones and Tommy and Greg. According to Morris, they were all high-maintenance people, adding that the comedy performance ensemble would undoubtedly say the exact same thing about the musicians. In any case, the math wasn't working out as it became impossible trying to drag the whole ensemble all the way across Canada, adding to the complexity of irregularity of bookings and gigs.

"You couldn't sustain it on the island alone," says Morris.

With that, everybody went their separate ways. Ron started doing his solo career, and then Ron's album came up, his first album which was originally independent. Some members of the band ended up playing on it, including Morris and Glenn Simmons.

"Not all of us," says, Morris, "just a bunch of us, and then we toured to support that with Ron. We took the whole thing on the road. Again, a huge big band."

As it turned out in terms of economics, they were just too big a band. But the wonderful die had been cast: the WGB had left an indelible imprint on Newfoundland, Newfoundlanders, and many other Canadians.

"The biggest show in the world on television wasn't from New York, or Los Angeles, or Paris, or Chicago, or Toronto, or even Halifax," says Newfoundlander and Great Big Sea frontman Alan Doyle. "It was from Newfoundland. The biggest stars in my young life were from Newfoundland, and they played Newfoundland music, and they played my songs [meaning the songs he would come to love and appreciate]. I didn't know any of that at the time, of course. This is in retrospect.

"The WGB show was running hard in the late 70s and early 80s, and I was born in '69. So in retrospect, the whole Grand Band thing was huge. Before we started playing music at all, we were looking inward and not outward, which is amazing for a place as big as Petty Harbour, where I grew up.

"Everybody in the Grand Band was a rock star to us when I was ten years of age. The three big stars of the show were Ron, because he was the leader of the band, Greg Malone, and Tommy Sexton, because they were the funny guys. Different groups of people I think, like the serious musicians, would have guys like Sandy Morris because he was like a guitar god. And all the young girls liked Ian Perry because he looked like a Bay City Roller. Boomer [Stamp] was always the goofy chum. It was the perfect TV band. It was perfect. It was like the Muppet Show band or something. It was fantastic. They were like cartoons to us."

Guitarist and singer Chris LeDrew was also part of the cult following of the Wonderful Grand Band at that same time. At just twelve or thirteen years of age and learning how to play guitar, he used to watch the WGB on TV. The show used to come on once a week on Monday nights.

For the several years the show ran, Ron and Glenn Simmons and Sandy Morris were all like early heroes for local kids, and especially any who were aspiring musicians.

"Seeing someone like Ron, Glenn, or Sandy was always like seeing a major rock star," according to LeDrew. "These guys were already built up in your mind as sort of icons before you met them, so years later, after I had been a musician for seven, eight, or nine years, I had sort of gravitated toward downtown and I ended up meeting Ron at Bridgette's."

Bridgette's Pub was up on the Cooks Town Road, just down from where Ron was living at the time. It's called the Peter Easton Pub now, a mere shell of what it used to be. It used to be a music venue. Ron used to play there quite a bit. LeDrew says that one day he went in and Ron was behind the bar on the telephone, and LeDrew remembers being taken aback and thinking, "Oh my God, there's Ron Hynes."

For LeDrew, it was like running into Lennon or McCartney.

In the same way that music is all Ron ever did, drumming is all WGB drummer Paul 'Boomer' Stamp has ever really done.

"God yeah. That's all I've ever done. I worked, I think, one job. I worked on the dry dock when my dad retired and I took his job for a couple of years. Then I left there and I went to Toronto."

As far as Stamp can recollect, he first met Ron in Toronto at the Caravan festival. But Stamp thinks it was in the revolving restaurant atop the CN Tower, which is where the WGB had set up once during the festival.

"It was '79. I think that's where I met him. Now, I'm not sure if he was involved with CODCO at the time," says Stamp. "I knew CODCO. I was living in Toronto then of course, right? I was playing in a band up there called A Foot in Cold Water."

Stamp had originally gone to Toronto in the early 1970s with Brian MacLeod, who later went on to join Chilliwack. His going to Toronto, however, wasn't part of some grand master, well-thought-out career or business plan. Far from it. He was just following the stream of Newfoundlanders who, like a lot of Maritimers, were caught up in the latest exodus to central or western Canada.

"We were playing the Legion in Pleasantville [Newfoundland] and I got home and here was Brian, and he's like, 'You're booked on a flight tomorrow morning at six.' So I put all of my clothes in the bass drum and brought it along to the airport."

Once in Toronto with his funny luggage, Stamp was in demand as a drummer and did stints like touring with the band Trooper. When Morris and Ron and the guys came to Toronto, he had to go see what the Wonderful Grand Band was all about.

The genesis of the WGB: (left to right) Kelly Russell, Sandy Morris, Rocky Wiseman, Bryan Hennessey, Bawnie Oulton, and Ron Hynes.

"And I just loved it, you know. I fell in love with it. I thought it was a fabulous show."

After Caravan, he eventually got a call from Morris, who said to come up and join the band.

"I mean, the whole band thing with the comedy, it's pretty weird stuff. You think about it now, why did anybody think that formula was going to work? But that's the thing. That was the genius of it."

And they were all fearless.

"Oh, we were definitely fearless," says Stamp. "There wasn't much we wouldn't do. At CBC it was insane because we pre-recorded all the shows musically, so when we were actually shooting the show, you had to keep it back to just look like you were playing and not hit the cymbals hard."

The cameraman kept complaining about the cymbals shocking the cameras, but Stamp would just keep on doing it anyway. And smoking and drinking and carousing even during production periods.

"We would go out and have a little swalley, and the audience came in and we just mimed the tunes. If we did it well, we did it well, and if we didn't, we would do it again."

The studio audiences were so enamoured of the WGB they would stay if the crew asked them to. Stamp jokes that they would have stayed for breakfast if the tapings went really late and the producers asked them to. Newfoundlanders fell in love with the band and the show.

"It was huge here. We were The Beatles in Newfoundland," according to Stamp. "It got to be crazy for popularity. And that was it. Everybody just loved the Grand Band. When that album dropped, *Living in a Fog*, that was it. We owned this town, and the island and Labrador, especially Labrador. We couldn't go to Labrador but it was like The Beatles showed up. It was insane, because that's all they had up there was CBC. It was Grand Band mania absolutely with Tommy, and all the acting and all those characters, and then the band being like a separate thing within the show, and everybody having their favourite performers. It was fabulous.

"We went to Labrador City and places like that and the place would be blocked. You'd be expecting like 900 people and there would be like 2,000 show up. They just swarmed the place. It was insane. The lounges we would play there, you know, and people would come at 4:00 and have supper there just to get a seat. We were definitely on a big high, that's for sure.

"We'd walk around town and there'd be like twenty or thirty kids following you everywhere you went. A little tiny town. It was a lot of fun. Really nice."

Of course with all that regional touring, there was always the complication of transportation. The way the gang got around really took a toll on the vehicles they had.

"One of those Beatlemania touring stops was in Stephenville," recalls Stamp, "and the entire band and hangers-on all crammed into one of Ron's cars, which they kicked the shit out of.

"I think we did an ad for Host Rent-a-Car here [in St. John's]," he says, "and as a payment they gave us two Pontiacs. A Pontiac Phoenix and a Citation, I think. We're talking '80 I'd say, '81. We took those cars on tour, and just about destroyed them of course. Ron took ownership of one of them. I remember leaving Stephenville, and I am sure there were twelve or fourteen people in that car, and I was driving and I didn't have a license back in those days. It was just one night after the other, having lots of fun, lots of partying. I can't specifically say what trouble we got into, but there was trouble."

And the buzz wasn't just in Newfoundland.

"We could tour in Canada and did really well. Really well. Everywhere we went, Newfoundlanders came out of the woodwork because the biggest export Newfoundland has is its people. So we had a lot of exciting times back then. And it didn't stop at the Canadian border, with gigs in Boston and Philadelphia, for example. CODCO played in Philadelphia, the last night there was bought out by the Newfoundland Club of Philadelphia. Everywhere you'd go there'd be these Newfoundland clubs."

There were no PEI clubs, no Ontario clubs, no Yukon clubs; just the proverbial Newfoundland club.

"As Newfoundlanders, we're travellers. We stick together a bit or something. You don't get that at other places. We were a country. We weren't like Nova Scotia which had been part of Canada for a long, long time."

Stamp admits the whole WGB thing made them believe they were larger than life.

"Oh God yes. Your shit didn't stink and that's the truth. I was already like that when I got to the band after being in Toronto with [the band] Private Eye, which had management and were hooked into Capitol Records. Yeah, talking the walk and full of shit, but we were having a great time."

The WGB was a great band for a drummer to be in, says Stamp.

"Oh God, indeed it was. That's the thing about Newfoundland. Figgy Duff and all those bands that started to cross over, that started to take folk songs and jigs and reels, putting life to it and putting like Fleetwood Mac to it. And it was great to play, even though I couldn't tell a jig from a reel, and honestly, I really can't even now. I have to think about it… jiggity jiggity or whatever the feel is."

It's the kind of high-energy movement and feel that the Newfoundland band Rawlins Cross popularized, but Figgy Duff long before that, according to Stamp.

"We put the walls to it. That was it. It was like kick the shit out of it, nail these songs to the wall. And it was fun."

The guy drumming before Stamp had a style of a really fine jazz drummer, which meant he gave the band a light touch with a lot of great footwork.

"I just added a bit of muscle to it."

WGB manager Mary White agrees that the band's popularity was off the scale, driven essentially by the exposure on television.

"I know the *Dukes of Hazzard* was on opposite us," says White, "and we beat them by a long shot, right? So we had like over 80% of the viewership."

The group had their digs into the CBC in St. John's but also elsewhere through the network, like in Toronto. They played a New Year's Eve gig at the Royal York Hotel's Imperial Room, jazz man Moe Koffman's room essentially, where a very young comedian named Jim Carrey opened up the show. The group did nine minutes on CBC live. Based on what they were paid, Stamp estimates the band got $100 a minute, as if they were a taxi with a meter. But they had beautiful hotel rooms, so that made them feel like stars, at least momentarily.

"The things that made the Grand Band different from every other band in Canada," according to Sandy Morris, "or anywhere else for that matter, was the fact that we did traditional jigs and reels and Newfoundland music, plus we had Ron's original tunes, and we had comedy. Record labels got involved and they were trying to sign us to a record deal, and they said, 'We really love those jigs and really love the comedy, and we know how to sell them. We want you to focus on the rock part of your act."

Of course, Ron was not a rock writer, being more of a folk or country artist. In fact, his first album was considered a country album even though it was not what anyone would consider to be hard-core country.

"So," says Morris, "we were trying to influence Ron to write a little more rock," which never really came to be.

There was a point at which White was actually fired from being the WGB manager as precipitated by a couple of the band members.

"They didn't understand really at the time what was involved," says White, "and I guess it was a heady thing to be that popular and that kind of stuff, and I guess they felt that my fee could have been better off in their pockets."

Within a year or so following that debacle, the band asked White back into her role. By this point, the WGB had grown into a small conglomerate of four actors and six musicians, a very expensive company to move around for television or for live gigs.

"I don't know any other band that toured like we did or any other show that toured like CODCO did in Canada," says White. "I mean, there were things like the Royal Winnipeg Ballet," who of course would have Canada Council grants coming out of their ears. The company was touring from one end of Canada to the other. Youthfulness, she believes, is what kept them going, not to mention "the fumes of their popularity."

STRAIGHT MAN

ALTHOUGH FOR RON IT WAS ALWAYS primarily about the music, he also had the knack for acting and for comedy. Greg Malone says that when it comes to good raw, satirical and spoof-driven Newfoundland comedy, Ron could play the part of the perfect straight man.

"We'd do a live show and Ron would be very good to work with on stage because he liked having the Mickey taken out of him," says Malone. "I can insult Ron day and night and he would just laugh, like you know what I mean? I would come out and bamboozle Ron, after him singing 'Sonny' and the crowd going wild. I'd come on and cut Ron right down to size."

Malone attributes Ron's straight-man capability partly to the fact that he's simply a good performer all round.

"You can give him any role to act and he'll act it, and be good," notwithstanding that he always had a hand in musical theatre.

"He's done a lot. So he's a good performer. So that was great, and I used to do most of my stuff on stage with Ron. And then Tommy [Sexton] joined, and me and Tommy did a lot of stuff as much with Ron, but we always used Ron. He was a good straight man. We wrote him into all the shows."

Malone says Ron liked being the straight man and, just as much, being the target of humour.

"He would do anything. He's game. And I mean, he was compromised then too, and I had to really work with him to make sure he got his lines right. But he did.

"So, me and Ron, we get along wonderful on stage actually. We were just like that on stage. And we don't really see each other off stage. Our interests are different."

A plethora of the show's segments which aptly characterize the freestyle tone of the production and how the WGB so uniquely combined music and comedy are available on the Internet. One of those classic segments features a bearded, long-haired Ron playing himself, entrapped in a bar by a vivacious female plainclothes RCMP narc posing as a tourist from Regina. Her cover is to decline his gentlemanly offer to buy her a drink. Instead, she convinces him to find her a joint from someone in the joint. When Ron leaves and returns with a jay, he tries to give it to her for free, but she stuffs money into his coat pocket against his will, as she and two accompanying narcs (two boys from the band in narc clothing) nab him and throw him in jail.

In the next scene, Ron appears locked up in a cell next to one occupied by grimy Greg Malone and Tommy Sexton, both in the roles of townie lowlifes who have extreme Newfoundland accents. They cajole and mock Ron about his father, about being a snooty celebrity, and being too good for them. In the scene, all Ron wants is be left alone and to make a call home. They badger him until he produces a couple of cigarettes and then, of course, they love him. When the next scene shows him on the phone with his mom, explaining that he's in jail, his tone-deaf father and senile Nan harp on in the background, creating total confusion and havoc. This episode was standard WGB fare.

Ron says he's never been in jail in real life, although he's apparently come close, even apart from the time he burned down Charlie Freeburn's meadow as a boy.

"Way back when I was young and stupid I got caught shoplifting a Bob Dylan cassette," he admits. "The judge gave me a choice: a $100 fine or ten days in jail. I had stuff to do so I couldn't take the ten days and I paid the fine. But I really wanted to go to jail. Sadly, I didn't. I've never been in jail, but life ain't over yet."

Thankfully, Ron's jail fantasy never did happen.

WGB guitar player and vocalist Sandy Morris says a huge part of the WGB bit involved Greg putting Ron down on stage, constantly making fun of him.

"Ron's kind of a foil for all of this stuff," says Morris. "He was the butt of all the jokes and people love him for it. That's just how the dynamic works between Mr. Budgell, who's Greg's character, and Ron. He's always putting Ron down or making fun of Ron or showing up Ron's gullibility. If you watch any of the shows, you'll see it right away and Ron loves that and eats it right up and plays right into it and does a really great job. And what I am getting at is he takes direction from that point of view too, in terms of being on stage and under Greg's hand."

Ron's had more than his share of being the butt of the joke off-stage too.

"On the last tour, Boomer, the drummer," says Malone, "oh my God, Boomer is the funniest person. If I was ever writing a sitcom, I'd have Boomer in the room to come up with one liners and lines."

It's almost as if he should have been in the CODCO company.

"Oh my God. He's like the frog in the box," says Malone, referring to the *Bugs Bunny Show* cartoon in which the seemingly closed-mouth frog in the box is really a dynamic, dancing and singing entertainer replete with top hat and cane.

"*Hello my honey, hello my baby!*" sings Malone, mimicking the famous animated frog.

"Boomer would do any character on stage. He'd do a nun, a woman, anything he'd do, and he'd do a great job on them. He's a tremendous actor. A tremendous straight man. So, we were in Gander. Ron was with his girlfriend and stuff. He bought a whole bunch of shoes, right? He had these gorgeous new boots. He just loved them, and so we were off at the hotel, and Boomer took them and hid them the day before, the night before we left. Ron got down to the lobby in the morning, asking Boomer if he'd seen them. He asked the three of us, Boomer, Whitey, and me. We were sitting and Ron came over and complained about the boots."

According to Stamp, Ron was going on and on about how he'd paid six hundred bucks for them.

"That's three hundred bucks a foot," Stamp taunted him. "You're losing it man."

"Boomer was so straight," says Malone, "that me and White burst into laughter. I couldn't believe how straight Boomer was. He was so good he had me convinced.

"He's a better actor than I ever was. So me and White tried to keep a straight face. Finally, as we were leaving, he dropped Ron's boots on the ground."

Stamp teased Ron about his clothing on more than just a few occasions.

"I'm glad he stopped wearing the high heels and the thongs, you know," he jokes. "I remember he bought this jacket, I think down in Nashville. Jeez, the man was walking around in red and black, looking like a bumblebee. It looked like a Michael Jackson jacket, and it was like $900. They saw him coming, you know, that's for sure, before he put that money down."

But Ron was fully capable of getting back at Stamp as well.

The two were playing a pre-Christmas gig one year in front of a small St. John's crowd. Ron had marked "The Man of a Thousand Songs" as the first song off the top of the first set, a song which has a certain pace. Stamp could tell he was in "One of those Ron Moods in which he seems like he's floating. You could see that there was a gap between the floor and his feet," Stamp exaggerates.

As they began the number, Ron turned to Stamp and counted the song in like normal, but then suddenly turned and stopped and told Stamp to hold back the cadence. Ron was pacing the song from its norm to a slow crawl, which for a drummer is terribly off-putting, especially in front of a crowd at a live gig.

"The song was so slow, I could have went home and came back and the song would still be going. I was going to choke the life out of him. He didn't realize how close to death he came. I don't know if Ron had trouble enunciating the words and that's why he wanted it slow, or if he was just plain out of his mind, and that's why he wanted it slow, or if he just wanted to start a fight with the drummer, and have death by drummer."

Of course, it was all about creating hilarity.

On the point of acting, according to Malone, Ron's use of substances never got in the way of his ability to perform whether as straight man or singer or musician.

"Well even when using and stuff, he did a good job. He always delivered performance wise.

"For the reunion show a few ago, and I was doing some older bits getting him up, the new and old stuff. And I said, well, what about that line? Oh and he knew everything. He knew more than I did and it was mine. I did it every night. I don't have that kind of mind, but Ron remembers all the lines from all the shows. He can remember all the lines from all the scenes we did. I can go into the middle of the scene and Ron will give me the next line.

"He just knew all the scenes. He knew all the lines that me and Tommy did because he listened to it every night, and he would just go ahead. So if we missed a line, he'd be on it. Oh, he's got quite the brain. He's got quite the brain."

It truly is amazing how Ron can remember endless reams of lyrics. He can recall practically anything he's written on the spot.

"Plus Ron's a good guy," said White before his death. "He's a great guy. I'm the one who named him the poet laureate, even though he's not official but I call him the Poet Laureate of Newfoundland and Labrador. Ron is it. He's got a great turn of phrase. His lyrics are fabulous; his melodies are great. He's a great writer. He's done a lot of writing. Ron too is a bit of a crossover because he's done lots of theatre shows too."

Ron's growth as a performer was linked to the hundreds of rooms and stages he'd played. As time went on and the WGB faded into the distance, he became, more or less, in spite of periodic accompaniment, a one man grand band.

In the early 1970s, he began in earnest performing in public by singing soft ballads in loud bars. Then it was the full WGB. And in his final years, the agenda turned to his amazing compositions—back to many of them being soft ballads—in loud bars and small stages across Canada.

Malone and others would agree that as his ability to perform matured, Ron learned to use virtually anything in his life as part of his act. Because he was such a great storyteller, he knew how to take advantage of whatever situation he was in to add to the legend or myth or whatever, so when he contracted cancer, he did not hesitate to use it. This doesn't mean in a self-exploitive or stupid or bad way. He used it on stage, and would use anything else that came to him to frame a story or to frame his story because his performances were his story. It was his life on stage in front of you and in his songs, his yarns, his banter, his jokes. He knew how stage craft works. He learned which shtick worked best with audiences and he would use them over and over and over again, like his frequently used line that he'd only recently discovered that there are two eight o'clocks in one day, poking fun at the unorthodox lifestyle of a musician. Ron had a valise full of these lines that he could repeat over and over again no matter where he went. He loved repeating the one, depending on the makeup of the audience, that he says originated with Boomer Stamp, that goes, "Do you think it would be abnormal if one of your testicles was larger than the other two?" With that one he got a laugh, or at least a nervous snicker, every single time.

It's like Abbott and Costello doing their famous "Who's on first" sketch or the

Smothers Brothers routine where Tommy complains that "Mom always liked you best," a routine they've been performing since the late 1960s. Such techniques are rooted in American burlesque. It's like Henny Youngman saying, "Why, take my wife, please." These routines always work no matter how many times you hear them simply because the comedic timing is beyond perfection. Repetitive comedy that works every time is the highest standard of effective comedy. Ron had become so adept at being the straight man for the WGB that, at some point, he actually developed the ability to be the straight man for himself.

Ron was more than a performer and straight man for the WGB and in his own stage role just being Ron Hynes. He had true-blue thespian blood pulsing through his veins along with those other addictive narcotics. Not surprisingly, most of his work as an actor goes back to music. In 1977, he starred as the famous Newfoundland songwriter Johnny Burke (1851-1930) in a musical called *The Bard of Prescott Street* in St. John's. And well he should have, for the parallels between Burke and Ron are striking.

Burke was a St. John's balladeer, and a number of his songs, including "The Kelligrews Soiree," are folk staples across the island. Burke's father, a sealing captain, would have been away from home much of the time. While Burke wrote as a poet and for the stage, he became best known for writing songs that immortalized contemporary events or personalities. And like Ron Hynes, Burke was a member of a prolific songwriting and performance community that included T.M. Lannigan, James Murphy, Michael Power, Johnny Quigley, and Johnny Quill.

Given their childhoods, their singing and songwriting parallels, their ability to work across genres, and their involvement in a wider community, the comparison between Burke and Hynes is truly uncanny.

Eleven years after portraying Burke on stage, Ron played the lead role in *Hank Williams: The Show He Never Gave*, both in Ottawa and in St. John's. Ron had an obsession with Williams and his alter ego, Luke the Drifter, and was equally obsessed with creating his own. Later, Ron had a principal role in the feature film *Secret Nation*, winning the Genie Award for best song with "The Final Breath."

THE GIRLS AND THE STYLE

RON'S INTRODUCTION TO GIRLS MAY HAVE very well began when he received an SS Stewart Archtop model, which Gibson made for a short time, from his travelling father.

"I learned Beatles songs to impress local girls, who could sing along and loved doing it," said Ron. "Everybody wanted stardom then and they all knew the lyrics. The Ferryland/Calvert area had several good girl singers and I went out with every one of them."

Ron immediately learned that playing guitar and singing was a sure-fire bet for attracting members of the opposite sex. According to Sandy Morris, being the lead singer of the band meant he was guaranteed to entice loads of girls.

"Mr. Popular, right!"

According to Morris, Ron was not just predictably popular as lead singer, but he was a legitimate "babe magnet," the guy with true curb appeal which every band needs.

"Ron was our ticket to tail," says Morris. "That's a quote from the Grand Band show."

Morris says it wasn't all about Ron, however, and in fact there was a little competition going on within the ranks of the WGB. Boomer Stamp was the other babe magnet, Ron's closest competitor, or vice versa, depending on who you talk to.

"He had Jordache jeans and long hair and the physique and all that stuff," Morris says of Stamp. "He was the drummer and just the coolest guy," says Morris.

But in spite of the natural competitiveness, the guys got along really well.

"A little competition, and a little collaboration sometimes," Morris insinuates. Whether this simply means they acted as one another's wingmen or engaged in three-ways remains unsaid. One can only use one's imagination given the wildness of the times and the antics of the WGB and the whole culture, really the subculture, that they were part of or even partly responsible for forming in St. John's.

While Stamp was prancing around in his Jordache jeans, Ron was developing a style that is really all his own. His lifelong affection for hats, scarves, boots—really clothing of all types—is linked to his desire to attract women's attention.

"He likes clothes," said Greg Malone. "He likes new shirts, new cowboy shirts, and new pairs of boots."

Ron's love for cool and different clothing could be seen in his daily attire, not just as part of his onstage persona. He would shop virtually anywhere, but one of his favourite places to go was William L. Chafe and Sons on Water Street in downtown St. John's. He was as loyal there as he was at O'Brien's Music, just a few doors down.

Derek Chafe thought of Ron as a good man. Chafe is a latter-day member of the family who've been operating out of this store (as their website says, "On one of North America's oldest streets") for more than eight decades. The family did business with Ron for many years and even displays hats in a niche called the Ron Hynes Corner, an area showcasing fedoras and similarly styled headwear. Ron's preferred fedora typically had a slightly wider brim, almost a western look. Chafe estimates Ron must have bought between sixty and seventy hats there over the years, all of various colours but of similar style. It's not that Ron was hoarding them. Given that he wore a fedora almost all the time, most of them simply wore out.

"We get a lot of people in looking for Ron Hynes hats. We'll point up to them and show them, and they'll always chuckle and remark, 'Geez, that's Ron right there,'" meaning the style of hat.

Chafe talks about how Ron was extremely loyal to the store for a very long time. He was always around looking for some new hat or other apparel, so he was top of mind with the staff. When something came into the store they anticipated he would like, they would even put it aside for him.

"We'd see him twice a year for sure on hats. But he loves the boots too and the blazers and sports coats. He likes all that. We deck him out whenever we see him. He's very distinct in what he wants, and he knows he can usually find it here."

Malone thinks the way Ron dressed made him popular, not just with women, but with cowboys and other musicians.

"They like the boots. They are all very boot fetish-like."

And Ron also had a penchant for scarves, which he would wear as traditional around his neck or bandanas which he liked to wrap around his forehead; there was a little bit of the pirate in him.

Girlfriend Susan Brunt spent lots of time and fun shopping with Ron. She tells the story of an incident only Ron could have gotten away with.

"We were on tour together and in New Brunswick and Ron loved to shop, so we stopped at a local mall for something. I turned around and there was Ron sporting a pair of rubber boots with the most garish and tacky picture of horses on them. He was beaming and thought they were everything.

"But I couldn't stop laughing, and he was completely bewildered as to why. I didn't exactly think they were an amazing fashion statement. These boots were really, really, really ugly."

Ron's and Brunt's love for shoes made them known amongst friends for their outstanding collections.

In 2012, Brunt had to undergo some unexpected surgery. The day she was to go receive her results, she was extremely anxious. To kill time, she and Ron were wandering around The Bay in downtown Toronto and of course they gravitated toward the shoe department.

"I saw a pair of boots I loved and Ron kept saying, 'Get them Suzy. Get them,' but I was too overwhelmed by the day to make any decisions. About two weeks later I came home and Ron was there. A suitcase was sitting on the floor and Ron said to me casually from the kitchen, 'Can you check in that suitcase? I think I left something or other in it.' When I opened the suitcase, there were the boots I had admired in the store."

The hat and boot and scarf themes fit too with the fact Ron loved old westerns to the point that he could closet himself away for hours on end to watch them. From Malone's perspective, it's the fabric and the texture of westerns which appealed to Ron, movies like the old Sergio-Leone-directed 1968 classic spaghetti western *Once Upon a Time in the West*; so pure and realistic you'd swear you were inside the celluloid. The classic westerns not only had an effect on the creation of Ron's wardrobe, but they also helped shape some aspects of his creativity.

"I love stealing from film," said Ron.

He quotes Oscar Wilde, who said, "Talent borrows, genius steals" or "Talent imitates, genius steals" or "Talent invents, genius steals," depending on which source you read.

"Every now and then I'll hear a line of screenplay and I'll drift away from the film completely and start writing in my head based on what was just spoken in the film. Books too, magazines, or some chance remark. Whatever, but mostly film. I love to steal from film."

Another inspiring film from Sergio Leone was *My Name is Nobody*, starring Henry Fonda. To Ron, the line is also linked to the way people introduce themselves at AA meetings: "My name is…and I'm an alcoholic." It was also linked in Ron's mind to Legion, the demon of Gadarenes, referenced in the gospels of Mark and Luke which describe an incident in which Jesus meets a man, or men, possessed by demons who, when asked what their name is, respond, "My name is Legion, for we are many."

Although there could frequently be a serious or meaningful source of origin to Ron's song writing, he was not above having or poking fun at his own material. Boomer Stamp would be one to precipitate such humour, but just as often it could be Ron himself.

"We were at The Ship [a popular downtown pub] one night," says Stamp, "and I was just in the back room and I'm humming away and I was singing 'My name is Noseworthy.' So, low and behold, we had a few drinks, we got up on stage and it just came out of him. 'My name is Noseworthy.' He cursed me that night. It just came out of him. I had it burned in his brain."

My name is nobody
I'm a weary traveller out upon a lost highway
I come all the way from hell with this tale to tell
Like many here before me
Longing to be set free
My name is nobody

And I am lately blessed
I heard a voice that cried out inside the wilderness
When I awoke, my heart and soul were in in despair
Like a sailor lost at sea
No ship to rescue me
My name is nobody

So I take it one day at a time
I walk the hard line
Above this blessed sod
And I'm still living with this fear
But I'm still here
With all these children of God
My name is nobody
I'm a weary traveller out across a lost highway
Every night as I lay down I say a silent prayer
That morning light will find me here
Without this cross to bear
My name is nobody

So I take it one day at a time
I walk the hard line
Above this blessed sod
And I'm still living with this fear
But I'm still here
I'm still living with this fear
But I'm still here
I am still living with this fear
But I'm still here
With all these children of God
My name is nobody

O'BRIEN'S

RON ALSO HAD A LONGSTANDING OBSESSION with O'Brien's Music on Water Street in St. John's. And no wonder. The place is connected to everything in Ron's life that matters most: one of the guitars he first learned to play was purchased there by his Uncle Thomas 'Sonny' O'Neil, a 1962 Gibson 375 J50 ordered from the Gibson guitar company catalogue. There came a later point when Sonny had decided to sell the guitar, which took Ron off guard.

"When I heard Sonny was selling the guitar," said Ron, "I was disturbed, as it was the instrument I'd learned to play on and had been in his possession for many years. My mother was aware of how much I wanted the guitar kept within the family."

O'Brien's Music had offered Sonny $6,400, essentially buying back what they'd sold many years previous, but Sonny ended up selling it to Ron's mother for $5,000.

O'Brien's is the one place on earth you are virtually guaranteed to find Ron Hynes music and items associated with Ron and his music. And O'Brien's is symbolic, in a sense, of Ron's transition from innocence to adulthood.

"He's been coming in since he was a little fella," says Gord O'Brien, whose storefront is a firm fixture of the city's retail scene and as synonymous with St. John's as towering Signal Hill, you might say. And the love affair between Ron and O'Brien's continued for three of the four generations during which the store has been operating. Their building actually used to be a hotel and confectionary store run by Gord's aunt Ivy. Gord's father, Roy, started the music business when she died.

"The old man used to talk to him," says Gord. "My dad used to talk to Ron all the time."

"Ron was coming in," says Gord, "probably before he was a teenager and he was buying guitar strings, he was looking at guitars, he was talking music with Dad. You know, we just have this common area. So every time Ron came to town, he'd be in chatting it up with Dad. The next thing, he buys a guitar and he's writing songs."

Gord says the longevity of the relationship probably has to do with the personal relationship, the personal touch, which the O'Brien's do their best to offer.

Gord and his son, Mike, had a lot of time for the boy from Ferryland. You might say that at times they had a barter system going on with Ron and at other times they would buy CDs from him for cash. Normally with local artists, the O'Briens would accept CDs on consignment. Once the first ten were sold, they'd take in another ten. But when Ron went in and put his hands on the counter, he'd say, "What do you want?" And the O'Briens would respond with, "Well, what do you got?" This back and forth could take place whether it was for a book or DVD or CD, because they could never predict what Ron might have.

"The last batch that we got from him, we actually opened all the CDs and had him sign every one of them, and then we dropped the price."

Dropping the price, of course, is counterintuitive to normal retail activity. Typically an autographed book or CD would go at a premium. According to Mike, however, Newfoundlanders are gung ho on having things wrapped and packaged, even though the world is going towards non-packaging.

"So, it's fairly simple, but that, to tourists or the music industry, is worth a lot more wrapped and that's his newest album that we have," he says, pointing to a new release. "But there are three or four other older CD's that we are still getting calls about that we cannot get any more. And if we can't get them, and Ron can't get them, then they are probably un-gettable."

Sometimes Ron would just randomly arrive at O'Brien's with five CDs in his hands. They could be loose in a bag, which was emblematic of Ron's sometimes disorganized life. And there was no such thing as calling Ron or getting in touch with him as you would with other people. Instead, according to Mike, "You would send the word out on the street and it would just get back to him."

Sort of a St. John's way of sending out an all-points bulletin.

If the O'Briens really needed some replenishment materials, they would send out messages through Sandy Morris.

Anything on O'Brien's shelves or showcases with the name Ron Hynes on it will sell.

"Guaranteed. No matter what year it was released or even the one *11/11* which Ron produced years ago with eleven Newfoundland women doing eleven Newfoundland songs. I'm still getting calls for that today. And that's been gone off the market for twelve or fifteen years."

Morris played on *11/11*, which he personally considers to be Ron's greatest album. "That's the whole concept," says Morris, referring to the eleven women and eleven songs. "In fact, I went up on my own to play on *11/11*. There was no budget. But it was, as far as I'm concerned, it was the strongest writing of Ron's career. Notwithstanding 'Sonny's Dream,' 'Atlantic Blue' and all the stuff that he has done completely on his own that have been really fantastic tunes, but the collection of those eleven songs were just brilliant and I thought the high point of his career."

All eleven were co-written by Ron and his wife, Connie, who is from and currently lives in PEI.

Morris talks about the album which includes songs like "Maybe She Went Crazy," which he believes is about one of Connie's relatives. A song called "Picture to Hollywood" is about Connie's aunt from New Brunswick who sent her picture off to Hollywood when she was young because she was a pretty girl. She kept waiting for the reply which never came.

Ron considered Connie to be perhaps his greatest collaborator, both in music and in life. In the MacGillivray feature film, *The Man of a Thousand Songs*, he talked about how she was the best thing that ever happened in his life and that he still had a hard time computing, after years of separation, that he wasn't still with her. The two spent eighteen years together.

Gord O'Brien says it is a simple case that Ron's music appeals to the masses because of the themes he wrote about, themes people can associate with, like events that actually happened, communities, and people.

"The man is a myth, a legend. There's a lot of stories, but a lot of them I don't want to tell you."

Even when pressed, Gord will not relent, except about the relatively innocent story of Ron coming in to use their phone. Reflective of the fact that the O'Briens, like everyone else, could never reach Ron by phone and that he was so generally disorganized, he would sometimes arrive in their store and ask to make a few calls on their phone. They saw it as exciting whenever Ron came in, because they never knew what he was going to do or say. Or if he was using the phone, everyone would wonder and make a lighthearted game of it, as in, "Who is he calling? Who knows?" The O'Briens never really knew. It could be long distance to Tokyo and they didn't care, because they loved him and he'd only be there for five or ten minutes and be gone again.

While Ron would often drop by to either buy or sell, he would sometimes appear just to be social.

"He could be buying strings, checking on stock," says Mike. "Sometimes he would just open up the door and say hello. Or just wave to us. That is probably when he would be on his way to Billy's to get his cat or something and say hi to us."

"A lot of musicians have a little running tab here with us," says Gord. "They'd stop in on the way to a gig or a concert, get a couple sets of strings, picks, or capos or whatever. So, Ron had been picking up some goods over a period of time, I can't remember now because it was too long ago, and he owed us a bunch of money, and he came in one day, and he said 'Gord, I still owe you money?' 'Yeah, you owe us, you know, $100 or $150 or whatever it was.' 'Oh God,' he said. 'I got no money on me now,' he says, 'would you take some records for it? The Wonderful Grand Band?' I says 'Yeah, sure'. So he brought in three boxes of LP records for me to sell."

It wasn't long before they were all sold and gone.

"So he was happy. He got his debt paid. He got his receipt. I was happy. I got my money."

" I love my audience
but sometimes
that gets me in trouble."

RON HYNES

PART III

THE TROUBLES

CRAZY

I FOUND OUT FIRSTHAND THAT RON HYNES was crazy.

I learned firsthand and from others that he was crazy talented. That he was crazy about writing songs, that singular thing he most lived and breathed for. But I also learned firsthand that, at times, he could be just plain crazy. And I learned that it had to do less with Ron's normal nature than with what substances might have been flowing through his veins at any given time.

This book does not overstate the things Ron said or did. Rather, it tells it just as it was, which he was fully cognitive of from the get-go. Some readers may take offense at the degree of candor, feeling that he is being biographically attacked. But there is no malice involved. In fact, it was hard not to become wrapped up in and learn to like Ron Hynes. He grew on people in a manner that is irresistible, which is one reason why he had, and still has, so many loyal, loving fans and friends. But rest assured, he and all of his accompanying alter egos could, in one way or another, be absolutely crazy.

Ron liked to talk about his alter egos or that there were actually three of him. There was Ron, the human being who lived on the planet; there was Ron Hynes, the performer, the man with the act; and then there was the dark, troubled creature who always wanted to be in charge, who was impossible to deal with, who took over everything. Ron would say he had to get that third person under control because it was he who wanted to kill the other two Rons. This is pretty close to how Ron's nephew Joel described his uncle— that the figure who was The Man of a Thousand Songs was always the addict talking, the figure who continuously told Ron that he was not sick, even while he was trying to kill Ron. One voice in the film, *The Man of a Thousand Songs*, talks about Ron's inner turbulence as being required in order to play his craft and his art.

Another individual, in an anonymous part of their interview, said that at least ten percent of us are addicts. Ron happened to be one who acknowledged his addiction, owned it, and never glamourized it.

"Just as someone with diabetes lives and dies with it," this person said, "an addict lives and dies with their disease."

It's clear by now that this is not a typical biography, with all the standard "Ron Hynes was born in…," and "Ron Hynes went to this university." This is simply an account of a man who relished saying his "name is nobody," who enjoyed being seen as *out there* and eccentric, who loved to tell stories, and a man completely driven mostly by one singular thing: songwriting. Ron was a man whose life experiences and stories come from some place far, far away from most of us—experiences and stories which are riveting, fascinating, and in some cases, just plain outrageous. Ron Hynes lived only a fraction of his life within the bounds of what most of us would consider normalcy. Rather, he lived most of his life inside the music subculture, what Hunter Thompson referred to as "a cruel and shallow money trench, a long plastic hallway where thieves and pimps run free, and good men die like dogs." And Ron lived parts of his life in the most precarious underbelly of all, the drug subculture. As a result, it was hard to predict which Ron Hynes you were going to get at any given time, depending on the time of day, the place, whether he was performing or not, and his general mental and physical state.

He was an accomplished Canadian songwriter, singer, and musician who, oddly, thought he could just as easily have enjoyed being a Toronto cab driver. Talk about crazy.

As St. John's musician and collaborator Chris LeDrew accounts, he was once told by Ron, "If I wasn't a songwriter, I'd like to be a Toronto cabbie."

He told LeDrew this when the two were driving in downtown Toronto along Queen Street.

"He used to really enjoy weaving in and out of heavy traffic. We were going one place or another, and it was like a game trying to get in and out of the traffic."

"The thing about Ron," says LeDrew, "is that Ron always said, and I think he has said it in interviews too, this is all he's ever done," in deference to his music. "This is his only skillset. This is it."

He didn't spend time fixing anything except the mechanical parts of a guitar. He didn't cut the grass. He didn't punch a clock. He never had a paper route or worked at Tim Horton's or McDonald's. He didn't really finish school. It's not to say he couldn't have. He simply just didn't. He didn't spent much time in the kitchen, except to make Chai tea and to take on what girlfriend Susan Brunt said were his three culinary specialties: two of which were scrambled eggs, which he prepared well and ate often, and mashed potatoes, which he consumed in prodigious quantities because they were so easy to swallow after his treatment for cancer. The other was not something he prepared, but rather bought. He loved buying grocery-store barbequed chickens and sharing them with his dog Iris.

"We were staying with friends in Florida one year and went to the grocery store where he bought an entire chicken as a snack," says Brunt.

The magic elixir of the music underworld could have seized on LeDrew as well, but unlike Ron, LeDrew came to the timely realization that music and music alone would never see him through life. So he went back to clean up his degrees at Memorial University and became an educator.

"Well, I had to go back," he says. "I realized at thirty that this [the music business] was a one-way street," although he still performs as a sidebar to his normal life.

"That life is very neurotic. Very, very unsteady. I found when I finally got away from it I could get a better sense of why Ron was the way he was, to a certain extent, because of the pressures, the daily pressures that come with only having one skillset."

LeDrew says that music is analogous to sports in the sense that the business tends to be more of a young man's game, especially if you don't reach the upper echelons, if you don't become a Rod Stewart or a Bono with a private jet and tons of money.

"When you're twenty-five or thirty or whatever, you can endure anything. You can sleep anywhere. But then you think at a certain point, you don't really want to be living that life, but you find yourself looking back and saying 'Holy shit!'"

LeDrew means you can be trapped in it with no way out, without even recognizing it. This is essentially what happened to Ron, the difference being that Ron needed this life to function whereas LeDrew could not have continued to function in that way.

This is not to say that his life was exactly mirroring Ron's, but his story gives one a sense of the music subculture and where it can lead someone if they're not careful.

"At thirty," he says, "I made a conscious decision, and I feel that it saved my life."

He had experienced a transitional moment. He found himself living in his bathrobe, with no money, writing songs in his apartment, surprised that he even had an apartment.

"I've always argued with people about the whole artist's life, and the artist's life being, you know, people say artists are so sort of neurotic, but because they're artists, I'd always say, half the reason they are neurotic is because they don't work nine to five. They don't get up every morning at the same time. Because human beings, even as pastoral creatures about 200 years ago, they were meant to get up, do this, go to work. After a while, it is finally going to get to you. Then your neurosis can make you creative, but I find there is a certain aspect of that that comes from just, well—I am going to be an artist now and I'm just going to fiddle about."

Ron attended Memorial for a spell, too, in his earliest of days, but after one term in which he did well, he discovered O'Brien's Music on Water St. and took the rest of his student loan to buy a guitar. From there, he "majored in coffee houses," as he said, and never returned to academia except to receive his honourary degree. Instead he quickly found himself busking, sleeping on pool tables, and playing small coffee-house venues. When he walked through the doorway of that first coffee house, he was walking through the looking glass into the world of music, and there was no going back. He had always been a musician and songwriter and that's pretty much that.

HOW THICK IS BLOOD

GREG MALONE SAYS THAT RON DID tell about his past. He did talk.

"I'd get him to talk about the past because that's what I'm into," says Malone, sitting at a window seat of Coffee Matters on Military Road in St. John's.

Malone is a student of what shapes people's personalities.

"All the traumas in your childhood that shape your personality, and what you can deal with and what you can't, and what it makes of you and all that stuff."

And with Ron, as much or more than all of us, family and his past definitely shaped him.

Malone has depth which goes far beyond making people laugh. He is a writer, politician, activist, and philosopher. And he is clean and seems very together. Not a word gets by him that doesn't have a rapid-fire, witty, logical response. He is an amazingly easy, breezy interview. Not everyone, especially celebrities, is. The only challenge was the fact we were sitting in such a public place where everyone, due to his television and other forms of fame, knows him like he's their brother, and stops momentarily to pay brief homage.

Malone is too busy these days being things other than the *Wonderful Grand Band* and *CODCO* comedian: he is a best-selling author, actor, political candidate, and husband. His on-line bio describes him as a "cynic philosopher in the tradition of Diogenes and Lenny Bruce" who is one of the founders of the hit comedy television series *CODCO*, known for his impersonations of George Bush, Barbara Frum, Jean Chrétien, and Queen Elizabeth II. He's won more than a dozen Gemini awards and, like Ron, received an honorary doctorate from Memorial University. But prior to *CODCO*, Malone wrote and performed in a number of shows for CBC Television—including of course *The Wonderful Grand Band*, *The Root Seller*, and *The S and M Comic Book*—and appeared in the film *The Adventure of Faustus Bidgood*. In recent years, he has enjoyed a recurring guest role in the hit series *The Republic of Doyle*.

After the death of his *CODCO* co-star Tommy Sexton in 1993, Malone devoted some years of his life to raising awareness of HIV and AIDS.

Malone met Ron when the two were very young, attending Memorial University. He recalls that they were about nineteen at the time, towards the end of Malone's time at university. They were at friend Jennifer Mercer's apartment where they always collected to attend Sunday mass together. Like Ron and Sandy Morris, and others in his midst such as comedian Andy Jones, Malone had his Catholicism, but went from being an altar boy to being a rebel pretty quickly; he left the church when he was in grade eleven.

"This one evening, we dropped into Jennifer's, me, Sandy Morris, and Whitey, and low and behold, there was Ron Hynes."

Everyone mixed around and kind of knew who everyone was, even though they weren't best friends or anything. Ron might have been there with Sandy, Malone thinks. He vaguely remembers having a discussion that day about backing up Ron's songs because they thought he was the best songwriter around. He was playing at coffee houses and had a reputation for being a songsmith and for having good, solid songs.

What Malone remembers very clearly is that Ron was enjoying himself on some substance. He went to the bathroom, and he couldn't get out. "I think he was on acid or something, but everyone was doing something in those days, right?

"So, Ron was trapped in the bathroom."

Malone and Jennifer decided they needed to save him from being locked in the bathroom. They tried to explain he should turn the door handle this way or that way, but Ron couldn't compute enough of what Jennifer was saying to get the door working.

"You know those handles, you go to the left, then you press a button," recalls Malone.

Malone says that because he and Jennifer were on the opposite side of the door, it was like trying to do something in a mirror, which can be perplexing.

"So I got on the door, and I said 'Ok Ron. It's Greg.' But we had just barely met. 'Calm down now,' I said.

"I went step by step through it: 'You see the door handle. Ok. That's the door.' And he's getting more and more excited, because he's on something. 'To the left, you're gonna take that and you're just going to turn it slightly,' and finally we got him out the door."

When Ron was saved from the perilous bathroom caper, according to Malone, he was like, "Man, we're best friends, right?"

Which of course, since they'd just met, they weren't. But they were about to be.

"Me and Ron were best friends from then on, since I got him out of that bathroom. So we had a good laugh and got him out, and that became the famous story of how I talked him out of the bathroom."

That was the one and only time Malone recalls *saving* Ron's life as it were. But Malone's wife, White, saved Ron's life quite literally by helping him day in, day out during his cancer episode and especially by trying, in 2012, to shield him from the people trying to sell him cocaine.

"That's the one who really saved his life," says Malone of that time.

It's important to understand the context of Malone's own life beyond *The Wonderful Grand Band* and *CODCO* before exploring his relationship with Ron. He was performing at the time of our interview (early July of 2014) in the Shakespeare Festival at the Perchance Theatre in Cupids, a dramatic seaside community just over an hour from St. John's where the first English settlement in Canada occurred in 1610. Modelled after Shakespeare's famous open-air Globe Theatre in London, the venue features some of the province's best stage actors performing both traditional and tongue-in-cheek interpretations of Shakespeare and other classic writers. Malone loves how automatically Newfoundland accents can sound like old-English pronunciation which, of course, is requisite in Shakespeare stagecraft.

He's been busy over the years on a number of creative and political fronts, part of which focused on his own family and early life. The first book Malone wrote came out in 2009, entitled *You Better Watch Out*, an account of his own personal drama of growing up in St. John's. It ends in grade nine, but captures the whole childhood episode of his life in town with everyone he knew. The sequel was going to happen, focusing more on the public performance era—with Ron, the late Tommy Sexton, Andy Jones, Cathy Jones, and Mary Walsh—but was interrupted by the death of a key influence, a good friend and mentor who had led Malone to a wholly different literary theme, a book he wrote titled *Don't Tell the Newfoundlanders*, published by Random House. Malone calls it "the true story of Newfoundland's confederation with Canada," which deals with what Roosevelt and Churchill and Maynard Keynes were up to in Newfoundland. Newfoundlanders, says Malone, were sold quite a bill of goods over the whole Confederation thing.

ONE MAN GRAND BAND

Malone slips easily in and out of topics seriously political or funny. Finally, he arrives at the not-so-funny topic of Ron's family and the fact that his father was often absent.

Ron himself spent time reflecting on this arrangement while walking through his boyhood home in a scene from *The Man of a Thousand Songs*:

> I remember that there was a photograph of her, and she just holding my sister and she was smiling into the camera and she is, how should I describe her? She is drop-dead gorgeous. Absolutely beautiful. And when I think about that photograph to the point where, you know, she marries my father, you know, and has all these kids, and he just disappears from our lives. And she inherits this job of being mother and father to all of us.

According to Malone, Ron got along with his mother, but she wasn't always nurturing. And Ron revealed this as well as he continued his tour of the Ferryland home in the film:

> This was Gary's room, and it eventually became a room that he shared with Keith, and then it just became Keith's room when Gary moved out. And there is a grand view through this window of what was a gorgeous blue spruce that my brother Gordon took a bullwhip to. God he was a bad boy when he was younger. I like this room. This is my mother's room here on the right. And this was my sister Evelyn's room in here. I used to rehearse up here. I practiced a lot of guitar here. I used to stand in front of this mirror right here. Stand in front of the mirror and hold the guitar and try to see how a guitar should be held and how a performer should look like on a stage. I remember being here one day, and I was trying to learn how to play the "Canadian Railroad Trilogy" from Gordon Lightfoot, and Mom came to the bottom of the stairs, and she yelled up at me and said, "Ron, Ron, stop that racket." And it occurred to me afterwards I should have said, "It's Gordon Lightfoot for God's sake. It's Gordon Lightfoot's racket." You know, so it wasn't like there was a great amount of encouragement that went on.

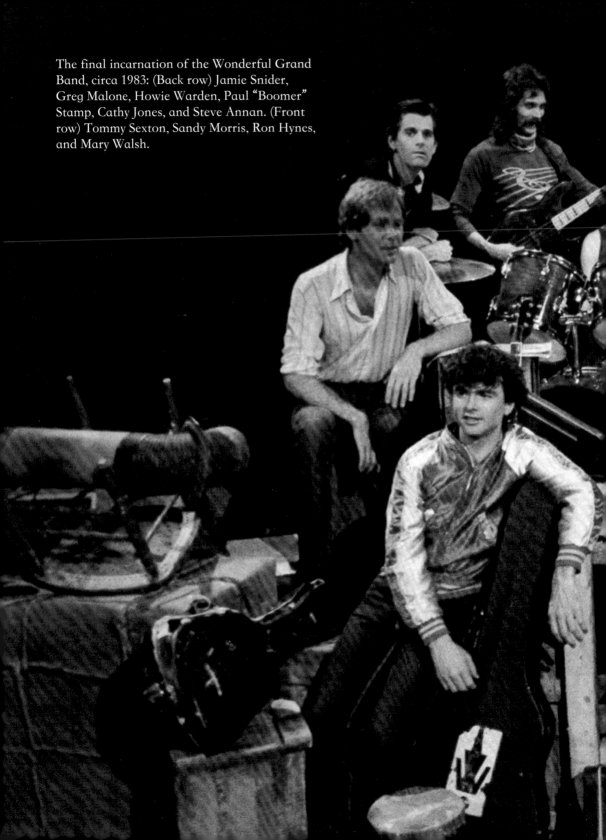

The final incarnation of the Wonderful Grand Band, circa 1983: (Back row) Jamie Snider, Greg Malone, Howie Warden, Paul "Boomer" Stamp, Cathy Jones, and Steve Annan. (Front row) Tommy Sexton, Sandy Morris, Ron Hynes, and Mary Walsh.

Ron's story in the film about the lack of musical encouragement from his mother seems to fairly match Malone's version of how things were. Before he died, Ron said, without being explicit, that he had come to terms with and had forgiven his mother.

During one of my sort-of interviews with Ron, he managed to open up a bit about his father.

"My father was one of the First 500," said Ron, referring to the first men from North America to join with England against Germany in World War II.

"We were the first overseas colony of the British Empire, Newfoundland that is, so they came to us first. My father joined up along with several other men from Ferryland and the southern shore. When the war was over, he opted to stay at sea instead of coming back home. I was never sure if this was his decision or Mom's or something they both decided upon. Maybe she didn't want him home or he didn't want to come back. Who knows? Anyway, he stayed gone for all of our childhood lives, and we were all grown and gone by the time he finally retired.

"I never knew him well, but have always felt that my life mirrored his in that I ended up with a life that took me away from my children as well. I've written several songs about him: 'My Old Man,' 'Be There Christmas Eve,' and a few others that were never recorded. He passed away in March, 2006, after a long fight with Alzheimer's."

Ron wrote more than just *those* lines about his father. He also wrote a pretty mind-bending poem about him. And having learned about Ron, it becomes clear that the mother's lament in his most famous song, "Sonny's Dream," about a sailor who never comes home and pleading with her son not to go away, was never his Uncle Sonny's mother. The entire story is about Ron's mother, Ron's father, and Ron.

Atlantic Canada broadcaster Eric MacEwan has heard the poem about Thomas Hynes from the horse's mouth. Ron's performance of the poem happened in the seaport town Canso, Nova Scotia, while he and MacEwan were attending Stanfest, the Stan Rogers Folk Festival, where Ron was a fixture for several years.

Canso had long been a very busy fishing port, that is, up until the cod-fishery moratorium was announced and as the Newfoundlanders say, "after the arse fell out of her." It devastated the port, and all along the shore fishing factories closed, a tragedy of epic proportions. But the people of Canso and the surrounding area, like their counterparts in other areas of Atlantic Canada, are nothing if not resilient, and created and built the folk festival as one pathway to their survival. It has been voted one of the top five summer music festivals in all of North America, and attracts an audience from around the world by the thousands who wind their way to this tiny coastal town.

Although Rogers hailed from Dundas, Ontario, he spent considerable time around Canso with his aunt and uncles; in fact, it was an aunt who first suggested he write songs that reflected what he saw around him while there, places like Fogarty's Cove, which became the subject of one of Rogers' best known song and album titles.

"This festival was a place that Ron really felt at home," according to MacEwan.

Amongst his many other accomplishments in broadcasting and supporting east coast music, MacEwan considers himself very fortunate to have been a main stage master of ceremonies at Stanfest for most of its nineteen-year history. During the festival, while most attendees parked their trailers and pitched their tents, MacEwan and Ron typically stayed at the only motel in Canso, the Last Port Motel. The two would laugh over the name of the motel as an apt place for two aging men to stay.

"Ron and I would have breakfast together there and regale one another with our tales.

"One day in the motel parking lot, on a sweet summer day," says MacEwan, "he recounted for me a recent trip to Ireland, when he had realized it was the first anniversary of his father's passing and had retreated to a pub for a glass of Guinness and wrote the most powerful poem for his father. Absolutely riveting. And he recited it to me without any notes of course. I only heard it the once and can't wait until he records it."

MacEwan says Ron "performed" the poem right there in the parking lot for him and Father Ora McManus, a colleague of MacEwan's from Cape Breton University in Sydney.

"We were both blown away by his performance in the warm morning sunshine of a Canso summer day."

Ron says the poem came to him several years after he penned and recorded "My Old Man," a cut on the 2003 Borealis label release *Get Back Change*. The poem was written as he sat in three different pubs in Kilkenny on March 1, 2007.

HOW THICK IS BLOOD

Kilkenny in the cold sun
And a year ago today
As the winter's cruel wind held sway
My father passed away
So all day long I think of him
And I go and have a drink for him
And then I have another
And a thought for her, his wife, my mother
It was a military funeral
Flag folded, passed to my younger soldier brother
And he before my mother
And she with eyes of adoration
Hands held in supplication
To you ma'am from a grateful nation
And how he managed that without a tear
I will never fathom in ten thousand years
He the easiest to grieve
Heart forever on his sleeve
All straight, tall and a smart salute
The old enduring warrior's truth
Kilkenny in the cold sun
And a year ago today
As the winter's cruel wind held sway
My old man passed away

The folded flag referred to in the poem was presented to Ron's brother, Keith, the youngest in the family, who'd served in the army as a master sergeant.

"He was in full military regalia at my father's funeral, and when Dad's overseas army buddies did their ritual of flag-folding, they passed it to Keith who presented it to my mother. It was a very emotional moment for me, I do recall."

"My mother raised all five of us," says Ron, referring to his older sister, Evelyn, and three younger brothers, Gordon, Gary, and Keith. "We have little or no contact and even less since my mother passed in 2013. I suppose I could fill this book with my relationship or lack of one with parents and siblings, but what's the point. It's another story and one I need to write myself," which of course, he never did.

Whatever else Ron was prepared to talk about, which apart from music wasn't much, family was not high on the list. This applied to both his family growing up and the family he helped create. From Ron's early home life, to adulthood and himself as a father, he talks sparingly about his own four daughters and what's left of what he can actually call *family*.

In the end, Ron's family consisted almost solely of his nephew, Joel Thomas Hynes, and much further afield, his Uncle Sonny and his four daughters: his youngest, Lily, and differing degrees of relationships he had with the other three girls, including the oldest, Lori, followed by Rebecca and Elena. So there are four daughters in all who survive Ron and who can, if they so desire, find a way to enjoy his musical legacy.

The story of Lori is told for the first time to a camera in MacGillivray's film *The Man of a Thousand Songs*. She was the result of a momentary relationship between Ron and her mother, Marg, and Lori with no idea that Marg's husband was not her real father; living outside of St. John's in a place called Swift Current, Newfoundland, she was raised to believe otherwise.

But like other girls her age, the WGB television show was a point of fascination, especially a certain singer named Ron Hynes. Lori would walk around the house talking about Ron Hynes and humming "The St. John's Waltz."

Finally her mother broke down and told her daughter and then made herself call Ron to tell him there was a ten-year-old girl who wanted to meet him.

"Lori found me on TV," said Ron, a concept that he could hardly come to terms with believing. "I mean, how thick is blood?"

Ron called those ten lost years the sorrow of sorrows in his life, of not having had the chance to be close to her those years. He recalled in the film that the night he received that call from Lori and her mother was the first good sleep he'd enjoyed over all those years. He rewarded her for the lost time by telling his side of the story—how else but with a song?—co-written with Declan O'Doherty.

Sorry Lori

You were the one in my heart
The one from the start
And now that it's all said and done
Who would believe you'd come home
As all the years would pass
I thought I'd never last
It's nice when you come through clean
If you understand what I mean

I'm sorry, Lori
It was all just a big mistake
That's my side of the story
I meant to give I could only take
So I got away scot free
No one could put chains on me
But then you come back to me
clear out of the blue
So I won't put chains on you

I guess you could say we were young
In need of help from someone
And it's true it was wrong for me to run
But it's far too much now to dwell on
Still it's been like a dream sometimes
One that stays on your mind
And though it was so long ago
I only thought you should know

I'm sorry, Lori
It was all just a big mistake
That's my side of the story
I meant to give I could only take
So I got away scot free
No one could put chains on me
But then you come back to me
clear out of the blue
So I won't put chains on you

So I won't put chains
I won't put chains
I won't put chains on you

The fact that Lori never discovered Ron until she was ten years of age, might be why he seemed to overcompensate by doting heavily on Lily, including a stint in 2014 where he paid for her to attend the Toronto Trebas Institute's forty-eight-week entertainment management program, which guides students through many of the legal and other complexities of the entertainment industry, including the oversight of intellectual properties. It was a fantastic idea they shared, which unfortunately did not see fruition; unfortunate since she might have learned to control and manage firsthand where Ron's musical legacy and royalties would end up.

So the concept of family in Ron's world is very limited. One member of the family who more or less hung in there with Ron is his nephew, Joel. Back in the 1990s, Ron was in Toronto, and the two hadn't seen one another for several years. It took Ron's moving back to Newfoundland for Joel to get up the impetus to pursue his uncle. He first saw Ron perform live at The Ship Pub, off Duckworth Street in St. John's, somewhere around 1996 or 1997. He was sixteen at the time.

He'd found out that Ron was living in St. John's and hitchhiked out from the Southern Shore community of Calvert to watch him play. He remembers feeling very anxious about talking to him after the show, experiencing an expectation that he wouldn't be welcome, that he'd be an imposition. It's not like he was meeting Ron for the first time, but certainly it was his first time being in Ron's company on his own, away from the politics of his family. Ron welcomed Joel with open arms and an unconditional loyalty that Joel had never known before.

"I was a bit of a hell raiser in those days, fucked up and angry and depressed and stressed. Always in some kind of trouble, couldn't quite find my footing. Ron became a lifeline for me. He put me to work, lugging guitars and breaking down stages, brought me around everywhere with him, introduced me to the whole town and other towns."

Two years later, Joel was selling CDs for Ron at a show one night in Gander and Ron told the crowd to say hello to his nephew when they had a chance.

"He said I was a really funny guy. That's all, he just said I was funny. But as simple a compliment as that was, it gave me such a boost of confidence. I started to think differently about myself. Then one night sitting around his kitchen table on Queen's Road he asked me what I was planning to do with myself. I said I didn't know and he asked me whether or not I knew I was an artist. And I think from that moment on something was unleashed in me. I was young enough then that I think I needed permission to be a creative person. I mean, I'd been writing for years and I was singing in bands and was a voracious reader, but it all felt like something rebellious I was doing. It always felt like a part of my *fuck you* to the world. I didn't realize that that's who I was or who I could genuinely become. But I think Ron gave me permission to become what I am today."

Joel is still struck today by Ron's early realization that he saw himself as an artist and how he would not turn his back on that realization. Joel observes that growing up in Ferryland, on what he calls "the hockey-crazed Southern Shore," a pursuit of the arts was unheard of or openly scorned at the very least.

Ron admits in *The Man of a Thousand Songs* that it couldn't have been any tougher growing up on the Southern Shore given his distance from his peers.

"I wanted to be Gordon Lightfoot and everybody else wanted to be Frank Mahovlich."

"I can't imagine how stifling it must have been for Ron in his day. But he came out of it uncompromising in his pursuit of the next song. He didn't do anything else or aspire to be anything else. He never had any other job." Joel is no different from Ron in terms of having had any other work apart from being an artist. "I think to this day, other than a very brief bartending gig in a downtown bar, I haven't worked at anything outside the arts myself. And I doubt I ever will, for better or worse. And as complex and heady as our relationship had been over the years, sometimes it scares me to think what might have become of me if that connection with Ron hadn't been there, or hadn't worked out."

In *The Man of a Thousand Songs*, Ron and Joel go back and forth about one another.

> "When he was young from the time he was eleven," says Joel, "he had a one-track mind and it was all music. So, he recognized himself as an artist very early on. He was always this distant character who would show up like a tornado, would get ties and fancy outfits and hats and boots and the whole deal for me. By the time he came into my life,

and by the time I came into his life, he was already Ron Hynes. He already had the Grand Band behind him. Hank Williams. He was with EMI. He was then The Man of a Thousand Songs."

"I just always thought Joel was more my son than he was my brother's son," says Ron. "We are both kind of, you know, the dark horses of our respective families 'cause he seems to be, in the immortal words of my own brother, 'You're just like your Uncle Ron, why don't you go live with him?' So, he did."

And Joel reciprocated.

"It's funny being asked to speak about him in a documentary about him. A part of me is feeling like, yes, now all I can say are all those things on camera that I can't say to his face. You know what I'm saying. With Ron, it's really difficult to break through to the man you want to talk to. I remember I ran into him yesterday on the street, and I had something to ask him 'cause I knew I was coming to do this documentary, and I wanted to say I need to talk to you before I go on camera and talk about you. I want to know what's cool and what's not. And I told him, you know where my fucking heart is. I'm not going to sell you down the river, but I don't want to sugarcoat you. You know, but by the time I got to him and started talking to him, we were standing up in that alleyway, and I realized, God I can't. It wasn't the camera. I've been on camera lots of times. It wasn't that. It was just this awkward thing I knew, I could tell by his energy that I couldn't reach him. So, I knew I had to bullshit to get something out of him, right. We just shot the shit. So there is a lot of that in real life with Ron too. And so you have to build up your defense for yourself. If you're in a position like I am, and the position I'm in is that I love him, and I worry about his health, and his harvest, all that old shit, right? And I want him to do well in the world. Yeah."

HOW THICK IS BLOOD

Family to Ron, for the most part, was a distant concept, like they were a group of people *over there* and that he'd come from some other place. He conveyed the notion that there was nothing he could do about his lack of family connections, that you can't change people. And family, including daughter Lily and nephew Joel, surely felt exactly the same way about Ron.

THE DEVIL

" If crack cocaine and free base won't kill him, cancer doesn't stand a chance. "

PAUL 'BOOMER' STAMP

RON WASN'T EXACTLY ENJOYING THE CRESCENDO of his career in the summer of 2012. He was still writing and recording, but gigs for performers of his ilk were increasingly hard to find. The music business had changed so much over the past few decades; soft-seaters in small concert venues, whether bars or concert halls, threaded together across Atlantic Canada and and the rest of the country, had become the norm, but they were sporadic and the market was limited. There was the odd festival too, but for anyone trying to make a serious living, it had become very tough sledding. Ron's manager, Charles MacPhail, working from his home office in Perth, was taking it on the nose from Ron consistently over what Ron said was MacPhail's failure to find him gigs. MacPhail, however, wasn't having any of it. He would just as consistently put Ron right back in his place on the phone. He was never one to put up with Ron's dramatics. At the end of the day, the two of them were harmonic and could always make well with their world. This was a pattern that went on for years.

In truth, MacPhail was at times more busted up and frustrated over his inability to keep Ron busier and earning more money than Ron was. Loads of Canada's best performers have experienced difficulties finding decent bookings. In Ron's final years, for example, you could walk down Water Street and see a chalkboard outside the Rose and Thistle advertising Ron Hynes performing for just a $5 cover, which, of course, was crazy for a man of his caliber. He was one of the great singer/songwriters in Canada, and you could pay $5 and watch him perform in a half-empty bar. One of the sad truths was that near the end, Ron was taken for granted. It was as though people assumed they could always see and hear him perform some other night down the road.

THE DEVIL

Early in 2012, Ron had been having increasing difficulty with his vocals. The symptoms didn't exhibit noticeably during the CBC Gene Maclellan tribute taping, but increasingly for Ron, certain syllables weren't clear and his pronunciation was off. At first, he dismissed it as a joint condition in his jaw, but when he began to suspect it was something more serious, he went to see a specialist. The doctor discovered a growth on his epiglottis, an area of tissue that's next to the vocal chords.

Ron announced his condition during a show he played at the historic St. George's Church in Brigus, Newfoundland. Then the fear really kicked in as he began treatment.

When Ron was going through his cancer, and was out in Ferryland, it was not a great time. There was a small handful of people who nursed him through his entire cancer episode, essentially Greg Malone, Mary White, and Boomer Stamp.

Malone says that when Ron was in treatment, White was the one who got him through it. She was the one who stationed herself outside his hotel room to keep him away from the coke.

"This was down at the Delta St. John's when he was out of the hospital, trying to get through the chemo and still having to go back for more chemo. He was in pretty hard shape. He had a really hard session of chemo. It was really hard, pushed all these buttons."

Stamp's role mirrored what White was doing day to day.

"When he had his radiation treatment, I'd come and get him," says Stamp. "I just had to nod yes to everything," because Ron was so congested and could hardly talk. When he could utter something, he would call Stamp the biggest prick in the world, and Stamp would just respond, "Yes, Ron."

"Oh, we're brothers, you know," says Stamp, reinforcing how they could get away with almost anything with one another. "I could be away from Ron for a year, but then when you see each other again, you pick it right up. There was never anything angry or hurtful between us. It was always fun. I could blaspheme Ron's songs and make my own lyrics. I do that quite a lot."

The whole treatment process was rough as hell on Ron.

"It was just horrendous," says Stamp.

It began with radiation followed by four rounds of chemotherapy.

"I remember his last chemo," says Stamp. "I didn't go into the hospital to get him, I just waited in the car. And he came out of the hospital door, and reached over and opened the door, and I said 'Get in Chemo Sabe.' And he just sat in the car, he didn't have the strength to tell me to go fuck myself."

According to Stamp, Ron needed that little injection of humour. And he knew it.

When things were at their worst, Ron couldn't eat anything, so Stamp was also making him food.

"He was staying at the Delta, and he couldn't swallow a fly. So I'd be making spaghetti and meatballs, and I'd throw it all in the blender. And just making it mush, and put it in a plastic container or in a Tim Horton's cup, and I'd do the same thing with fruit cocktail. And then I'd take it down where he stayed on the ninth floor. You had like a little kitchen area you could go over to, and he had a fridge there he'd put shit in, and that would be Ron's food, you know. So, all we could do is hope and pray that he'd eat it. Me, White, and Greg were doing this. Because he wouldn't eat much, right, and he had the Ensure, and he had to do this, and he had to drink this orange crap to keep the swelling down.

"So he had a lot of work to do," Stamp says, to try and get his health back. "And he used to let himself get dehydrated and he wouldn't go to the hospital. You had to fucking drag him in, body and bones, you know, and lie to him and say it would only be ten minutes, Ron. And then when I got him in there, they would hook him to a slow dip to get rehydrated. And I would find a movie or a room with a TV and VCR and I'd slip in a couple of movies and we'd sit there and watch them. I'd be watching a movie and he'd nod off, and I'd just try to pass the time waiting for that to end because he was impatient and a bastard to get to go to the hospital.

"It is just brutal and just being in the hospital, of which I'm not a fan, because I went through prostate cancer myself. About five years ago, but I was lucky. I had early detection. I knew all the nurses at the Health Science Centre, especially Suzy Power, who I'm sure, if you saw the woman naked, there would be wings on her because she was definitely an angel."

Power works at the Dr. H. Bliss Murphy Cancer Centre in St. John's where she has been an oncology nurse for fifteen of her thirty years in health care.

"She was Ron's oncology nurse, and she was mine too," says Stamp. "And she is a super human. She has two hearts in her body. Definitely, one on the left, one on the right, you know? She's an amazing woman. Friggin' amazing. It's just how she treated Ron, like kissing him on the forehead. I did well up, you know, just with the care that she had. Yeah, she was a fan, and she loved Ron. She just blew me away with how much she used to phone me and check up and say Ron has to do this, and he has to come in."

Suzy Power, Stamp, White, Malone, the Murphy Cancer Centre doctors, and others got Ron through his treatments. From there, Ron wondered of course if he'd heal well enough to ever perform again.

"To get through it," says Malone, "he went back on the coke, right? Which we think is crazy, but that's how he got through it.

"He had chemo brain, and he was driving without a license. We had to call the cops on him to stop him on the road. We had to get the car impounded to get it out of his hands."

The cops cooperated as much as they could given Ron's driving antics, but given the matter of public safety, they had a limit as to how flexible they could be.

Ron's had more than one run-in with the law since the day he burned Charlie Freeburn's meadow, most of it having to do with cars and driving.

"He asked me to find him a car because he was back on the road driving again, so I found a Volvo for him," says Stamp. "So I'm driving around and I get up to Petty Harbour and I see this one for sale. Nice car. I said, 'Ron, I found a car for you. It's a '95 with low mileage.' And he said, 'I'm going to up and buy it.' So he goes up to this woman, Sherry White, who owned the car, and who happens to be the mother of Ron's nephew, Joel Hynes' child.

"This is the woman that's selling the Volvo. Ron gets a family discount then, right? So he got it for a lot less money than she was asking. And went off with that, and let it rust to death."

With the Volvo rusting away in the yard, Ron then turned around and bought a Buick for his daughter Lily and the Buick sat around and rusted out.

"With the Buick," jokes Stamp, "it was great to look at, but if you stopped fast, the body would just keep going and the chassis would be behind it. That's how much rust was underneath this fucking car. He's a riot."

Then Ron came across a Nissan Frontier down around Witless Bay.

"He liked that truck," says Stamp, "even though it had no dash. So you didn't know if you were going forwards or backwards. There was nothing on the dashboard, right? All the stuff was gone, but it ran. It could go forward or backward, but you didn't know how fast, or how much gas, or how your battery was charging, or any of that information. You could drive it, if you dared.

"He had his own fucking car lot in Ferryland," says Stamp, except during most of that winter, you could hardly see the vehicles for snow.

During this recovery period, when everyone was trying to save Ron from himself, he decided one day, even though he wasn't permitted to drive, to take the Buick on a run (Stamp believes Ron was intent on a drug run) and he got stopped by Constable Danny Williams, which just adds to the story because the constable shared the name of Newfoundland and Labrador's former premier, which Stamp and everyone else thought was just hilarious. Williams let Ron go with a warning. But as soon as he got home, Ron took the Nissan and made another attempt at the drug run. Williams nabbed him again, however, and Ron was issued a plethora of tickets.

"I think he got so many tickets," says Stamp, "that he won a turkey that Christmas Eve," a joking reference to the stereotype of a police association raffle.

Even though he probably set some new kind of record for most highway traffic fines in a single day, including the loss of his license, Stamp says Ron continued to drive after that.

The motor vehicle antics were around the time, according to Greg Malone, when Ron had left the Delta Hotel in downtown St. John's, and White was going back and forth from St. John's to Ferryland with food. She was trying to keep him going physically and sometimes staying there just to keep the drug dealers away in an effort to get him back on track. It went on for months. All the while, White was managing a trust fund that had been built up with money sent from people in communities where Ron had played over the years, including about $10,000 raised in Toronto. People just wanted to help Ron so he wouldn't have to work right away. There was also a large event staged at Mile One Stadium in St. John's, which he actually attended.

"Ron will always go if he can," says Malone. "He likes the scene. He likes the public, really, even though he can turn on his own audience and tell them to shut up when Mr. Hyde comes out. One minute he's Dr. Jekyll, and then Mr. Hyde comes out."

It's estimated that about $70,000 found its way to Ron's trust, which enabled him not to have to work for about a year and to be able to go to Toronto and visit his girlfriend. Surprisingly he didn't spend it all right away on hats and clothes and instruments and drugs.

East coast music broadcaster Eric MacEwan could identify with Ron and his bout with cancer. About ten years before Ron's diagnosis, MacEwan was in the same position, although from a different form of the disease.

"It was swift and brutal and I soon entered the hospital and things were dire and my time on earth appeared imminent," says MacEwan today. The word quickly spread throughout the east coast music community and several benefits were planned for MacEwan, one to be at the Confederation Centre of the Arts in Charlottetown.

A hoard of the region's top musical artists appeared on MacEwan's behalf: Dennis Ryan, Lennie Gallant, Rita MacNeil, Jimmy Rankin, the Barra MacNeils, and a host of others. Ron Hynes was among them.

"I was too ill at this time to attend," recalls MacEwan, "so I and the doctors thought. But, my brother, Allison, was insistent I be there and arranged an ambulance to drive me to and from and have a wheelchair ready for me as I couldn't walk on my own at this point. I was to watch the show from the wings and appear midway through the performance and address the audience and thank them for everything and my special friends there on my behalf. There wasn't a dry eye in the place when they wheeled me onstage to speak."

Ron took the stage at one point during the evening and talked of his long friendship and how MacEwan was the first person to play his music on-air. He then performed MacEwan's favourite song, "Sonny's Dream," to which MacEwan was emotionally overcome.

"Ten years would pass," says MacEwan, "when I got word from Ron's manager at the time, Lynn Horne, that Ron had been diagnosed with cancer of the esophagus, which must have scared him senseless as it could mean the end of his singing career. I dropped what I was doing and hopped on a flight to St. John's and had a friend there drive me to Ferryland. I wanted to let him know I was there for him, like he was there for me.

"I told him I brought him the secret sign, known only by the artists of our time, the true Gods of sand and foam, so he would know he was loved by all of us at home. Ron answered me: 'And I have promises to keep, and miles to go before I sleep, and miles to go before I sleep,'" quoting the immortal words of Robert Frost.

Before long, MacEwan had his chance to reciprocate for Ron's appearance at his Charlottetown benefit with a Ron Hynes tribute planned for Halifax's Rebecca Cohn Auditorium. Stanfest executive director Troy Greencorn asked Eric to perform a monologue for Ron.

"He had the tech crew at the Cohn install a large screen above me on-stage so we could show various pictures of Ron to the audience while I spoke. This was all communicated via social media so Ron could be there vicariously. And so began MacEwan's bit for the benefit.

> I bring you the secret sign, known only by the artists of our time, the true Gods of sand and foam, so you will know you're not alone. You and I have been entwined like branches on a tree, two native sons brought up alongside the sea, and I want you to know how you are loved by so many of us here at home. Come with me to where the river bends, where love begins and never ends. It's time to go and I can't bring myself to say goodbye, so I'll just say, hello, my old friend, so good to be with you again. The woods are lovely, dark and deep, but you, you have promises to keep. And miles to go before you sleep, and miles to go before you sleep.

"The audience was as caught up in the emotional moment as much as I. You could hear a pin drop. It was enough to bring a tear to a glass eye."

The tribute concluded with everyone on stage joining hands and singing "Sonny's Dream."

"It had become," says MacEwan, "a night to remember."

When the trust money ran out, Ron started getting back to work.

According to Malone, White basically saved Ron from himself. "He would not have gotten through, I don't think, if White had not been there." But at the end of the day, Malone says, Ron had to run his own life. "You can't live someone else's life for them and if he is going to kill himself, fill your boots. You know what I mean? You have to make your own decisions."

Along the way and even during the Mile One benefit, people tried to keep the jokes going, even about Ron's cancer, and all that went with it. It was either laugh or cry. Malone adds that, after all, Ron was past sixty when the cancer was found. So if he'd died, it wouldn't have been as tragic as if he'd been younger.

"It's a little before your time," Malone told Ron. "'But you've made your mark. You've done something. You've had a chance. Jesus died when he was thirty-three. What chance did he have?' So we laughed at him of course. So it was fun."

"When I was sick, I really started to believe that I would never do this again and that bothered me as much as the cancer," said Ron. "I've been doing this for thirty years and it's all I know how to do.

"But I guess God smiled on me again."

Ron was referring, as he always did on stage, to the idea that God smiled on him back in Saskatchewan in 1976 when the melody and lyrics for his signature tune, "Sonny's Dream," first filled his head.

The treatment for Ron's throat cancer was successful enough that he began performing again on July 31, 2013, when he took to the stage at Hugh's Room on Dundas St. West in Toronto to play his first gig in over a year.

Contributing editor to the *Toronto Star*, and a host on the Fashion Television Channel, Jeanne Beker wrote a piece on Ron after interviewing him in July of 2013 (truth of the matter is she's a friend of Ron's girlfriend, Susan Brunt). Her piece fairly characterized where Ron's head was in the aftermath of the surgery and recuperation.

> "The thought that I might never sing again was very scary," Hynes reflects. "I kept reassuring myself that I could always continue to write and do other things like film or theatre or whatever. But at the end of the day, I'm a one-trick pony, a performing songwriter. It's the only thing I've ever done and the thought that I'd have to leave it behind and move on to God knows what was becoming a constant concern…I never thought I'd get through it," he admits. "The radiation is just killer. It leaves you weak and useless, and the chemo leaves you nauseated, so they give you steroids to combat that. Those things make you crazy…you try and stay positive. That's all you can do," he says. "But in those moments, at the darkest hour before dawn…well, you just can't help but wonder: 'Will I survive this? Will I live? If I do, will it come back?' Just lying there, knowing you've got this thing living inside you, is terrifying. I'm sure everyone who's ever had it and beaten it lives those moments. They make life all the more precious," he says.

Beker wrote about his back and forth between hope and doubt.

> "It felt like God had given me a second chance," Hynes says. "But again, in the darkest hours, you wonder, 'Did they get it all? Did a few cells slip to your brain? Your throat? Your lungs? Your testicles for Chrissake?!' All my checkups have been good so far. But the radiation does a job on your vocals, so that recovery is still ongoing."

He told Beker he was as terrified in the recovery period as he was when he found out about the cancer. However, he reconciled himself to a degree that if the performing side wasn't possible, then he could at least continue his first love, song writing.

"The songs might be miserable, self-pitying works to begin with, or angry, hate-filled pieces of shite, but I'll get past that," Hynes says. "And nobody will ever hear those songs but me. Ya gotta console yourself somehow. Jeez. But ... let's pray that doesn't happen and my voice holds up."

"It's been a year and the expectation is high," he said to Beker. "So there's the added pressure of that."

Though he'd been working with a Toronto vocal therapist to help him get back to where he was, Ron told her that most of his efforts then were concentrated on just singing "when there's no one around."

"I lost a lot of my vocal strength," he told Beker. "I'm still only good in certain ranges, mostly the high, soft ones. But it's slowly coming back," he says. "So, I look to the future. I'll roll with what comes and learn to live without what doesn't."

There's no doubt that, vocally speaking, the Ron Hynes who emerged from throat cancer was not the same Ron Hynes as before the affliction. Even though things gradually improved and he plowed forward relentlessly, friends and audiences couldn't avoid noticing the difference.

"He's having more trouble speaking than singing, at least that is what I find," says Mike O'Brien, the fourth generation member of O'Brien's Music in downtown St. John's. "What amazes me about him is his will to keep going. I mean, I think a lot of us would probably decide to either give it a rest and see what happens or to give it up all together, or I don't know what, but Ron, he's undeterred."

There were times in the aftermath of the surgery, chemotherapy, and radiation that Ron believed he sang better than he talked. He spent time early on trying to limit how much he did of either until things drew back to normal, which they never really did. He struggled continuously on both fronts. But because it was everything he had, he was overjoyed that he could still perform. He needed to be back on stage. And it was clear he gave everything he had to give.

One of those places he gave it his all was at the Marigold Cultural Centre in Truro, Nova Scotia. He'd played there just a month before I'd pitched the biography project to Charles MacPhail and met Ron. It was an interesting place for Ron to perform at that time, as he encountered others who were confronted with throat cancer.

The centre is an intimate, 208-seat house with state-of-the-art audio-visual support, a venue which forms part of a larger cultural role in the town, including an art gallery and a social calendar that goes beyond concerts. Ron's was one in a series of concerts during the spring and early summer of 2014 which included other artists such as Joel Plaskett, Rose Cousins, and the Sons of Maxwell. Marigold General Manager Al Rosen had just begun in his role.

"When I first got here six months ago, I heard a lot about Ron because they had just booked him. So I didn't really get to book Ron. They had just booked him. I didn't know who he was. In fact, being an ex-banker, I didn't know who any of them were. I loved music, but don't ever ask me who's singing, or who wrote it or whatever. But I was fascinated about Ron because everyone here was excited that he was coming. The connotation was we would fill this place up."

Rosen learned a lot about Ron in a short time: "That he is a living legend, that he has a devoted following, and new fans too. There is a mystique about him; there is a curiosity about him. Everyone knew he had throat cancer. Everyone seemed to know. They wondered what does he look like now? What does he sound like now? They knew something was going on. They weren't sure whether it was drugs, was it alcohol, that there was something else in his life that affected him [besides the cancer], but it didn't bother people. They loved him for the great songs that he wrote and the performances. So we had a crowd that really wanted to find out what's he like now and there were new people in there. The way he sang, he struggled with some notes, but it was so heroic. It was so courageous. You knew something was different. He was just barging right through."

Rosen more or less understood what head space Ron might be in more than most people. He had his own bout with latter-stage throat cancer in 2012, the same year Ron was diagnosed. The minute Rosen had finished his rounds of chemotherapy, radiation, and blood transfusions, he decided to come out of retirement and get right to work.

"The greatest moment was really at the end," Rosen says about Ron's concert. "Everyone wanted him to come out again and do another song. They wouldn't sit down. They wouldn't stop clapping and they forced him out. He didn't really sing another song. He did something really unusual. They got something that they never experienced before.

THE DEVIL

He sat down on the stage, let his legs hang over the edge and he had a heart-to-heart chat with them. He told them how much he appreciated and loved them. Finally, without any musical accompaniment, he rattled off some lyrics, partly singing, partly talking. He sort of did a little toast to everybody: a salute with everybody like hey, I love ya, I always loved ya, I still love ya, and I'm glad I'm here with you tonight. It was unbelievable. It was incredible."

When it was over, people wanted another small piece of him.

"They were in love with him. They waited for him outside. They waited for him to come out."

Rosen knew then and there he wanted Ron back the following year and wrote Ron's manager Charles MacPhail to tell him as much.

"I want him back," he told MacPhail. "I want him next year and maybe we can show *The Man of a Thousand Songs* movie upfront. Maybe we can make a special event of it."

During the show, Ron had taken the time to introduce one of the Eliot brothers, a couple of men who are well-known musicians in their own right in that part of Nova Scotia. One of them was in the audience, another person recovering from throat cancer. Ron acknowledged him from the stage, and Ron acknowledged Rosen because all three of them were recovering from similar health challenges. The next day he wanted to go visit the Eliot brothers at their home in Bass River.

When MacPhail heard from Rosen following the Truro gig, he was equally enthused about re-booking Ron at the cultural centre.

"He communicated with me right away but then asked, 'By the way, do you know somebody who is going to Bass River because Ron needs a lift.' So, I said 'Yeah, I'm going.'"

Rosen wasn't really going to Bass River but decided to fulfill MacPhail's request and make the offer anyway.

"I picked him up, and took him to Bass River. You know, I didn't bug him in the car. We chatted about a few things, but mostly it was silence. He was relaxing. He didn't know me, and I didn't want to be a gushing new fan kind of thing."

I knew immediately what Rosen was talking about, what this drive was like for him. I knew which of the various *Rons* Rosen had driven to Bass River.

ON THE ROAD

AFTER MY EARLIER-MENTIONED BRIEF INITIAL encounter at the Trailside Café in Mount Stewart, PEI—the introduction when I was suffering a cold and Ron was terrified to be within a mile of me—the next time he and I met, we spent some serious time together, me in the role of chauffeur with him in the role of the constantly complaining passenger. I picked him up at Robert Stanfield International Airport outside Halifax with the agreement, through manager Charles MacPhail, to deliver Ron to the charmed community of Chester, on Nova Scotia's south shore, for a concert the following evening at the Chester Playhouse.

After a handshake at the airport arrivals area, I offered to take his guitar or his bag and he looked at me like I should take both. He looked okay, but he was in a nasty mood, whatever the combination of substances was streaming through his body. I can only attest to alcohol and nicotine, two elements not necessarily recommended for a guy on the mend from throat cancer. There's a strong likelihood he was using something harder at the time as well, which according to most accounts was probably cocaine.

The first order of business was to find and deliver Ron to a nail salon. He played guitar with either acrylic or gel false nails on his right thumb and three fingers, depending on which of the two applications he can find while on the road. He was begrudgingly polite at best and I could tell that our three-day sojourn was going to be a mighty test. In my early life as a reporter and my later life as a consultant and facilitator, I've learned how to manage all kinds of people and personalities, but Ron would push me to my limit over the coming days, not to mention in some of our later encounters.

Once in the car, as requested—should I say directed—I Googled and found him the Asian-owned Shades of Pink salon at the Sunnyside Mall in the Halifax bedroom community of Bedford. Even though I was chauffeuring him for free, when I could get him to talk to me at all, it mostly involved an angry rant. He did not want to see my digital tape recorder even though it's a very slim and non-intrusive apparatus. I kept the conversation moving by asking casual, benign questions, trying to get to know him at least a bit. He was terribly reticent to talk, but then he would suddenly say something fascinating, like that he is a huge fan of Hank Williams and Williams' alter ego, Luke the Drifter. Or that he likes watching old westerns, and hearing songs from old westerns like *Cool Water* by cowboy movie star Roy Rogers and his backup singing ensemble, the Sons of the Pioneers. I asked him at strategic intervals to repeat what he'd said and he did to a minimal degree, allowing me to tape him only in fleeting thirty-second bites before scolding me to shut it off. The whole thing was like pulling teeth and was very combative, not a pleasant atmosphere when you're sitting so close to someone in the front seat of a car. Especially a stranger. Of all the interviews conducted for this book, Ron had the least to say on tape. Putting his voice into the book has been, at best, like a patchwork quilt of those short sound bites and scores of e-mails. He told me later about his wider viewpoint concerning interviews (essentially that he shuns them and lies throughout them), although I compartmentalized all of that and convinced myself he was referring to typical media interviews and not so much to this exercise.

"In truth I've never told the truth in an interview in my life," said Ron. "It's just the same answers to the same tired questions. I don't care enough about interviews, and the interviewer is essentially filling a quota and doing the media job. I'm the fodder. I just give them what I know they want to hear so I have the same pat answers for all of them. In reality your best work should be what you're about to write."

But to be clear and fair, as time moved on and as he straightened himself out chemically, Ron grew more and more collaborative, if not giving and generous, in his responses to my questions.

My secret ally—my only reason for thinking at this point that I would stay committed to the biography project—was Ron's manager, Charles MacPhail. His association with Ron was, at the outset, no more intentional than mine, which had stemmed accidentally from the request to include him in the Confederation Centre of the Arts 50th anniversary commemorative book.

"It started in '92 or '93," says MacPhail. "I was a small promoter from the Kawartha

Lakes area who knew of Ron, but very little."

MacPhail certainly had the music and entertainment industry bug, having had a hand in promoting or working with such artists as George Jones, Tanya Tucker, Michele Wright, George Fox, Ernie Toombs as Mr. Dressup, Rita MacNeil, Leahy, Burton Cummings, Lawrence Gowan, Valdy, Blue Rodeo, Long John Baldry, Lynn Miles, and on and on. He went on to be nominated once as promoter of the year by the Canadian Country Music Association, one of fifteen nominated, and he made it to the final cut of five.

"So that," he quips acerbically, "together with a buck and a half, may get me a coffee somewhere."

A Toronto agent that MacPhail had worked with called to see if he would be interested in promoting a Ron Hynes show and sent him a CD. After a few times through, MacPhail loved what he was hearing and contacted a local radio station for their support. They had a show.

"I met Ron and we immediately got along. He had a four-piece band and they were all just fabulous. Fast forward to 2006 with me now living in eastern Ontario. I decided to bring Ron in for another show and another and then another. Ron ended up being unhappy with booking agents, so his manager at the time asked me to book his shows. Then his cancer hit in 2012. His relationship with that manager deteriorated late 2012 and I was elected to take on that role.

"I had never managed anyone before. It's hard enough managing myself, but I have been involved in the industry one way or another since doing my first show at an old farm in Markham, Ontario, in what I believe was 1974."

MacPhail's connection with Ron was partly due to Ron's art, but there was more to their relationship than just the music. There was a bit of Felix and Oscar going on there too, an odd couple kind of yin-and-yang thing happening. Plus, they enjoyed having the odd joint together. MacPhail talks about spending some recent quality time with Ron in MacPhail's backyard where they had a toke or two during a visit when Ron crashed at his place. Ron told him it was one of the most peaceful and beautiful situations he'd been in in a long time. Ron found that while the sea off Newfoundland can perform its magic on one's soul, there can also be something wonderfully soothing about a quiet Ontario backyard in summer, with the heavy, humid air, the manicured lawn and hostas everywhere, bursting with colour, all supported by the subtle delirium of grass.

"My love is of the true Canadian singer/songwriters," says MacPhail, who admits now to obsessing at times over Ron's music. Riding on his lawn mower, resting in his yard, relaxing in his house—wherever he can listen to a playback device—MacPhail will sometimes play one of Ron's songs dozens of times in succession. When a song is audible in the house instead of through a set of headphones, his wife, Brenda, can barely stand the repetition. He tells her, as he does others, that in order to get the fullest appreciation for his artistry, she needs to invest the time to really listen more intently to what Ron is saying through his lyrics and how he brings the lyrics to life. She's not having it, however, having been precariously over-exposed to Ron Hynes as though he were musical second-hand smoke.

There is no getting around the fact, whether he likes to admit it or not, in between the times that he grumbled about Ron's frequent complaining or about Ron's weaknesses in managing his personal affairs, including everything from phone bills to what he owed MacPhail, that MacPhail had become a Ron Hynes fanatic.

Far less fanatical and far more practical is guitarist and frequent Ron Hynes accompanist Chris LeDrew. He begins by comparing Ron being dry (drug and alcohol free) to being dry sometimes with the people around him.

"There's a lot more going on being dry as far as not getting into drugs. Being dry in many ways. Dry emotionally. Ron has been in an emotional conundrum. You know what I mean? People don't quite understand Ron that way."

And neither did LeDrew profess to understand Ron really in any way.

"I think a lot of people would probably feel that way," he says, adding that anyone who says they understood Hynes are probably bullshitting.

"I would never pretend. I've known Ron since '92 or so, but I haven't known Ron consistently since then because not many people get to know Ron consistently for any period of time except, I guess, for family maybe, or musicians that played with him consistently. And they switch up quite a bit. Sandy and Boomer are exceptions to that. Also Glenn Simmons. He's had other people that played with him for good periods of time.

Barry Hilliard played bass with him for a long period of time. Barry was also a bass player, but he was confidante, travel companion, drug partner, you know? They had a relationship that was sort of half musicians' relationship, half friendship, half co-dependency.

"Like I would be comfortable to talk with Ron, but then again, I would not be surprised the times I've seen Ron, he's like 'Hey Chris, how's it going?' Other times I've seen Ron when he's walked right by like he doesn't even know you. And that is what you have to get used to with Ron."

To cope with that attitude in a relationship, LeDrew simply had to learn to ignore him. Eventually, it didn't mean enough to LeDrew to get emotional about Ron's moods and interactions, or lack thereof. Though he used to be bothered by it.

"But now, I see him and I don't expect anything from him. I just know that it is not me he is ignoring. It's just whatever is going on with him. It's not me. I think it is just a matter of everybody being at the mercy of how Ron feels or how Ron is and everyone having to negotiate that all the time."

LeDrew says it was always hard to communicate with Ron, to express anything personal to him. He saw being interviewed as a vehicle toward overcoming that, believing that Ron would be able to read what people had to say about him, which, of course, didn't come to pass.

"I think what you are doing is an important thing," LeDrew told me, in deference to writing Ron's biography.

Like most, he may have had difficulty communicating with Ron at certain times, but according to witnesses and a YouTube recording, LeDrew can do a pretty good Ron Hynes impersonation. At a benefit for Ron during the 2012 cancer episode, he took to the stage and performed a kickass impersonation of Ron. From the hat to the personal mannerisms to an exaggerated rendition of his singing and playing style, LeDrew had him down pat.

The feature-length documentary about Ron, *The Man of a Thousand Songs*, is a no-holds-barred exploration of his creative process, the genesis of his songs, the meaning of performance, and the vulnerability of an artist obsessively compelled to bare his soul through his music.

ON THE ROAD

The world premiere of *The Man of a Thousand Songs* played to capacity crowds at the 2010 Toronto International Film Festival and subsequently garnered Atlantic Film Festival Awards for Best Documentary, Best Director, and Audience Favourite.

The film mostly consists of Ron performing his music (pointedly live for the camera), interwoven with very intimate black-box interviews in which he discusses the songs and the life that informed them: late nights, dark alleys, marriage, children, divorce, his near death and recovery from drug addiction, and punctuated with backstage moments, insight from the street, and Ron's coarse and jagged nephew, author Joel Thomas Hynes, who takes on the role of chorus of the people. When I asked Joel if he would interview for the written biography, he simply responded with a curt but understandable, "I don't know, man. I ain't got much left to say." True enough. Although he finally relented and broke his silence following Ron's death, Joel really had said it all in MacGillivray's film, as exemplified in this excerpt:

> He always had the fact that he was Ron Hynes to save him, right? And he could go here, or there, and be recognized and everybody wanting to buy him a drink and… and you can really get trapped in that whole celebrity aspect of it all too. And there is something else about Ron, whether or not you know he's Ron Hynes the songwriter or not, even if you have never heard of him before, when he walks into a room, or down an aisle on a plane, or wherever the fuck, you'd say "Who's that? What does he fucking do?" But Ron, when he refers to The Man of a Thousand Songs, that's his own addict. That's what it boils down to. In all that addictions jargon, The Man of a Thousand Songs, for Ron, is the addict talking, right? It allows him…it can be defined, and I'm not saying I define it this way, but it can be defined by some as a disease that the very nature of the disease tells you that you are not sick while it is at the same time trying to kill you. And I think he is just misnamed, or given that persona the wrong title, and it is another way of dancing around the fact that he's got a fucking sickness that he needs to take care of.

MacGillivray's film truly does strip down to much of the true Ron Hynes, but as Joel suggests in the film, Ron was an actor and knew full well how to play for full dramatic effect to the camera or on stage, or when he was being chauffeured around the Maritimes by me, his would-be biographer. It's as though he manipulated MacGillivray and the camera; although that might be overstating it. As Joel put it, "It's as if the camera is always on. Do you know? And, it doesn't matter if there is a camera around or not, there is always an element of the performance barrier up. You never know which side of him you're gonna talk to."

Still wondering myself how in the name of God I'd gotten caught up in the idea and pursuit of Ron, I was curious to find out from MacGillivray why on earth he wanted to risk so much more time, money, and personal capital in order to film and produce *The Man of a Thousand Songs*.

"Of course, being a Newfoundlander, I was well aware of Ron," says MacGillivray, "but one night, Terry, my partner and I saw him in a bar in St. John's. We were amazed at how the audience was so fully in his thrall. It took about a year to convince him. And the deal was he had to agree to go the distance or not at all. He went the distance."

It took me a while, although not a year, to convince Ron that his biography was timely and in order. Charles MacPhail, not so. He'd known immediately when I posed the question that it was timely and in order. But in spite of MacPhail's reassurances, and in spite of being Ron's manager, I learned that he couldn't completely manage Ron, as it were. God knows, no one could, least of all Ron. So while in the early throes of taking the project on, I wondered whether he might not bail on me. But I found out slowly, over time, that Ron's word is his word and that once he had finally said yes, I could move forward with the project with the assurance I was not wasting my time and money.

"Ron is a consummate professional," says MacGillivray. "Personal troubles aside, when he is on, he is on. We shot the main interviews over three days. We shot the rest scattered over probably ten days. The hardest part was the edit, constructing the arc of his story. But our construct—using his songs as the spine of the film, weaving his songs with the recollections and comments they triggered—was right on the mark as far as we were concerned. We shot the whole project with that construct in mind."

"I think there is little doubt that Ron Hynes is a master," according to MacGillivray. "He has given his life over to his music. Probably there are times when he regrets this, but he has left a legacy that I think is undeniable. He is the songwriter's songwriter. Never trendy, never really popular in a big way, but some of his songs border on the perfect: 'Godspeed,' 'Atlantic Blue,' '1962,' etc."

There was no movie camera on in my 2013 Highlander as we drove through Nova Scotia and New Brunswick, but you'd think there was.

There was more than one Ron Hynes. This became clear instantly when I met him at the airport in Halifax and during phase one of our little Maritime auto tour. Once he got his nails done in Bedford (with me waiting patiently in the car in the Sunnyside Mall parking lot), I soon found out which Ron Hynes was in the car. It was the heavily addicted, pissed off, self-entitled, ego-inflated, totally broke Ron Hynes. I would come to know the other Ron Hynes, or one of the others—the warm, caring, nice one—at a later stage, but this version was not at all pleasant company. I will admit that in a completely bizarre way, it was, however, entertaining and daring, like bungee jumping or taking on a new extreme sport; this crazy idea of trying to manage Ron Hynes and Mr. Hyde and Jack Torrance in the front seat confines of my car.

I think that early on Ron was under the mistaken impression that I was caught up in his celebrity, from the idea of taking his bags at arrivals to everything else he more or less demanded of me. Certainly he was completely caught up with himself. As he explained honestly, making no apologies or bones about it in *The Man of a Thousand Songs*, Ron defined himself as a "selfish creature" with a "huge ego," but that to do what he does, to get up in front of crowds and bare his soul, you have to have a large impression of yourself. It goes with the job.

He had no sense that over the course of my career as a writer and performing-arts publicist, that I'd interviewed, worked with (and driven around) numerous so-called celebrities to gigs or media appointments, people with strong egos. I think he thought there were stars in my eyes when I'd met him at Halifax airport, but that was certainly not the case.

Over the next three days, he would order me what to do, tell me where to take him, what to buy him, yell at me for wanting to write this bio in the first place, and inform me he has not yet decided whether to cooperate with me or not. There's not a lot of space between the driver and passenger seats in a Toyota Highlander, so when someone is yelling at you, it has a certain in-your-face effect. There is nowhere to go. I somehow found a way to put up a wall which deflected his rants. I must have fallen unavoidably I guess, like Ron's manager Charles MacPhail, under Ron's spell.

Like MacPhail did from time to time—wondering why in the name of God he became involved with Ron at all—I began cycling through the question why in the name of God I'd put myself out on this limb attempting to begin a biography with a subject who basically refused to be interviewed. And crazier yet, why was I driving this guy around the Maritimes when at any minute, he might not agree to this biography project at all?

72 HOURS

EVERYTHING ABOUT THE FIRST 72 HOURS we spent together was about anteing up or paying my dues for the right to take on Ron's authorized biography.

With his new acrylic nails intact, Ron and I drove from the Shades of Pink salon to Chester, where our first stop was the local liquor store. It was late Friday afternoon. We had more than an abundance of lead time for his Saturday night gig at the Chester Playhouse, but with Atlantic Canada's unpredictable weather and flight frequencies, or lack thereof, it's always safest for musicians to give themselves a good bit of travel leeway. I offered to get him something to eat, but he wasn't the least bit interested in food.

With a bagged pint in his hand, I delivered him to the roadside Windjammer Motel, a location too far from Chester proper to walk to a store. The place was no screaming hell.

The front desk clerk, no doubt the owner, welcomed Ron but warned him in black-and-white terms there was to be no smoking in his room or there would be a charge of $200. Ron assured him he would do no such thing. The owner looked disbelieving, to say the least. You could tell instantly there would be more to this story.

After unloading Ron's guitar and bag at his motel room door, I offered again to get him some food, but he wasn't interested in that form of nourishment. I stayed at a coastal resort a little further down the South Shore Highway. Although I didn't need to see or talk to him about anything specific (and he certainly didn't need or care to see me) until sound-check time on the Saturday afternoon, I had this odd feeling that he needed checking up on. But over the next twenty-four hours, Ron went into complete mute mode. I couldn't raise him by phone, text, or e-mail to confirm anything. Manager MacPhail, operating from home, couldn't raise him either and we both wondered aloud to one another if he'd offed himself. He was in a state where anything was possible: he had no money, he was un-enthused about doing this tour, he was having difficulty managing the affairs of his youngest daughter, Lily, who was attending school in Toronto. All in all, Ron was not having any fun in life.

But sure enough, he fooled both MacPhail and myself, and by late afternoon, Ron was up for doing his sound check and needed a drive to the playhouse. The check went okay though he was far from talkative. In fact, the techs at the playhouse would probably attest to the fact it was the shortest sound check in their history. Ron either didn't care or he loved the levels he was getting. He was rude to pretty much everybody, especially me.

As I drove him back to the Windjammer, I offered once again, in spite of my patience running low, to pick up some food. Yet again, he wasn't the least bit interested. There wasn't even a vending machine in sight, let alone a convenience store or restaurant.

I picked him up at 7 p.m. that evening for the gig and as I dropped him at the door, he suddenly seemed changed. He seemed extremely vulnerable. He turned to me in a much softer state and declared that he was as "nervous as hell." He'd had a bit to drink but he was in control. I actually felt for him in that moment, reached out a hand to shake his, and told him he was going to have a great show.

The gig was sold out and Ron performed fine, struggling at times with both his speaking and singing voices as he continued to heal from the trauma of his cancer treatments. Apart from the fact that he struggled with his voice, it was an unremarkable evening. He carried the show off as best he could, but the two couples seated next to me in the theatre remarked to themselves a couple of times during the show about the stress on his voice.

"It is a cruel irony that this singer of songs now suffers from the effects of cancer of the throat," says filmmaker Bill MacGillivray. "But it has not diminished his passion for performance, nor the love his audience continues to offer him. It can be difficult to be in a concert and see him so diminished, but he soldiers on."

Keyboardist Paul Kinsman has experienced a number of people who talked about Ron's voice after hearing him in post-treatment performance. Kinsman says people would say almost anything: "My God what a poor looking man" or things like "I can't stand his voice, it absolutely grates on me."

But as much as people were criticizing what they were seeing and hearing vocally from Ron, there was one area which remained sacred.

"You would never hear anyone say anything bad about his songs, man."

Greg Malone has an interesting way of framing how health and well-being can muster one's ability to do their best work. Not only did Ron keep focused on writing in the aftermath of his treatments and recovery, but according to Malone, he wrote the whole way through his chemotherapy.

According to Mike O'Brien, Ron pushed on, in part, for the money, but it was not just about the money, even though he had to find some way to keep some cash rolling in. "He has to be in front of an audience, I think," he says. "I think it's for him, it's not just financially rewarding, but he kind of needs the feedback and support from the audience."

Truer words were never spoken. Ron Hynes did not live for money. He lived for music.

When I wheeled around and picked him up at the door following the gig, Ron was back in sour mode and just wanted to get back to the Windjammer. I couldn't convince him to eat anything, so now for at least thirty-six hours, he'd gone without sustenance, save for his pint of liquor and whatever smokes he had.

As for the motel room and the cigarettes, I found out a year later in casual conversation with MacPhail that Ron was not welcome back in Chester because he'd not only smoked in the room, but had left burn marks on the furnishings. The owner was furious about it and obviously let the playhouse manager, Erick Vickerdike, know. MacPhail had to pony up the money from Ron's earnings to pay for the damage.

SUNDAY MORNING COMING DOWN

RON HYNES AGREED WITH HUNTER THOMPSON who wrote, "The music business is a cruel and shallow money trench, a long plastic hallway where thieves and pimps run free, and good men die like dogs. There's also a negative side."

He said constantly that he actually hated the music business. I mean he emphatically stated that he really, really, really hated the music business. At that point in his life, at sixty-four, he hated the paltry one-night gigs and a shortage of work. The only thing worse was having no gigs at all because it left him idle and more susceptible to getting into trouble.

"That's never a great time for me," Ron said, knowing full well the evils of having too much time on his hands. "I'm easily lost down some dark hallway."

He talked like he hated the agents. He hated the record companies. He hated the music publishers. He told me he hated the fans, which of course wasn't really true, because he loved the adulation. He just hated stupid fans.

Shortly after his cancer had been diagnosed, Ron bumped into his sister, Evelyn, on a street in downtown St. John's. He hadn't seen her in a year. As they were talking, a fan came up, thumped Ron on the arm, said they'd met two summers previously and asked how he was doing, meaning in regards to the cancer. When Ron told him he was doing okay in spite of the disease, the guy quipped, "Oh well you've already had your kick at the can."

As the man and his wife were walking away, she scolded him, "I can't believe what you just said to Ron Hynes."

But Ron was used to those fans who didn't know where the line was between being a genuine fan and being downright ignorant.

"This kind of thing happens to me a lot, and especially in those years when I was a bad boy," said Ron. "I'd be walking down the street late at night and these guys would come up and start yelling at me."

The man responsible for Ron's booking at the Chester Playhouse had no inkling that Ron felt this way and he certainly had no knowledge of the motel smoking problem at the time I interviewed him.

Erick Vickerdike has been the general manager at the Chester Playhouse for eleven years. The playhouse does a lot of theatre in the summer but in the spring and fall they turn mostly to youth music programs, community events, and touring artists such as Ron.

Vickerdike had booked Ron at the Playhouse once before the 2014 gig.

"He's big. He's big. You know that he speaks for Newfoundland and I don't know if there is any better known musician coming out of Newfoundland than him. Maybe Alan Doyle. They are on the same par. I think he has a sound that is all his own. He loves to perform, he loves to tour, and he connects well with the audiences. I think he can go anywhere in Canada, and people know him."

Vickerdike was happy that Ron was in recovery mode from the cancer and back touring again. The show in Chester was sold out at the second highest ticket price in the Playhouse's 2014 concert lineup, so Vickerdike was not complaining.

For a house the size of Chester's Playhouse, getting the right artist and the right market price is a great outcome for a guy like Vickerdike.

"It's perfect," he says.

Vickerdike wasn't aware at the time, of course, about the Windjammer, and he likely wouldn't ever have known about a minor fan encounter I would witness the morning after his show. Only I knew.

The morning following his Saturday night gig at the Chester Playhouse, I was trying to communicate with Ron via e-mail. We'd agreed the night before, as I dropped him off at the Windjammer, that I'd pick him up at 10:30 Sunday morning for our trek to St. Andrews, a good seven-hour drive through parts of Nova Scotia and New Brunswick, after which I had to turn around and drive back to Prince Edward Island, all in all a long day behind the wheel. At 10 a.m. he wrote to tell me he wouldn't be ready until two. Thirty seconds later he wrote telling me to pick him up at eleven. Twenty seconds later he wrote and demanded I pick him up right away. At 10:30, I entered his motel room to help with the guitar and bag and smelled the stench of cigarette smoke. I knew immediately that we hadn't heard the end of the Windjammer story.

I drove us to Chester's Kiwi Café and parked out front on Pleasant Street. A not so pleasant Ron Hynes sat irritably in the seat next to me. I went in to grab a couple of coffees as a sixty-ish man, one of the foursome sitting next to me in the theatre the night before, was paying his tab at the cash. He was the guy who remarked to his wife and the couple they were with about the strain in Ron's voice, which Ron, of course, had no knowledge of. However, in spite of his comments during the show the evening before, it was clear the man was a Ron devotee. He noticed Ron in the car outside and pointed him out to his wife. As he left the café, the fan tapped on Ron's passenger-side window, wanting a chance to adulate, to thank him for the show he'd put on. But Ron was having none of it. He couldn't bring himself to even turn and look at the man. He simply stared out the windshield. Dispirited and embarrassed, the man slowly shied from the car and walked down Pleasant Street with his wife and the two other friends they'd attended the show with.

As I got into the car, part of me wanted to dump his coffee in his lap rather than place it in the cup holder. I knew then and there, as I turned left off Pleasant Street toward the South Shore's Route 1, that it was going to be a long unpleasant ride to St. Andrews, New Brunswick.

According to frequent accompanist Brian Bourne, some of the fans can really bug the hell out of Ron, especially the people that come up to him and say, "Ron, do you remember me, you played for my graduation, or my wife's coming-of-age party."

"They are actually offended when he doesn't because, you know, they have no sense that he might have met 60,000 people that year and they have no sense of appreciation for that."

Bourne said that at times Ron has been so absorbed with his art that it's been to the detriment of his social life.

"Sometimes he might seem like, well, geez, he don't want to talk to me, you know?" Reflecting back on his time in the band house or the apartment in Ottawa nearly forty years ago, "He was always busy. He was working twenty-four hours a day in his head."

But according to Bourne, Ron absolutely loved his audience, even if it didn't seem so on a hungover Sunday morning in Chester. Bourne insists that at the end of the day, it really was all about live performance for Ron, as it is for anyone else who's a true musician and performer.

"It is with anybody, I think. That's what you do it for. Impress that girl down the street or whatever, you know? Half the show is the audience. It's just a vague human give and take, push and pull arrangement. I think he'd want to play until he's gone."

Ron would have probably rolled his eyes at this comment, even though it's almost certain to be true. Everyone you talk to who knows Ron at all will attest to the fact that it is his songwriting, yes, but performing too, which makes Ron go on.

"I think art has kept him alive," says Greg Malone a year and a half before Ron's death. "It's the art that keeps Ron alive. Otherwise he'd just be another guy destroyed by his childhood, right? Know what I mean? He's not. He has made something.

"You know, he probably would not have survived this long. He's survived this long because he has to get on that stage. He's got to do the thing, and you have to have a certain amount together for that because he loves the words, and he's still trying to formulate what's going on inside of him, trying to, you know, define things and to work out that big problem."

"I think Ron's a survivor," says Malone, "and he's survived art. Art. Art. Oh my God, art. It is like Janice Spence told me one time. She was a great actress. She said—I was thinking of going into politics, or I had been in politics, I was halfway between each, thinking about going back into theatre and stuff, and trying to decide—and she said, 'Well, Greg, art will never let you down.' And it doesn't either. Your friends might, your fellow actors might, but your art will never let you down."

"Politics will let you down, of course," says Malone, a man who knows first-hand because he ran and lost federally.

Over the course of our sporadic talking, Ron basically told me, about three of four times, and he actually said it on stage to the audience in Chester too, that he really hates performing.

"I don't believe that," says Malone. "I think Ron loves performing. I think he'd die without his audience. He only lives when he's on stage. He has no other life. When Ron was sick down in that house down there [in Ferryland] with cancer, it was a mess. His life was messy. He doesn't know how to live other than performing. He doesn't know how to buy groceries, cook a meal, clean a house. He's not that guy."

Even people on the fringe of the true music business understand Ron's need to be on stage.

"He wants to perform all the time," says Mike O'Brien. "You can't stop him from performing. Ever."

Ron had pretty much had his fill of the music business and with silly types of fans, but let there be no doubt, Ron Hynes was still in love with writing songs. He loved the crafting, the symbolism, the fleeting moments of inspiration. More than anything else, he loved reminding me over and over, pretty much any time, especially in the early going of our relationship, that "explanation is the ruination of art." In those first days spent driving through Nova Scotia and New Brunswick, this was tantamount to scolding me with the sense of *why the fuck are you asking me all these fucking questions about my fucking songs*. When in fact, in the supposed role of biographer, that really was the job at hand.

It would take me months to learn that it wasn't Ron Hynes who was sitting in the front seat next to me driving through The Maritimes. It was one of his alter egos—the dark one. The suspicion between myself and Charles MacPhail is that Ron wasn't just hard at it in terms of cigarettes and alcohol, but that almost certainly cocaine was involved. This is not to say he was using, but that we suspected he was; not to suggest for a minute that alcohol can't completely change a person's personality. To say the least, and for what are now obvious reasons, I never out and asked him.

Greg Malone talked about how too many people have been sidelined by coke.

"Everyone's on coke and crack aren't they?" Malone asks facetiously. "Like the whole country?"

Ron, like many of us, has spent a lot of his life drinking, and that's how WGB alumnus Sandy Morris explains their younger days together.

"We spent a lot of time drinking, a lot of time hanging out in bars," says Morris.

SUNDAY MORNING COMING DOWN

"Laughing together and all that. There was a time when we would get up in the morning and phone each other and see what we would do for the day. We were that close. During the Grand Band and shortly after and all of that. Yeah like what are we doing tonight? Do you want to drop down? Do you want to do this or that?"

That was at a time when the drinking and partying was fun. Today, it's not necessarily as much fun or pretty to watch. What seemed funny in those days, at that age, for various reasons, is less funny today, and as often as not, tragic.

As Malone likes to say, one minute Ron can be Dr. Jekyll and the next he's Mr. Hyde.

"He likes the public really, even though he can turn on his own audience and tell them to shut up when Mr. Hyde comes out. When Ron is on the coke, he's Mr. Hyde, right? You know what I mean? When he's not on the coke, he's the good doctor.

"You know, he gets bad," according to Malone. "And then he gets better, he manages a bit better, and then he gets bad again, you know what it's like. Musicians!"

Stamp had seen Ron at this best and at his worst.

"I don't know when Ron fell into that, you know, that prescription drug and this shit, this crack cocaine. But it just pisses me off. Like I get really pissed at Ron, but I don't show it. It frightens me more than anything else.

"I get scared because I know what that shit does, and when Ron lights up that pipe and he has that first rock, and his face turns into Woody Woodpecker and his eyes are…, you know, it frightens me. He's been out at my house and would light up that pipe, and I'd be so freaked out because the paranoia would just go over him like a wave, and he'd be telling me that there are people coming into my apartment through a back room. He used to say there's a staircase out there, and people are coming down there from upstairs. And I'd say Ron, there is only one way into this friggin' apartment, this basement apartment, and he'd be so paranoid. I'd be so pissed off, you know. I'd be frightened. I'd leave."

Stamp can't really say when Ron first encountered hard drugs, but whenever it was, it was from hanging out with the wrong bunch in St. John's.

"When Ron was really in that underbelly of St. John's, I was sort of absent at that time. I wasn't hanging with Ron. I wasn't playing with Ron. I was just aware of his existence down in these bars, you know, late at night running a huge tab for fucking cocaine."

"He seems like he wants to be a dead guy sometimes," says keyboardist and sometimes accompanist Paul Kinsman.

He makes a mild comparison between Ron and an artist named Johnny Burke, who was known as The Bard of Prescott Street.

As Kinsman put it, much more prophetically than he knew at the time, Burke "bought his ticket" and died, but his songs live on. He had often been concerned about Ron in a similar light. It's similar to how guitarist Sandy Morris talked about the once-famous Newfoundlander Harry Hibbs, who had his own show on TV. On screen he looked clean, but he apparently actually drank himself to death. Kinsman says Hibbs sold more than a million records and could have been a millionaire when he died.

The weird thing is that when Ron and all of the guys he was hanging with were younger, he was not the party animal in the crowd.

"Ron wasn't really that much of a party dog like that," recalls Stamp. "He was a gentle soul. He wasn't outgoing, no fisticuffs in a bar, toe to toe and sideways with somebody, you know. I never saw him drink. He didn't drink like I did, that's for sure.

"You didn't see Ron get out falling around drunk. I can't remember any of those nights. That's because I probably passed out long before he got to that point. But you know, lots of good times. He was very serious, and I guess that's why he wasn't partying because he was doing what he does, and writing songs in his hotel room while I was out throwing booze in me, and the rest of us, you know. Ron was probably inspired by and more focused on his writing."

But the fact is that Ron had a significant problem with addiction, a battle he did not hide but rather wrote about in one of his most moving songs, "Dry."

Mary White, of course, loved Ron, but she was not naïve about what he was capable of when he was on a high or on a bender.

"Don't fly too close to the flame," is how she put it, in deference to the scary possibility of becoming quickly absorbed in the alcohol and drug scene, which at times surrounded Ron.

To most, *bone dry* derives from an allusion to the dryness of bone after being left in the sun, of long-dead creatures whose bones have been picked clean by scavengers; typically this image is depicted by the skull of a steer in the sun of a crackling hot western desert. The equivalent phrase is *as dry as a bone*, which we often associated with an alcoholic in sorry need of a beer or a whiskey.

When Ron sang "Dry," you'd swear you were inside his body at the very time when all the toxicity in the world was bearing down on his soul. It is rough and, well…dry. Bone dry. In spite of the rain pouring into his eyes.

The song was written while Ron was in detox in Ontario. He'd been sent to Barrie still juiced up even though you're supposed to be two weeks clean before you start recovery. Innocently, on completing his admission sheet to the Barrie facility, he gave a flawed answer to their first question: How long since he'd last used?

"My reply was, the night before; one last hurrah."

They admitted him anyway. Ron suffered from several addictions, including alcohol, cocaine, and nicotine. It was his lifelong sorrow and he knew it well.

"It's part fiction and part truth," he says, about the requirement to be clean.

"The second night I was there, an old gentleman approached me outside while I was enjoying a thunderstorm: 'Come with me, young fella, and I'll find what you need.' I did not go with him. When he said 'I'll get you what you want or need,' he was probably conning me. He probably just needed money so he needed someone to con. He showed up back at the detox centre about seven hours later. Shortly afterward an ambulance came for him and I took over his room. I heard afterward that he had died."

Ron took over the man's room but fortunately not the same sad outcome. He had been in detox a few times and in recovery twice. "Neither actually worked," he told me. The typical rehabilitation program for alcohol and other forms of substance abuse follows a stream of intake, detox, rehab, and recovery. Most people with alcohol problems do not decide to make a big change out of the blue or transform their drinking habits overnight. Recovery is usually a more gradual process. In the early stages of change, denial is a huge obstacle. Even after admitting you have a drinking problem, most people make excuses and drag their feet. It's important to acknowledge your ambivalence about stopping drinking. Ron freely admitted to everything he'd ever drank or tried.

Bellwood Health Services, a fifty-eight bed facility located in Toronto, is another example of rehab, considered to be a centre of excellence in the treatment of addictions covering the whole gamut from alcohol and drugs, sex, gambling, and eating. Bellwood is based, Ron said, on the twelve-step program and "you have to have that religious bent to you to make it work. I don't. Recovery works for some. It never has for me."

Much more therapeutic for Ron would be writing a song. He wrote "Dry" after taking life-saving treatment to rid him of his addiction.

Whenever Ron sang this song, you could feel the toxicity and dryness in your own bones. He sang it raw and real, like he'd just come out of treatment that day. As keyboardist Paul Kinsman says, "It just tears the guts out of me."

It's a song that was best performed by Ron solo, according to Kinsman. With the band in play, it tended to overwhelm the rawness of his performance.

It was not the voice of God
But was only rolling thunder
I stood outside the detox
And the night was rent asunder
Lightening lit the midnight sky
Rain poured into my eyes

And the morning came
And I said goodbye
I went back into the world
Back into the shadows
Down the darkened alleys
With a disappoint⋯
And I searched out a familiar friend
And he reached out a welcome hand
And we set out to find our
favourite poison

We were dry
We were bone dry
The darkness takes forever to die
When you're bone dry
This highway runs on for a million miles

I knew a man who walked in fields of gold
With the wind in his sails
And the sun on his shoulders
Down the line his heart and soul
It got colder, now he's the windshield king
Now he's the unknown soldier

It was not the voice of God
It was only rolling thunder
I check back in the detox
And I shook my head in wonder
Moonlight lit the midnight sky
I tried to close my eyes
And the morning came
With the same sad surprise

I was dry
I was bone dry
The darkness takes forever to die
And I crucified no longer cried
This highway runs on for a million miles

When your bone dry
Bone dry

When Ron and I left Chester on our way to St. Andrews, it was 10:45 in the morning. There was no *thank you* for the coffee I'd just bought him and no mention of the fan who'd tapped on the car window. It was a lovely, warm, early summer morning, but there was a chill in the car. We headed up Highway 103 towards Halifax in determined pursuit of twelve noon, the time when Nova Scotia's liquor stores open on Sunday. As life would have it, we arrived at the Enfield, Nova Scotia, Atlantic Superstore parking lot at twelve on the dot. You could see the store supervisor unlocking the electronic sliding door. Realizing this was the only way to make Ron comfortable or happy, I went in and bought him a twenty-six-ounce bottle of rum or whiskey (I forget which). I was now biographer, chauffeur, and enabler.

Using a paper cup, Ron enjoyed his drink without any mix and he began to ease back and relax. As we chatted, he began to reveal morsels of thoughts that I needed to record or they'd have been gone forever. He did not want the recorder on, so at several strategic intervals, I asked him to repeat what he'd just said and, in violation of Nova Scotia's distracted driving laws, I turned on the recorder and held it out in front of him. At first, he scolded me for having to have it my way, as though recording his thoughts was an illogical way in which to write his biography. Nevertheless, there were some things he couldn't resist repeating, especially anything to do with his favourite artists, like Hank Williams, Del Shannon, even Paul McCartney, whose Halifax Commons concert both of us had attended a couple years previous. This more relaxed discourse went on as we crossed the Nova Scotia-New Brunswick border.

Then, unpredictably, he became exasperated with me and my questions and flew off into a wild, roaring rant about not really wanting to do the biography project at all, about all the stupid effing agents and managers and anybody else he could deflect blame towards. Of course the booze had seeped in enough that he was now an altogether different Ron Hynes from what I'd so far encountered. He was, as Greg Malone put it, completely trans-formed into Mr. Hyde, only this wasn't some book whose cover I could just close or some movie I could simply switch off.

So I had to intervene and have my say. I forcefully reminded him that I was devoting my weekend to driving him, my money toward gas and liquor, and that it was time for him to trust me. It quietened him down enough for me to persuade him to get something to eat. I was pretty certain he had eaten nothing since before I'd picked him up at the airport on Friday afternoon.

Finally arriving at the Irving Big Stop in Salisbury, NB, I ordered him a hot turkey sandwich to go, got a sandwich I could eat while driving, and headed back on the road. He completely devoured it, practically nibbling on the Styrofoam container, simultaneously sipping now and then from his paper cup. For part of the rest of the trip, he shut his eyes. When he woke, he was more malleable and I reverted back to recording him at small intervals, nothing more than a sequence of thirty-second sound bites which I would later weave into the narrative.

When we arrived at his accommodation for the next few nights, he was still ornery as hell. He was in St. Andrews to play a gig during the annual Paddlefest Music and Outdoor Recreation Festival which was co-founded by Jamie Steel, the co-proprietor of Salty Towers, situated downtown on Water Street. As former director of tourism for the Province of New Brunswick through the 1990s, I'd known Jamie for years, a tall, long-haired, bearded, kind-hearted, latter-day hippy. As Jamie showed Ron through the property and to his room, I could tell Ron was not a happy camper with the place MacPhail had booked him into. Jamie is a good guy, but to say the least, Salty Towers is no Waldorf Astoria. Actually, it's a mess.

But I'd done my bit, including carrying Ron's guitar to his room while he carried his suitcase. It was time to bid adieu.

I spoke to MacPhail during my drive home. We spent most of the time on the phone commiserating with one another over our frustration in dealing with Ron. But at the same time, we were relieved that he was still alive and kicking.

NO SHOW

A MONTH AFTER MY FIRST ENCOUNTER with Ron, I'd gotten over the drive from hell and was in St. John's lining up and conducting interviews for the book with alumni of the Wonderful Grand Band, Alan Doyle, and others. Ron seemed, in his e-mails, to have sobered and softened up considerably, or so I'd thought. So I gambled on the flight, car rental, and hotel costs, plus a week out of my other life as a tourism consultant, to spend more mental and real capital on the book.

The day after I arrived, MacPhail called to tell me Ron could use a drive in from Ferryland for his gig that night at The Ship on Duckworth Street in downtown St. John's. Having failed so miserably to get Ron on tape during our drive from Chester to St. Andrew, I deluded myself into thinking this might be the start of my first real interview. The drive into town from Ferryland would be a fresh start.

I picked him up at the house in Ferryland overlooking the harbour and the archeology site of Lord Baltimore and the lighthouse and the rocks and, somewhere down there, long-dead Charlie Freeburn's meadow. The Hynes house is vaulted up in a way that is best described by Ron's friend and drummer Boomer Stamp.

"His house is on a fucking cliff. And all the lawns there are going uphill. He was telling me once he was going to go out and he was going to mow the lawn, you know. I hoped it was a gravity-defying lawn mower."

I was to drive Ron to his cousin's in St. John's where he was staying over rather than begging a drive from someone all the way back to Ferryland after the gig. After contending with his two dogs and several clumsy attempts to get them into the house, he finally succeeded, grabbed his guitar case and an overnight bag, and got in the car. He was in a state.

He barely said hello, and instead commanded me to head a little further south to the Ferryland post office so he could mail something to manager MacPhail and pick up a parcel. I bit my tongue and had an internal conflict over wanting him to simply get the hell out of the car. I decided to just grin and bear it, all for the sake of the elusive interview.

He wasn't in the post office thirty seconds when he returned to the car with the parcel, which turned out to be from a complete stranger. Wrapped in brown shipping paper, it contained a used fedora which was accompanied by a note. Ron read the note and flipped the hat over and tried it on. It was a fedora, but it wasn't his style. His hats tend to have a wider brim, a cross between a traditional fedora and a western hat. It was hard to tell if he was appreciative of the gift.

On the way into St. John's, he wrangled on about having no money, about all managers and agents being idiots and liars, and continuing still to question the biography. Yet again he wanted no part of any taped interview. It was now weeks into the biography project and it was beginning to feel as though he would never really speak with me. I remember tapping my fingers and thumbs on the steering wheel, feeling pretty close to deciding that I'd come to St. John's for nothing and that the whole project was a waste of time. Shaded in the background, which I knew about through MacPhail, was that Ron had no money whatsoever, to the point where his phone was being cut off.

I dropped him at his cousin's place in the city and briefly met the thin, thirty-ish looking woman who would put him up for the night. Surprisingly, out of the blue, he thanked me graciously before I drove away. Polite as he was as I departed, I was still in the midst of an authorized biography without benefit of an interview with the main subject.

I arrived at The Ship at around 9:30 expecting to see Ron milling about the room, but there was only his guitar on its stand on the stage. The guitar actually looked lonely. Because the guitar was there, it was clear Ron had made it to the pub for his sound check sometime between the drop-off at the cousin's place, around 4 p.m., and now.

Half an hour later, Ron had not materialized. Couples and clusters of friends sat at their tables chatting but also facing the stage for no good reason, staring intermittently at the lonely guitar and anticipating Ron's arrival at any minute. Another half hour passed and people were visibly quizzical, shuffling in their seats, beginning to wonder aloud why they'd paid a cover charge to sit in a pub with only recorded music playing. For some stupid reason, apparently because I'd driven him to town, I began to feel responsible. The girl who'd been taking the cover at the door was looking more uncomfortable by the minute.

After another half hour, customers began to return to the girl at the door, requesting their money be refunded. She complied without hesitation.

The pub's manager was at this point visibly upset, anticipating a backlash from the hundred or so people still waiting in the bar. Most were courteous, a few were completely pissed off, but their exodus was well underway.

At around 11:30 p.m., I e-mailed MacPhail in Ottawa asking if he'd heard from Ron. But to no avail.

Ron never did show up for the gig, telling MacPhail the next day he'd gone for a sleep, slept through, and missed the show. MacPhail and I had spent the night wondering if he was in a ditch somewhere on the outskirts of the city, the result of a cocaine entanglement of some sort, our imaginations running away with us. It's stupid that someone like me, so on the fringes of someone else's life, a passerby really, can become so entangled and concerned. But with Ron I fully admit, it was inexplicably unavoidable. MacPhail nor I ever found out what had really happened that night. We suspect it had less to do with sleeping through and more to do with getting in with a bunch of crackheads.

Missing gigs has never been Ron's thing; although, it's said that he can, at times, be ornery on stage.

"I've seen it go where he's kind of tossed it off and hasn't done very much, like he's left early, you know, done three or four songs, and walked off stage and left people frustrated," says Mike O'Brien. "And I don't know how to explain that, but when Ron decides to do a good show, he always blows my mind because you think he's in a bad mood, he's not sounding very good, it's going to be an awful night, and then he will just pull it out of the water and just be brilliant."

Being legitimately too sick to play has happened, but nothing quite like the no-show at The Ship. A few weeks earlier, Ron had been so sick with a cold, a horrible experience in the aftermath of his cancer, that his ability to perform hit a wall.

"One of the first nights we played [in the late winter-spring of 2014], I gave him the flu," says accompanist and long-time friend Brian Bourne. "We had to cut one of the nights in half. He just couldn't get his breath. And neither could I."

NO SHOW

The abbreviated show happened at the Carleton in Halifax. But unlike the disappointed customers at The Ship a few weeks later, there was an amazing response from the people at the Carleton. "Nobody wanted to refund their tickets," says Bourne. The response was, "Nope, it's okay. We hope he's okay."

"The audience didn't want a refund even though we only got half the show done. People just appreciated his work so much, and they know he felt sick."

MacPhail says that matters with the manager of The Ship resolved themselves. That's the one venue that Ron would book on his own, and things, believes MacPhail, went back to normal.

THE ANGEL

SUZY POWER HAS BEEN A REGISTERED nurse for thirty years and as an oncology nurse, she was on the front lines for a great deal of Ron's care as he went through his treatments for cancer. According to Paul 'Boomer' Stamp, she was Ron's angel.

Power's mother had a love of traditional Irish Newfoundland music, music which was a constant in her family's home and which she generally felt was "annoying." Thank God then, she jokes, that the Wonderful Grand Band came along.

"I was like any other fourteen-year-old girl forming crushes on musicians, wanting to see the world, and wanting my world to be okay or cool in some way. And then along came the Grand Band! Wow!"

Power thought they were the coolest, most gorgeous guys around, not to mention local and fiercely loyal to Newfoundland, making the place she lived better than any other place in the world. She recalls them also making all of the old songs she was familiar with, the ones she was never enamoured with, simply rock.

"Looking back, it was incredible," she says. "I think the boys did more for my generation's pride of place than has ever been recognized. Being from Newfoundland and Labrador, knowing the songs, knowing the references and belonging to that actually gave us a confidence that I'm not sure we would've otherwise. It has consequently impacted other generations of course. My own adult children have a cockiness about Newfoundland and Labrador that would not have been if not for the WGB."

Like thousands of others, Power's love affair with the WGB began with television and then she and her friends started sneaking into bars underage to hear them live.

"Ron's voice always moved me. It was different and sincere and not put on in any way. Even then, there was something about his voice, the lyrics and the manner in which he sang that made people feel connected to him. He seemed to be funny, humble, and familiar, so we all kind of felt like he belonged to us. We were proud of him and protective of one of our own at the same time. I don't remember ever having a crush on him per se, but I've always loved him in a way. He always felt like family to me, even though we hadn't met. I would swoon over some of the others as a teen, but Ron seemed removed from that to me. I believe that's part of his charm; everyone felt/feels like he belongs to them in a way. I feel like that continued, at least for me, throughout the years."

It's not like she was the type of fan who would traipse all over the world—or Newfoundland for that matter—to follow him for concerts and such, but whenever she had the chance, she would go to see and hear him.

"Whenever the stars would line up, I would go to see him. His voice touches me in a way that I find it difficult to describe. His song lyrics always seemed to speak to me and whatever situation I could relate them to. I think that is part of what makes him an amazing artist. Everyone can hear something different in a line and none of it is incorrect."

Power has seen both sides of Ron perform, the side when he is completely on and the side when he's been drunk and belligerent and heart-breaking.

"It was so horrible to observe that I swore I'd never go again. People at the venue then, or on the street the next day, would comment to strangers, 'Poor old Ron' and 'I suppose he's okay.' There was never anger or wanting their money back. It was always pity and worry and wanting to help, like as if it was your brother or cousin who kept trying and was truly a good guy but who kept fucking up."

Guitarist Chris LeDrew says that the remarkable thing about Ron is that even when he's drinking, he can usually pull the show off.

"Yeah, that's like muscle memory from just years of doing that. A lot of bar musicians have that, right? I'm about seven or eight beer in me before I experience any problems at all playing guitar. It's just from years and years of doing it."

But those times when Power has seen Ron perform when he's on, she says that he shines, he's charming, humble, personable, smart, connected, intimate, and "very, very funny." When he was in that state, she felt proud and happy for him. Power says that when he was on, he was extraordinary musically, lyrically, and through his on-stage persona, what she refers to as his "amazing gift."

"Maybe that's why I love him. He has always represented redemption for me."

With Ron, people have a tendency to forgive and forget, like he's family. For some, it's more than they ever would trouble themselves for family.

Manager Charles MacPhail found himself in this situation all the time. One minute he would want to kill Ron for his attitude, his belligerence, and his complaining. But the next, the two could be sitting amid the greenery of MacPhail's backyard, the hostas blooming wildly, and Ron thanking him for the luxury of the peace, the comfort, and the sunshine. One minute MacPhail could be questioning why he ever picked up the phone to talk to Ron at all, and the next he is on his lawn tractor with headphones on, listening to a Ron Hynes recording for the thousandth time, never able to get enough, never hearing the song the same way twice. MacPhail's wife thinks he's insane for it.

"We all have someone in our lives who struggles," says Power. "The difference with Ron and his struggles is that he owns them. He is brave and proud and honest and true enough to completely own who he is. Never any conniving or guile. No deception, ever, in my life experience with Ron. It just is what it is."

Power has seen Ron in many types of venues and met him dozens of times over the years. He could be distracted, friendly, joking, cordial, or sometimes flirtatious, depending on the day. But none of those encounters with her was memorable for him until the summer of 2012, the summer that changed everything in Ron's world.

"One of Ron's frequent jokes on stage years ago was how he'd like to pick up a six-pack of nurses on the way home. I believe he meant no offense. He was just being funny. Well, he got his six-pack all right," by spending so much time at the cancer centre.

Over those thirty-five years working at the clinic, Power has seen it all, the good, the bad, and the ugly. But the day Ron walked in, it took her completely off guard.

One day out of the blue, a colleague on the oncology team contacted Power to let her know that the Ron Hynes whose name was appearing on the new patient list was none other than "our Ron." The friend was just as much a fan as Power was, although her friends and colleagues were aware of her admiration for Ron to the point that she was occasionally teased about it. The guy was rattled with Ron's diagnosis and Power knew she would be too.

"I think we just knew that we needed to straighten up, lose the emotion, and do our best for him, as we would for any other patient."

The coming months would serve as a benchmark in Power's career in health care.

THE ANGEL

"Being Ron's nurse was one of the most precious, blessed things that's ever been laid before me."

After thirty-plus years of Ron Hynes being a present, but distant, constant in her life, he was suddenly inside *her* world, where she would come to know him intimately.

"I would have given a year off my life for it not to be so. I'm not even sure what words can describe the universe being that twisted."

She was confronted with the fact that "her Ron" had contracted a cancer that might affect his voice. She did not want to face the fact that he could suddenly need her that way.

"If he needed me though, there was no way I'd let him down. A lot of the staff felt that way, like we owed him somehow. It was really hard for us, for him to associate us and misery, but it wasn't about us. It never is and it shouldn't be."

Some of those clinic staff, being younger, didn't really realize who Ron was at first, except perhaps having heard of him through their parents. Some others, being mainlanders, hadn't heard of him at all.

Power's professional ethics dictate that she cannot and would not betray the intimacies of any individual's illness. But she does talk generally about his time in and out of the clinic. He was very much like most other patients: just as sick, just as vulnerable, just as courageous, and just as scared. Power says he was genuinely and completely unaccustomed to the world of health care, its conventions and the simple fact, for example, that schedules have to be followed. Scheduling is not exactly Ron's modus operandi.

"And like others, he slipped into a perhaps unintentional pattern of mindfulness, taking one hour at a time."

As he worked through the challenges of treatment, beyond the medical staff, Ron had Greg Malone, White, Stamp, Susan Brunt, and his nephew Joel at his side. According to Power, they supported him greatly and were quite moving in their love and devotion to him.

Arriving at the clinic for his appointments, his swagger and his hat constantly gave him away. Being such a household name and face in St. John's and across Newfoundland and Labrador, and with that signature fedora, he was constantly approached by other patients and families. He wasn't trying to be conspicuous, according to Power. It was simply unavoidable. Unless he was simply too sick at the time to linger, Power says Ron always made sure to spend a few moments with anyone who stopped him to chat.

"I think he was amazed and touched by the amount of sickness and suffering he witnessed at our centre."

Ron's experiences on the cancer ward were remembered two years later, in June of 2014, when he acknowledged the presence of former CBC broadcaster Mack Campbell during a performance at the Trailside Café in Mount Stewart, PEI. Campbell was in serious trouble with his cancer and the prognosis was not good. Within months, Ron managed to find his way back to the island to join Campbell and his wife, Edwina, at their house for homemade Newfoundland-style cabbage rolls, following which he sat and performed his song "Killer Cab" before an ailing but gratified Campbell, Edwina, and two curious cats, Jack and Bitzy, who crawled in and around Ron and his guitar case. The poignancy of the occasion is captured on YouTube under the title "Ron Hynes Private Performance."

Such poignancy was also evident two years earlier when Ron was undergoing treatment for his own cancer in St John's. According to his girlfriend, Susan Brunt, he was sick as hell but nevertheless found a way to be concerned about a fan.

"We were sitting in the waiting room at the cancer centre one day and he could barely sit up," says Brunt. "A gentleman approached him and sat down and told Ron that his wife was there and had a terminal brain tumour. He said that she was a big fan of Ron's and wondered if Ron would mind saying a word to her. Ron initially put him off and then as this fellow walked away, Ron said to me, 'That was unkind wasn't it?' Ron got up, though he could barely walk, and went and sat with this couple for at least twenty minutes, holding the woman's hand and chatting about whatever."

Months after Campbell's death, Edwina talked about Ron's visit and what it meant to her husband. Recognized in 2006 by the Canadian Nurses Association with one of five Order of Merit awards as Canada's Emergency Nurse of the Year, she too is a Newfoundlander who is more than mildly familiar with Ron and the WGB and health care. Edwina talks about how appreciative she is to have spent forty years with her husband, a calm, kind-hearted, popular guy whose name is known in every harbour of the Maritimes because of his long-time journalistic focus on the Atlantic fishery.

THE ANGEL

Mac Campbell was an avid music supporter, especially of east coast music. In his early broadcast years he worked for CHER radio in Sydney, Cape Breton, moving on to Newfoundland in 1974 to work with the CBC. He followed the local music scene there and wrote an entertainment column for a weekly newspaper which featured both known and unknown Newfoundland artists.

"He followed Ron in the early days with the Wonderful Grand Band and through the years," says Edwina. "He loved Ron's music, the lyrics, the great songs and the stories."

She says Mac loved them all as Newfoundland treasures, but his favourite song was "Killer Cab."

Whenever Ron introduced the song when playing live, he liked to talk about his favourite cab company in St. John's, Bugden's Taxi, and how all the drivers always, once realizing who they've picked up for a fare, think they've got the hook for the next possible Ron Hynes composition. Of course the most common gripe amongst taxi drivers involves the condition of the roads. Ron would break jokingly into a mundane melody and lyric about the roads being bad: "Roads are bad, roads are bad. Roads have never been this bad."

Ron wrote "Killer Cab" on a warm rainy day on the third floor of Andy Jones's house on Gower Street in St. John's. Banging away on a Stratocaster plugged into a twin reverb, Ron's second wife, Connie, arrived home from the grocery store and said, "You won't believe the story this cabbie just told me."

"That story is contained within the song itself. I went back upstairs and wrote it in ten minutes. I keep using the same phrase, I know," said Ron, "but when the inspiration's really there it practically writes itself. That guy drove that cab for God knows how many years and I wonder how many times he told that story. It would have stayed with him all his life."

Edwina Campbell has her own odd little connection to Ron by way of her mother.

"At one point in his life, Ron lived down the street from my mother on Campbell Avenue in St. John's. Now Ron is a handsome man and he had a cat named Chester who was even more handsome and charming than Ron if you can believe that! Chester would love to slip out of his own house and wander down to visit my mother, a lover of cats, who always had a meal for him and loved his visits."

Killer Cab

Taxied up and down this town
Since 1954
Wore out ten or a dozen cars
For thirty years or more
Drove the other side of midnight
To the clear edge of dawn
Heard a whole lot of what
wasn't right
And more of what was wrong

Man gets in my cab one night
I'm sittin' at the stand
Slumps down in the backseat
With his face down in his hands
A mumbled out-of-town address
Is his only remark
Until we're halfway out
the highway
And he speaks up in the dark

And he says…
I can find no comfort in this night
O friend, I believe I might have taken
someone's life
I remember screaming, I remember
a front door slam
Don't remember how I got these
stains upon my hands

I drop him at a dirty shack
He's the picture of despair
Can't remember what the meter read
Or if he ever paid the fare
All I recall is a sweet release
I was halfway back to town
There was a police cruiser
with a flashing light
He was flaggin' me down
And he said…where'd you take that last
fare, mister

And there are times I'll hear him
whisper in the night
Whisper friend
I believe I might have taken someone's life
I remember screamin',
I remember a front door slam
But I don't recall how I got all these
stains upon my hands

Taxied up and down this town
Since 1954
Wore out ten or fifteen cars
For twenty years or more
Drove the other side of midnight
To the clear edge of dawn
Heard a whole lot of what wasn't right

And even more of what was wrong

THE ANGEL

Edwina thinks Ron's keeping and caring for Chester was a good character trait.

"Anyone who loves cats is always a fine person."

Edwina Campbell is clearly in the same cat-loving stream as Ron's girlfriend, Susan Brunt.

"I have a cat who likes no one but me with the exception that he loved Ron," she says. "When my daughter got a kitten, my cat was not happy at all and Ron was firmly in his corner and concerned about my cat's welfare."

Ron apparently used to sing a silly song he made up about 'a little pussy cat who lived in the woods, and lived in the woods all day' which he always sang to the cats.

"He really liked all animals and children."

The loop with Edwina's mother was closed when she and Mac and her mother caught Ron's show at the Trailside Café (Mac always went to see Ron whenever he played the island). Edwina says that before the show and between sets Ron treated her mother like she was royalty.

Following Mac's death, the 2015 East Coast Music Awards (ECMAs) were held in St. John's, where he was posthumously awarded the ECMA Stompin' Tom Connors Award for Unsung Heroes. Ron showed up there too to perform a few songs in Mac's memory on Radio ECMA, which Mac had helped establish through his east coast music volunteer work.

Edwina says she knows both sides of Ron—the generous man who would go out of his way for an afflicted friend and the man she acknowledges had spent time on the dark side.

"Ron Hynes has struggled with demons, I am sure," she said about a year before Ron died. Still dealing with her husband's passing, Edwina wished and hoped Ron could continue to make music.

Suzy Power says Ron's sense of humour shone sometimes when he visited the cancer centre for his treatments, especially if Greg Malone showed up with him. The two would get into a silly Abbott and Costello-style routine with the oncology practitioners.

"There would often be seven or eight surgeons/oncologists and others in the room and the introductions would start."

Because both Ron and Malone received honourary doctorates from Memorial University, they sometimes broke into a skit in the personas of Dr. Hynes and Dr. Malone. Ron, Malone, or Boomer Stamp, when he visited, would return to some of the WGB gag lines from the 1980s. For those working at the clinic old enough to recall the show and its style of skits, it proved hysterical.

When Power reflected on Ron's time dealing with his afflictions, she thinks about his songs, but more so about specific lines from songs.

"It seems sometimes that the score to my life's movie could be all his lyrics. That's his talent though, isn't it, how it relates to everyone? Everyone feels that he is part of them. But who does Ron feel he is part of?" she wondered and, it seems, worried.

One thing she knows in her heart of hearts—Ron was the most non-judgmental person she has ever met. Susan Brunt said exactly the same thing.

"We all tend to be a bit cynical and often have fun at another's expense," says Power. "Not our Ron. Never. He will always stick up for the other guy and will speak up to put a stop to gossip and badness. His true character is golden."

Brunt said pretty much the same thing. She liked Ron's intellect, his sense of humour, his kindness and generosity, but it was his complete lack of judgement of anyone which stood out. This quality in Ron was more apparent when he would point out to Brunt that she was ranting on about somebody.

"Suzy, Suzy," he would say to her. "We're all children of God."

Brunt found this terribly humbling coming from a guy who was judged so often.

Keyboardist Paul Kinsman speaks to this side of Ron as well.

"Guitarist Glenn Simmons's wife, Lillian, got mad at me once, for kind of taking the piss out of Ron one day we were talking about him and had a laugh. She said, 'You know what? Ron Hynes would never say anything bad about you!' She kind of stuck up for him. And I think she's right. I don't really recall him saying too much negative about people. I can't remember him saying anything bad about anybody, you know."

By most accounts, this is true. Ron might have been prone to telling you to fuck off to your face for one reason or another, but he wouldn't talk about you behind your back.

"Ron knows the
world's secrets:
that's the art."

SUZY POWER

_____

PART IV

_____

THE ARTISTRY

GORDON, GENE, AND TOM

RON GREW UP WITH AND LOVED the singing of Del Shannon, with that other-worldly falsetto he was famous for, but when it came to combined singer/songwriters, there were only a select few pursed on Ron's lips when he talked about his favourites. They included Gordon Lightfoot, Gene MacLellan, Stompin' Tom Connors, Bob Dylan, and Paul McCartney.

These names were important in terms of Ron's appreciation for music, for their originality, for their sincerity and for their individual sense of genius. There are names in the popular culture of the music business, especially songwriting, who Ron thought were insincere in their approach, who didn't have the genuineness of a Lightfoot or a MacLellan or a Connors. These shall remain nameless or, as Ron insisted, to be shared only between our two computers.

One of Ron's very earliest influences was the legendary Canadian icon, Lightfoot.

"He's inspired more young Canadian songwriters more than any other artist," says Ron, adding that he was captivated with Lightfoot from the first hearing of "Early Morning Rain" from his first self-titled album. "Just a great song. Then there was the next record with a bigger sound and real magic."

Ron recognized Lightfoot, of course, as a great singer and songwriter but also as a brilliant guitarist.

"His twelve-string rhythm guitar was like nothing anyone had heard before, just driving and passionate and spectacular. I've never heard anyone play a twelve-string like that before or since. It is just relentless, like a driving wheel."

Ron first got to see him perform when he was just fourteen or fifteen in Renews, a small Newfoundland fishing town about an hour or so south of St. John's. Given his age, it's somewhat remarkable that he recalled Lightfoot being accompanied by Red Shea (who died in 2008), renowned for playing lead guitar with Lightfoot and for backing the likes of other folk artists such as Ian and Sylvia. The other accompanist was bassist John Stockfish who died in 2012. The concert left an indelible imprint on the young boy from Ferryland who was just beginning to experience the taste of music through his Uncle Sonny during summer visits down at Long Beach and Mistaken Point.

"He was vastly misunderstood by all the locals who'd been raised by country and Irish music," said Ron, "but it was a great night."

The last time Lightfoot played St. John's, Ron had a front row seat and was introduced by Lightfoot from the stage. The two spent some time together backstage and had a photo taken together.

"Someone gave him a copy of *The Man of a Thousand Songs* film for his birthday and he sent me a get-well e-mail when I was very ill with my cancer. In it he spoke of my trials and tribulations and wished me well. He had his demons just like I did and they took their toll on the both of us, but we're both still here and huggin' the spotlight."

One Canadian song-writing icon who is now huggin' the spotlight from further afar is Stompin' Tom Connors, who died in March of 2013.

Shortly after the release of Ron's first project with the EMI label, *Cryer's Paradise*, he received a call from the recording company saying Tom wanted Ron and his wife, Connie, to come and spend some time with him and Tom's wife, Lena, at their home in Ontario.

"He told EMI he wanted a limo sent for us," said Ron, adding that in no way were they to charge Ron for it and that absolutely no way was he paying for it either. They were to also send an EMI representative, which they did.

"Tom treated him [the EMI rep] with nothing short of disdain the entire weekend we were there."

According to Ron, Lena was a big fan of the song "No Kathleen" and several other songs on the *Cryer's* album, so it became apparent to Ron and Connie that it had been through her encouragement that Tom had extended the invitation in the first place.

"It was a really fun weekend."

Connors had a large recreation room on the main floor of his Georgetown, Ontario, house, with all his career memorabilia stored, almost haphazardly, below in the basement.

The recreation room had a horseshoe-shaped bar where Connors sat with a bottle of warm Moosehead lager perpetually in hand and cigarettes smoked through a holder, one continuously lit off the other. A jukebox dominated the room, filled with Stompin' Tom tunes. The coolest thing amongst his collection of Stompin' Tom retail novelties (which includes a large postcard-size piece of Stompin' Tom monogrammed wood with a hole in it from too much stompin'), was the bottle opener which played "The Hockey Song" every time you opened a beer.

"Lena and Connie got along just great," said Ron, "and Tom and I spent the weekend drinking and singing all our favourite songs. His favourite kind of music was actually 'Newfie Country' and he knew all the old country songs from the Nashville rhinestone era, which I also knew through my Uncle Sonny's influence.

"His favourite game was to play a Lefty Frizzell song or a Marty Robbins song or a Hank Williams song. I then had to sing a song by the same artist."

If one or the other of them couldn't think of a song by the same artist, then he had to down his beer.

"Then it went back to him. To my knowledge I'm the only one who ever won that game. I beat him with a Woody Guthrie tune."

The fact that Ron would have beaten Stompin' Tom with a song by an American legend such as Guthrie would have incensed Connors beyond all reasoning. He hated any and all things to do with the US, including, for example, what he considered to be the sell-outs to America by singers k.d. lang and Anne Murray.

"So we were able to match one another song for song and drink for drink. All in all it was a great weekend and I was honoured and pleased to get to spend that time with him.

"I suggested we get together again to look at some co-writing but this never came about."

Connors mentions this in one of his two autobiographies.

"The last time I saw him was at a SOCAN [Society of Composers, Authors and Music Publishers of Canada] awards dinner where he received a lifetime achievement award." Ron recalled Connors' speech as, "It seems that SOCAN would like me to go away, but I've no intention of doing that. I got Gordon Lightfoot sittin' there and Ron Hynes sittin' over there and I've got good friends and lots to do yet so I've no intention of going away."

Ron felt it was ungracious of Connors, but he also recognized that that kind of retort was simply Stompin' Tom Connors' style, always railing against the Canadian music establishment over the years, from SOCAN to the JUNO organization to the recording companies. And it's true. Although there was a genuine folksiness and friendliness to Connors' persona, there was also this omnipresent bitterness. While I was working on that Stompin' Tom commemoration project intended for Skinner's Pond, you never knew which Tom you were going to get during a given meeting or telephone conversation.

Ron experienced this of course too, with Tom complaining bitterly as he had to others privately and publicly about k.d. lang, Murray, George Fox, and others. Connors would not hold back either when it came to expressing his opinions about Ron's music, saying that he liked "Sonny's Dream" and "No Kathleen," but hated the title song on the *Cryer's Paradise* album.

"I genuinely miss him and like him. I fuckin' hate that limp-wristed song Valdy wrote about him. I've been tempted to write one myself but I know his ghost would haunt me for it.

"When we left with excuses for needing to be home, he rejected all of it and more or less told us to fuck off. He enjoyed good company as long as everything was on his terms."

Ron has an innate understanding of Tom Connors, the man, not the brand most Canadians think they know.

"The man had a hard upbringing but knew his audience and succeeded against impossible odds," said Ron.

According to Eric MacEwan, Ron was very much taken with Gene MacLellan's beautiful talent and expressed to Eric how very much he would like to meet the famous island songwriter. The two actually had much in common, not the least of which is that although Ron is referred to as "The Man of a Thousand Songs," he is rather selective and patient about recording his songs, an obsession comparable to MacLellan's, whom MacEwan called the ultimate craftsman.

"I received a phone call from Ron from St. John's," says MacEwan. "He was asking if it would be possible for him to meet Gene for an evening of conversation between two like-minded souls. I said to leave this with me and I'd get back to him."

"Gene was a shy guy and wasn't comfortable around crowds. He loved people but usually one on one. For example, you wouldn't find him seated and having coffee at Tim Horton's. He'd use the drive thru.

"About this time our fledgling efforts to form the East Coast Music Awards was about three years along. It began in Halifax, the brainchild of a wizard named Rob Cohn, a true visionary and extremely passionate and totally eccentric guy, but Rob had it all figured out right to 'the last of a shingle' as the late PEI poet Milton Acorn would say.

"There were about a dozen or so of us hardy souls piecing together like an old quilt the ECMAs with team members from the four east-coast provinces, actually five as we considered Cape Breton separate and worthy of being its own jurisdiction as it contributed so many heavyweight artists whom we looked up to in admiration as models: The Rankin Family, the Barra MacNeils, Rita [MacNeil], etc.

"There were an equal number of women and men on our initial board of directors, one of whom was Sheri Jones who would go on to be the top talent manager on the east coast.

"It was Sheri's suggestion that we needed more top names attending our event held each February in and around Valentine's Day—Rob's idea, as he felt romance was in our music, and as usual, Rob was right.

"Sheri mentioned at our board meeting that maybe I could get Gene MacLellan and Stompin' Tom to come play and be seen to give us a strong profile and attract more people to our event and asked me to look after this. Now, Gene and Tom were probably the hardest to get to leave their nest but I said I would try. It took a couple of months but I landed them.

"Our event had started out at a neat club named The Flamenco, and this particular year we were moving it to a much larger venue, the old Nova Scotian Hotel, now The Westin Hotel, built in the 1930s, a landmark old grand hotel.

"I told Ron to approach Paul Lannon at Air Nova and he would look after getting him to Halifax. We all arrived on a Thursday, the first night of our grand soiree with east coast musicians of all stripes, right in the middle of a winter storm which brought with it freezing rain. I was in the lobby when Gene came through the revolving door and just then the lights went out and all hell broke loose and the board had to meet urgently and come up with a plan. I welcomed Gene, shook his hand and thanked him for being there but I had to leave with my friends to some room where we could work things out. I spied Ron Hynes strolling down the hallway and immediately introduced him to Gene and asked Ron to look after Gene until we worked something out.

"The board and I contacted Nova Scotia Power and explained our situation with so many people arriving and expecting greatness and they prioritized us and had our power hooked up by early evening. Whew! A major sigh of relief swept over us and I went looking for Gene and Ron but couldn't locate them as they had found Tom and were together in his spacious room and stayed up all night long trading songs and stories. Kevin Evans, a superb musician from Ireland who had moved to the east coast and formed Evans and Doherty with Brian Doherty [a duo that is still recording and performing live] was also in that room and he told me he had never seen anything like this before, in the company of musical geniuses, and I missed out on the whole thing.

"At this time I knew Ron was very good but I was too young to realize that he is great.

"When Gene died tragically some years later, the first news came out on CTV National News that night, and when Ron heard this he went to his piano and within ten minutes the song 'Godspeed' came pouring out."

There was a mutual admiration society of sorts that existed between Eric MacEwan and Ron.

"Eric and I have been and always will be great friends," said Ron. "Eric spearheaded numerous artists' careers in Atlantic Canada through his in-home radio network long before there was the Internet. Folks like me, the Rankins, Rita [MacNeil], Terry Kelly, Figgy Duff, WGB, the Barras [MacNeils]—we all enjoyed our first taste of musical and creative notoriety through Eric's radio show. Without him, most of us might not have been heard at all. We all owe a great debt of thanks to Eric MacEwen."

Ron recalls hearing about MacLellan's death and being compelled to write a song in his honour.

"I'd been in St. John's working with Greg Malone and trying to write some work based on Tommy Sexton's career. Connie and my daughter Lily were in PEI.

"For some time I'd been acquainted with a friend from PEI named Bob Stright who was also acquainted with Gene MacLellan." Stright was a Summerside-based sound engineer who'd worked on dozens of recordings for island artists. "He'd visit Gene to say I was on the island or he'd visit me to say he'd seen Gene who said hello." So Ron and Stright had this back and forth. During one of those back-and-forths, Stright mentioned that MacLellan had expressed an interest in co-writing with Ron.

"I was very excited and looking forward to that occasion," said Ron. But two nights after being in St. John's to work with Malone, Ron received a call from Connie who said, "quite simply and sadly" that it looked like he would never get to co-write with MacLellan.

"Though we hadn't been close, we shared a common regard for the music biz," says Ron, "he through his shyness, I through an ever-growing mistrust and disappointment. But his tragic passing led to the 'Godspeed' composition."

MacEwan was correct. Ron had completed it in ten short minutes.

"I always felt that he was very close to me in those few moments, like he was at my shoulder, like that was our co-write."

Ron has since grown close to and is very fond of MacLellan's daughter, Catherine, a singer-songwriter in her own right.

"I consider her a fine songwriter and fabulous human being," says Ron. "The fruit didn't fall far from the tree."

As in his dedication to MacLellan, Ron reflects on MacLellan with the lines, "Godspeed. God bless. Goddamn." But more cleverly, he creates a lyrical connection to MacLellan's gospel-pop song (one of the most recorded and covered songs in the history of the world), "Put Your Hand in the Hand."

Godspeed

Godspeed, Godspeed
Forgive a sweet soul a desperate deed
His was a prison and he was freed
Godspeed, Godspeed

God bless, God bless
What's born out of sorrow or out of distress
Speculation is anyone's guess
God bless, God bless

God only knows
What takes a petal from the rose
What makes the dark rivers overflow
What makes a lifetime come and go

But God damn, God damn
You put your hand in the hand of the man
Must have believed he would understand
Forgive a sweet soul a desperate deed
Godspeed, Godspeed

God only knows
What takes a petal from the rose
What makes the dark rivers over flow
What makes a lifetime come and go

But God damn, God damn
You put your hand in the hand of the man
Must have believed he would understand
Forgive a sweet soul a desperate deed
Godspeed, Godspeed
Godspeed

THE RUINATION OF ART

I'D BEEN DEALING WITH RON HYNES for more than a year. As stated, there was one line he repeated over and over again more than any other, forever dead determined to make his point: "Explanation is the ruination of art."

Whenever he says this, he means he doesn't want to discuss the origin of his songs and the inexplicable origin of his creativity.

"God smiled on me," he told *Kingston Whig-Standard* writer Greg Burliuk in December of 2013. "He's smiled on me since 1976. I was driving down the road and he said, 'I've got a gift for you.' He gave me 'Sonny's Dream.' I asked him if it was a gift to last. He said, 'You're goddamn right it is.'"

This is proof positive that God swears.

Berliuk wrote,

> Indeed, it's impossible to bring up Ron Hynes' name and not mention "Sonny's Dream" in the same breath. The song has been recorded by numerous artists including Great Big Sea, the late Stan Rogers, and Christy Moore, Ireland's most celebrated folk singer. "I wrote it in 10 minutes," says Hynes. "It's partially about me and my mother and father and uncle."
>
> He doesn't want to explain any further. "To quote me: explanation is the ruination of art," says Hynes.

Whenever we discussed doing this book, he repeated what he said to Berliuk: "Explanation is the ruination of art." I've heard this line so often from him by now that I've nearly bought into this theory that no one should dare presume to break down the art of Hynes's or anyone else's songs. That is, I've nearly bought in. For there is a contradictory side of Ron which loves to talk about his musical ideas.

"Song writing should never be explained," Ron explained nevertheless. "Once you know what the work is actually about, it loses its mystery. The song means what it means to the person who hears it. If it communicates something to them that they feel or understand then it works. If not it simply doesn't."

I knew him well enough to know what he meant by this, even though I understood it as a perfectly logical viewpoint. But he couldn't resist talking about his inspirations. And I'm not so sure he was correct that we shouldn't try to understand what makes his melodies and lyrics click. Some of the explanations behind his inspirations are as fascinating as the songs themselves. And there is no doubt his audiences love to know where things come from. It takes us to the line from Leonard Cohen which Ron loved to reiterate on stage: "If I knew where the good songs came from, I'd go there more often."

This whole issue of explaining art takes us back to my first encounter driving Ron from Chester to St. Andrews as Ron scolded me and wondered why he'd agreed to cooperate on this biography at all. "Explanation is the ruination of art. So why the fuck am I doing this? My favourite painter in the world is Gerry Squires. You don't see anyone else's name on the work. It's solitary inspiration, the work of one heart, one mind, one soul."

Though you can't really explain creativity and art, can't really put your finger on it, there's an internal part of art, for the artist, that affects them emotionally, very deep down inside.

"I believe it coming from him, yeah, because he doesn't need it," says Great Big Sea frontman, and now solo performer, Alan Doyle, "especially when it comes to characters and stories, he doesn't need to explain. He never needs to say you shouldn't go to a bar with a girl or whatever. He just tells the story. Yeah. You know, in a way, he's the most visual songwriter."

But this topic is like everything else having to do with Ron. There are always two or more sides: one wanting to hold fast on the *ruination of art* notion and the other loving to let people in on how a movie or a St. John's cabbie or a marine disaster or a simple request from a friend inspired his writing. There are scores of stories about the origins of his songs, but some stand out.

For example, he was asked early on in the careers of the Irish Descendants to write them a song.

"So I wrote 'Leaving on the Evening Tide' for them in a cheap hotel room in Regina during the middle of a tour."

But the story has an unhappy ending. Ron was also recording the album *Face to the Gale* at the time and elected to include the song on that release. The Descendants, meanwhile, intended to call their next project *Evening Tide*—the song was to be their first single from that project and a video was also in the works.

"When my record label heard of this they contacted the Descendants label and put a stop to the whole plan. No CD title, no single, no video. It effectively sent the Descendants back to square one and lost me a good amount of cash and career points. There's the music industry for ya."

When Ron wrote "Dark Angel (The Mother Who Bore You in Pain)," in 2004, he was going into recovery at Bellwood in Ontario. He received a call from his mother, who called to wish him well.

"She said, 'Do this for me if you can't do it for yourself, do it for the mother who bore you in pain.' Then she started laughing at what she'd just said. 'You're writing this down aren't you, you bloody son of a bitch!' 'Yes, I am, Mom,'" he responded.

The song "Carry This Cross" is a Jesus metaphor from around the same time, with Christ basically saying to himself that this is a huge mistake: "I'm not the son of God, just a healer, you got the wrong guy."

"Atlantic Blue," the song which commemorates the sinking of the Ocean Ranger, was not something Ron just pulled out of his hat in some immediate reaction to the tragedy. He had resisted the urge to write something following the event even though the CBC was calling and asking for something.

"Some things are best left till a later date. It's a story that is still unfolding," meaning that the impact on families of the eighty-four men who died are still living out their lives without their loved ones.

It was actually written some six years after the incident. It came to him on much the same kind of a stormy day while sitting in the window of a Bond Street apartment watching the storm evolve through the Narrows (the precarious entrance to St. John's Harbour). It took the whole of a very emotional day to write.

"I was always afraid someone with a son or brother or grandson who was one of the eighty-four would approach me at some point to say, 'Great song, but could you stop singing it. It keeps opening the wound.' Blessedly, that never happened."

Many agree that if that song doesn't make you well up, then you probably don't have a heart. It's been said that it's hard to imagine how anyone who had family or friends on the doomed oil rig can possibly listen to that song. It could only be that it provides them some form of comfort.

Ron's beautiful song "House" was inspired by the work of Stan Dragland, professor emeritus of English at the University of Western Ontario and an author living in Newfoundland, whom Ron credits as the track's co-writer.

"It was written on a flight to somewhere," says Ron. "Lots of the work happens on planes. Perhaps it's a fear that there could be trouble and you haven't written your master-piece yet."

"No Change in Me" was co-written at the home of well-known Canadian singer/songwriter Murray McLauchlan.

"It's about the ex-patriot Newfoundlanders far, far, from home and it's a salute to the singers who have kept a love of their home sacred to them by writing and performing songs that address them and their world far from home."

It was an interesting collaboration considering McLauchlan is not a native Newfoundlander.

"He recorded it long before I did and we have totally different interpretations of the same work." Ron's would emphasize guitar while McLauchlan's would emphasize piano, but the two actually later toured the song together.

THE NEWFIE BULLET

THE *CARIBOU*, AFFECTIONATELY REFERRED TO AS *The Newfie Bullet* by Newfoundlanders, was a passenger train that formerly connected outport and interior communities in Newfoundland with both the capital city and the ferry service in Port aux Basques. Defunct since 1969, the *Bullet* was a symbol of Newfoundland ingenuity and independence.

One of the interviewees for this book said that Ron was affectionately referred to as *The Newfie Bullet*. When asked if this might have been the case, Ron went sideways about the use of the term Newfie as something highly derogatory against Newfoundlanders. "I detest the expression Newfie," he said. "You may as well say nigger."

It doesn't matter to him that the term is less derogatory today than in decades past when it carried connotations of ignorance or stupidity. More often than not, today the term is used in an almost affectionate context and sometimes it's used by expat Newfoundlanders themselves as a means of endearing themselves to one another while living away.

Greg Malone likely agrees with Ron about the use of the term Newfie. In his book, *Don't Tell the Newfoundlanders*, Malone confronts the whole aspect of how Newfoundland was situated in Canada and how attitudes were developed and how they prevailed.

"That book, or what is behind the book, we all knew it. We just didn't have it spelled out. We all knew it. Everyone chaffed on it. Everyone was bitter. Everyone hated going to Toronto. We all went to Toronto as Canadians and came back Newfoundlanders because of the way we were treated, right? We were citizens of the world. We were young people. We were all Canada and the rest of, you know, but we really quickly were put in our place in Toronto about where we were and who we came from. We came back Newfoundlanders. Fuck ye. We came back Newfoundlanders if you don't want us, right? You know?

"And that's what happened in those days. So everything that is in that book informs Ron. It's part of the rage, the dissonance that is going on there and forms all my work.

Cod on a Stick was about our reaction in Toronto. The first CODCO shows were about how Newfoundlanders were treated in Toronto, basically, and that whole divide. And of course, we had a different perspective. I don't think we were any better or any worse, but we were definitely different. You know what I mean? And I like the difference."

According to Malone, Newfoundland's culture was destroyed so that the Newfound-land party would be distributed to Canada and teach Canadians how to lighten up, and how to laugh at themselves, "How to have a joke, and how to treat life like fun, as opposed to an accountant's sheet, you know. Toronto. Toronto the good. That was our…try to help Toronto the good not be so fucking good. And we did it. We did it through culture and entertainment."

Part of which was a phenomenon which came out of the minds of Malone and Hynes and their friends.

CANADA'S DANNY BOY

"DANNY BOY" IS A BALLAD USUALLY set to the Irish tune of the "Londonderry Air." Most closely associated with Irish communities, the song's lyrics were penned by English lawyer and lyricist Frederic Weatherly in Bath, Somerset, in 1910. Weatherly gave the song to the vocalist Elsie Griffin, who made it one of the most popular songs in the new century. And, in 1915, Ernestine Schumann-Heink produced the first recording of "Danny Boy." That's an awfully long sojourn for any song to endure in order to make it into the musical vernacular of any country.

There are various theories as to the true meaning of "Danny Boy." Some have interpreted the song to be a message from a parent to a son going off to war or leaving as part of the Irish diaspora. The song is considered to be an unofficial Irish anthem, particularly by Irish Americans and Irish Canadians. The song is so popular and heart-wrenching in its tone and warmth that it is popular for funerals, even though it is far from liturgical.

Actor and Wonderful Grand Band cohort Greg Malone says "Sonny's Dream" is Canada's "Danny Boy." "It's the 'Danny Boy' of Newfoundland. And not just in Newfoundland, but to a lot of people." Malone says that wherever or whenever you hear "Danny Boy," you're hearing the story of Ireland.

He adds that the song is all about leaving and that hunger for where home is, a universal theme that many cultures have experienced as their story, including the Scottish and the Irish.

"It's true that people can get wrapped up in 'Danny Boy,'" says Malone, "because they love the melody, they love the lament, and because it touches them somehow deep inside. But people dismiss the song's lyrics.

"People don't understand the universality of that. It is astonishing to me that many people have taken possession of that song around the world. It's something about that song that strikes a very universal chord. It really does. It will continue to, I think. Oh, that Sonny song. It's like 'Danny Boy.' It's like a song that's always been there."

Performing at the LSPU Hall in 1977, (left to right) Sandy Morris, Ron Hynes, Bryan Hennessey, and Kelly Russell.

To many, "Sonny's Dream" is like a song that's just always been there, as though it were part of Newfoundland folklore or the Newfoundland musical vernacular from time immemorial instead of since 1976, a tune that seemed to exist well before it was first recorded with the Wonderful Grand Band on the 1981 *Living in a Fog* album.

Chris LeDrew believes there are some people who can't discern between "Sonny's Dream" as a traditional rather than a more contemporary song, even though the song is barely forty years old.

"It's the story of everything," says Greg Malone. "It's everyone's story. You have to leave. It's the story of Ireland. Ireland thinks it's their song. They don't believe Ron wrote it.

"A lot of people think it's old and admired and whatnot. It will be eventually, down the road. Ron's name will be attached to it, I'm sure for a long time, but then it will go into the annals of traditional music."

"I like a lot of his songs," says Malone, "but it's funny, you know, listening to 'Sonny' the other day in the car, and I got tears in my eyes. I welled up. I have heard 'Sonny' a fucking million times. It came on the radio. It was an earlier version of Ron singing, right? The words are so perfect in it. He doesn't say a lot, but they just say the right amount, and they hint at a whole life behind it."

There are many stories about "Sonny's Dream"—the stories of the story you might say.

In Newfoundland, you never know when or where you might hear it. There's a story about a taxi driver named Larry Clarke who worked for Bugden's for forty-two years and used to moonlight as a disc jockey down in Portugal Cove in a place called the Spruce Lounge. He was there one night playing tunes and he played "Sonny's Dream." All of a sudden a waitress came up and put a beer in front of him. Ron was sitting in the audience and had bought it for him.

There is practically no end to the number of artists from all over the world who have recorded and performed the tune live, including Terry Kelly, North Sea Gas, Irish Aires, The Clydesiders, Hamish Imlach, Stan Rogers, Valdy, Allison Crowe, Jean Redpath, Great Big Sea, Hayley Westenra, Gerard Smith, Piece of the Rock, Tom Courtney, Daniel O'Donnell, Carol Noonan, Steve Gellman, and Phil Coulter.

There is one such performance, when you see and hear it on the Internet, that you feel being in the hall must have been spine-tingling—a true musical happening. Emmy Lou Harris can sing anything and make it seem that way, but add Delores Kean and Mary Black, as this video does, and it's a magical combination of sweet harmonic vocals.

Ireland's Christy Moore, who made a hit out of "Sonny's Dream," says time alone will tell if the song earns "Danny Boy" stature, which due to its longevity, familiarity, and popularity, is very strong.

"'Danny Boy' has been around a long time," says Moore. "I saw a full-length film doc about it recently. 'Danny Boy' has crossed so many oceans into so many different cultures, but 'Sonny's Dream' certainly has all the elements."

"There is a lot of longing in Ron's songs," says Malone. "And nostalgia and also the idea of you not being good enough, so you have to leave. Like the fact that Sonny has to leave."

Malone says there are recurring themes in which people are in search of dreams in some other "golden place, a hundred miles to town, or standing on the train tracks wanting to go to Hollywood," always seeking something else, "which you know is tragic."

Chris LeDrew talks about "Sonny's Dream" in the same vein as Malone, suggesting people think the song has been around forever. It will become a traditional Newfoundland folk song and will be around forever. The question is, as with a lot of other traditional songs where the song outlives the association with its composer, whether or not Ron's name will, decades into the future, remain associated with the song.

According to Malone, it's more than just Ron's iconic song. It's not just the song *of* his life. It's actually the song *about* his life.

"Ron is Sonny, really, and you know he empathized with Sonny and that uncle and everyone else that I guess was in the same position as he was. He didn't go to Alberta. He went to St. John's and the musical world of Canada, right? That was his dream."

"And like the way North American Irish take 'Danny Boy' as a song of their own— their song—many other than Newfoundlanders do the same.

"I mean, what a perfect song," says Malone. "They all own it. Everyone takes ownership. Portugal thinks it's their song. Japan thinks it's their song."

Ron knew he had to sing that song at every concert he performed. He tells of an elderly couple who travelled to a concert of his in Prince Edward Island all the way from Miramichi, NB, a journey of well over a day. "It probably cost them $500 and they came all that way just to hear 'Sonny's Dream,'" says Hynes. "I put them on the guest list so at least they didn't have to pay for the tickets."

There are moments when audiences become engaged and express their love for both song and artist. At the Harmony House in Hunter River, PEI, you could feel the love in the room anyway, but when Ron sang "Sonny's Dream," magic entered the hall. When it came time for the chorus, every soul present began to whisper the lyrics. They sang in whispers as though it were out of reverence or respect or love or adulation for the words and the melody.

Sonny's Dream

Sonny lives on a farm on a wide open space,
You can take off your shoes and give up the race;
You could lay down your head by a sweet riverbed,
But Sonny always remembers what it was his momma said.

Sonny, don't go away, I am here all alone,
Your daddy's a sailor who never comes home;
And the nights get so long and the silence goes on,
And I'm feeling so tired, I'm not all that strong.

Sonny carries a load though he's barely a man,
There ain't all that to do, still he does what he can;
And he watches the sea from a room by the stairs,
And the waves keep on rollin', they've done that for years.

Sonny, don't go away, I am here all alone,
Your daddy's a sailor who never comes home;
And the nights get so long and the silence goes on,
And I'm feeling so tired, I'm not all that strong.

Sonny's dreams can't be real, they're just stories he's read,
They're just stars in his eyes and dreams in his head;
And he's hungry inside for the wide world outside,
And I know I can't hold him though I've tried and I've tried and I've tried.

Sonny, don't go away, I am here all alone,
Your daddy's a sailor who never comes home;
And the nights get so long and the silence goes on,
And I'm feeling so tired, I'm not all that strong

ONE MAN GRAND BAND

Eric MacEwen was brought up in the fishing village of North Rustico, PEI, right next door to the better known Cavendish, one of the friendliest villages on the planet, as he likes to say. Eric developed a liking for the entertainment industry early on. He would eventually pursue courses of study in this regard at Memorial University in St. John's and in Boston, Massachusetts. He also began his radio career in both cities and eventually all over the east coast. He heard the local music being made and loved it. He is a founding father of the East Coast Music Awards, and has syndicated his radio show of east-coast music all over North America for many years.

The first time MacEwan heard Ron's name was during a telephone call from St. John's from Denis Ryan of the popular Celtic group Ryan's Fancy.

MacEwan had first dealt with Ryan and bandmates Dermott O'Reilly and Fergus O'Byrne, who were all moving from Toronto to St. John's. Driving over Cape Breton's Kelly's Mountain in their Volkswagen bus, they tuned into MacEwan's East Coast Music radio show being broadcast live from Norris Nathanson's Cape Breton studio at CJCB Radio in Sydney (one of the first radio stations in North America), with such in-studio guests as Kenzie MacNeil, Leon Dubinsky, Allister MacGillivray, Winston Scotty Fitzgerald and Max MacDonald, amongst others.

MacEwan would come to develop a lifelong relationship with Ryan and his two fellow bearded Irishmen. Almost unbelieving that they were hearing local music live on the radio, the three convinced themselves to drive straight to the studio to meet everyone.

At a later point, Ryan called MacEwan to tell him about a new singer-songwriter from Newfoundland who was really starting to cut it up. Ron was just twenty at the time and had already written "Sonny's Dream."

"Denis was so excited about this song that he sang it to me over the phone. I had him send me a recording and I played it on the show."

This made MacEwan the first to play "Sonny's Dream" on the radio. MacEwan looks back on hearing the song for the first time and that first airing as music destined to be famous and to be heard.

Shortly after that first airing, MacEwan says he was at a weekend house party in North Rustico when a young singer nicknamed Bubbles started singing "Sonny's Dream" and everyone in the kitchen began singing along with her.

"I phoned Ron at home to tell him that his song was going to be huge, and it became so.

"Over my lifetime I have come to believe certain songs are just meant to be, songs like 'Somewhere over the Rainbow' or 'I Can See Clearly Now.'"

St. John's-based musician Chris LeDrew says "Sonny's Dream" enabled Ron to do everything else he did.

"That song looms over everything Ron has been doing or ever has done. It has allowed him to play the places he's played, and allows him to draw those people out. Even though that is no longer a favourite of a lot of his fans, it is the cement. It is the foundation of what Ron does.

"That song is what allows everything else to happen. That song has gotten him out of a lot of jams, right? Those royalties from that song. I think that song is responsible for Ron being alive now. Because of the share of royalties. I've seen and I've known those cheques Ron has gotten from those songs at times when he has needed that money. So, it is called *Sonny money*.

"'Sonny money. I'm waiting for my Sonny money. It's coming,' Ron might say. He bought a guitar off me one time. Rather than pay it off, he said 'Next week, I'm going to pay that balance when my Sonny money comes in.' So, I think out of everything he has done, that's been his main source of income for thirty years."

Keyboardist and accompanist Paul Kinsman analogizes the importance of having Sonny money to the funeral ritual on India's famous Ganges River where the rich 'burn bright' in cremation ceremonies, some 200 per day in modern times, while the poor are left to simply float down the river, left to the vultures.

"You need Sonny money to float your burning corpse down the Ganges."

"Sonny's Dream" is one of those few magical songs in the world that when the artist pauses from singing to let the audience chime in, they know every syllable and they always get it right. When Ron holds back from singing, subtly with a nod or a wink inviting the audience to take over, they do so in a loving whisper. According to Chris LeDrew, it's easier for audiences to do this because it's one of these few songs in which the melody of the verse is the same as the melody of the chorus.

"So, it is easy and straightforward, you know? 'Sonny carries a load. Sonny don't go away,'" LeDrew sings. "Same thing, right? You know that's a mark of a good writer. To make it different, you know even though it's still the same. A lot of people don't realize that.

"I actually had a chat with Ron about that, that this was one of a few such songs. There are a few out there. 'Born in the USA' is another one. You know. I love 'Born in the USA.' The melody is the same. The syntax or whatever you call it. It was different. 'Born down in a dead man's town, Born in the USA' is the same thing. Sonny's Dream is very much the same. It's the spacing of the words and everything is the same."

Eric MacEwan relates Ron to Gene MacLellan's work.

> "I remember in a conversation with Ron when I asked how he came to write this song and he explained how it just came to him one June morning while walking down a sunlit street with fresh leaves on the trees. The song just overcame him. Divinely inspired, magical really. Like Gene MacLellan's 'Snowbird.' Gene told me that song came to him one morning in March while sitting on an old tree limb in the field and watching a flock of snowbirds flitting in the air. He said he wrote the song in twenty minutes and couldn't explain it. Such is the case with 'Sonny's Dream.'"

And "Sonny's Dream," it turns out, would travel the world just like MacLellan's "Snowbird."

THIEVES FROM IRELAND

NO NATION IS AS COVETOUS OF "Sonny's Dream" as Ireland.

Broadcaster Eric MacEwan says Ron learned that when he went there, that he was welcomed to Ireland like a native son.

"They loved his songs and considered 'Sonny's Dream' one of their own. All the musicians were familiar with his songs and included them in their performances."

And no wonder. Christy Moore's rendition of the tune went to number one in Ireland for fifty-two weeks in a row, according to MacEwan. The song came into Moore's hands after the late folksinger Hamish Imlach, born in Calcutta but conceived in Scotland, had been in Canada and heard Ron singing the song.

"This made everyone in Ireland assume it was an Irish song because it sounded so much like their music, with such great lyrics and musicality."

The song became so beloved in Ireland (by some accounts it's played at every wake and wedding in Ireland) that it paved the way for Canada's Rink Rat Productions to embark on a concert/documentary film tracing a string of Ron Hynes performances there. Written and directed by Rosemary House, *Ron Hynes: The Irish Tour* aired on CBC Television and featured some of Ireland's most prominent musicians, including Moore, Dónal Lunny, Mary Black, Coolfin, and others.

But, in spite of the benefits associated with the song's popularity in Ireland, what happened to the integrity of the lyrics there impacted Ron in two ways: one, the royalties made him a nice little cash cow, but two, it pissed him off royally because the lyrics ended up being bastardized.

Imlach was responsible for modifying the song and playing it in folk-clubs in Britain. There it was heard by Christy Moore who recorded it and passed it on to other artists in Ireland. In essence, Imlach killed the woman in the song:

Many years have passed on, Sonny's old and alone
His daddy the sailor never came home
Sometimes he wonders what his life might have been
But from the grave Mama still haunts his dreams

There are two versions regarding "Sonny's Dream" becoming a hit in Ireland and what Ron's reaction was at the time of the song's release. Ron talked repeatedly as an introduction to the song on stage about how he lost it when he heard the lyrical change to "Sonny's Dream," saying he contacted Moore's agent in Ireland shortly after its dynamic release and demanded the song be pulled from the airwaves and the records dumped. In one version he said he stuck by his guns, regardless of the consequences. In another version, he says that when the agent told Ron, "No problem, we'll pull the song and just forego your royalty cheque," which was for some ungodly amount of money. In that version, Ron told the agent that there was no problem and to let the song run its course. The truth probably lies somewhere in between those two yarns. Although the story made for great stage-craft, the whole Irish affair really did frustrate Ron though, just as it did when Canadian singer/songwriter Valdy changed the line about Sonny's daddy being a "sailor" to being a "singer" who never came home.

Any bastardization of a Hynes composition was like an affront to Ron's art. It reminds of the story of the night Ron was playing a gig at a PEI venue and a drunk in the audience was mouthing off that he had the lyrics wrong to "Sonny's Dream," the patron having not a clue Ron had written the piece. Incensed of course, Ron roared back at the guy that he sang it the same way he wrote it.

Even today, thirty-two years after his initial release of the song, Christy Moore is still in love with "Sonny's Dream."

"It's a very beautiful song that touches the heart," says Moore. "The imagery draws me in every time I sing it. The same movie runs in my head every time."

The song remains hugely popular in Ireland.

"I learnt it from Hamish Imlach who carried it back to Scotland from Newfoundland. I recorded it here circa 1984 on an album called *Ride On*. A few years later, Mary Black had a hit with it. Audiences here love to hear it and always sing along very quietly. It always evokes an emotional response and is now part of our National repertoire." Moore still performs it regularly, although not at every gig. It's more like "every now and then, when the air is right, when the wind is blowing in the right direction."

According to Moore, there is a mystery over the change in the lyrics which killed off Sonny's mother prematurely: "It gained a new verse along the way and no one seems to know who wrote it," claims Moore. "It's a glorious mystery."

Giving credit where credit is due and getting it right has always been important to Ron. For example, the song "The Final Breath" was written while the film *Secret Nation* was being produced; however, the composition was in no way influenced by the film.

"But shortly afterward," says Ron, "I was offered a principal role as an actor in the production and while entertaining the cast and crew, I performed the new song as I felt it had something in common with the film. The producer heard it and asked to have it for the film. Then when the film was nominated for a Genie award, the song was the only one that won, which made me one of only two Newfoundland artists at that point to ever win a Genie, the other being Gordon Pinsent."

THE FINAL BREATH

E. DAVID GREGORY IS A PROFESSOR of history and humanities at Athabasca University in Alberta whose contribution in 2004 to the University of Calgary's History of Intellectual Culture comes face to face with Newfoundland and Labrador and Ron Hynes, the songwriter.

Gregory made a 2004 contribution to *The History of Intellectual Culture*, an international peer-reviewed open-access academic electronic journal that provides a forum for publication and discussion of original research on the socio-historical contexts of ideas and ideologies and their relationships to community and state formation, physical environments, human and institutional agency, personal and collective identity, and lived experience. His abstract from this journal, "Vernacular Song, Cultural Identity, and Nationalism in Newfoundland, 1920-1955," examines an extensive list of songs and Newfoundlanders who sought to collect and save traditional Newfoundland music, but his writing begins with Ron and his work.

The term *vernacular song* is used by Gregory in reference to songs which have survived longer than their initial spell of popularity, and have entered oral tradition, thereby demonstrating their appeal to more than one generation.

"Such songs vary in character," writes Gregory. "Some are traditional (in the case of Newfoundland, anonymous songs that were brought by immigrants from their original homeland, such as Ireland), some have new words set to traditional tunes, some are broadside ballads (the authors of which are usually although not always unknown), some are the work of (known) singer-songwriters, and some are texts set to music by a composer other than the writer."

To earn the cred as a vernacular song, a composition must not only possess a good tune, what Gregory refers to as "a vital melody," but must also have words that strike a chord in the hearts and minds of audiences. In other words, they need to have stood the test of time.

"Vernacular songs can tell us something about the beliefs, values, and opinions of those who were drawn to them sufficiently to keep them current for generations," explains Gregory, referring to collections of Newfoundland songs such as Gerald Doyle's *The Old Time Songs and Poetry of Newfoundland*, Elisabeth Greenleaf's *Ballads and Sea Songs from Newfoundland*, and Maud Karpeles's *Folk Songs from Newfoundland* and which he believes illuminate the degree to which by the late 1920s a Newfoundland song-culture had replaced earlier cultural traditions.

According to Gregory, these traditions stand for more than just musical tradition.

> Just as the separatist movement in Québec seems to be waning, the call for an independent Newfoundland appears once more to be finding resonance among sections of the province's population. Television images of Canadian flags burning in Newfoundland and former Premier Roger Grimes's insistent demand to renegotiate Confederation in order to regain control of the fishery may serve as a reminder of the strength of separatist sentiment. Newfoundland singer-songwriter Ron Hynes, the recipient of an honorary doctorate from Memorial University, has captured this spirit of rebellion and desire for independence in a more poetic but equally uncompromising manner in the last verse of his 1998 song, "The Final Breath":
>
> > This could be the final breath,
> > This is life and death,
> > This is hard rock and water,
> > Out here between wind and flame,
> > Between tears and elation,
> > Lies a secret nation.

Gregory writes that Ron's message implies that Newfoundland has one last chance to take charge of its own destiny.

But the bigger question for Ron always seemed to be, what about his own destiny?

ST. JOHN'S WALTZ

WHEN BROADCASTER ERIC MACEWAN MOVED TO St. John's, circa 1956, he considered that it was very much more continental Europe-influenced than North America and he found it "utterly fascinating."

The city was built around the beautiful, enclosed and intimate St. John's Harbour, the centre of commerce in those days as Newfoundland depended on its world-class fishery.

"The Portuguese White Fishing Fleet was on the go then and it was a common sight to see the harbour full of white sailing ships. In fact, you could walk across the harbour deck to deck on these great ships."

The Portuguese sailors would sit on the decks playing Portuguese waltzes, which the Newfoundland squeezebox players quickly adopted in their repertoire of tunes, and the local cooks would learn Portuguese recipes, like the Portuguese salt-fish dinner with its own unique twist to this already famous NL dish.

The old mercantile class pretty much ran things and there were huge department stores with Newfoundland family names of wealthy local merchants. At nights, the downtown streets would see a squeezebox player playing for the hordes of shoppers while the fish-mongers, the Molly Malone's of the day, would sell fish from the back of a horse cart right downtown.

"It was quite a scene to behold," according to MacEwan, "beautiful really, kind of like a Charles Dickens time-warp."

In the summer of 1979, Ron found himself on the St. John's waterfront watching the Portuguese sailors from The White Fleet playing soccer and flirting with the local girls. This inspired him to write "The St. John's Waltz."

"I went back to my apartment and wrote the first two verses in no time flat. The third verse took a year. Sometimes I eat the page," he says, meaning he writes long passages of verse quickly. "It's short and sweet, I know," he says of the Waltz. "Sometimes, that's all there is."

ST. JOHN'S WALTZ

For some fans, it's their absolute favourite, he adds, as it was his mother's. It might be for anyone who takes the trouble to watch the old footage of Ron and the Wonderful Grand Band performing on an outdoor stage before a grassy knoll at Quidi Vidi Lake, in St. John's. With his long straight hair blowing in the wind and the strumming of his mandolin (in spite of Greg Malone and Tommy Sexton hamming it up for the camera in drag, frolicking in and amongst the crowd), it makes for a magical musical moment, frozen in time.

St. John's Waltz

Oh the harbour lights are gleaming
And the evening's still and dark
And the seagulls are all dreaming
Seagull dreams on Amherst Rock
And the mist is slowly drifting
As the storefront lights go dim
And the moon is gently lifting
As the last ship's, the last ship's coming in
All the sailors got a story
Some are true, some are false
But they're always wrecked and they're up on the deck
And dancin' the St. John's Waltz

And we've had our share of history
We've seen nations come and go
We've seen battles rage over land and stage
Two hundred years or more
For glory or for freedom
Or for country or for king
Or for money or fame but there are no names
On the graves where men lie sleeping
All the nine to fives survive the day
With a sigh and a dose of salts
And they're parking their cars and packing the bars
Dancin' the St. John's Waltz

Oh my heart is on the highway
And I'm sold on goin' to sea
All the planes fill the skyway
All the trains run swift and free
So leave the wayward free to wander
Leave the restless free to roam
If it's rocks in the bay, if it's old cliché
You'll find your way back home
But don't question or inquire
What's been gained, what's been lost
In a world of romance don't miss out on the chance
To be dancin' the St. John's Waltz

LUKE THE DRIFTER

RON WAS INFATUATED WITH AMERICAN COUNTRY-MUSIC legend Hank Williams. It's one of the first things he raised with me while driving from Halifax airport to that gig at the Chester Playhouse in June of 2014. Luckily, Ron lived thirty-five years longer than Williams, the latter dying at the age of just twenty-nine. Remembering that both Charles MacPhail and I thought maybe Ron had bought the farm that night in Chester, there have been some nights when some friends thought Ron was going to act out Hank Williams to the whole and worst possible degree.

In 1987, he starred as Hank in an Ottawa York Street Theatre production of *Hank Williams: The Show He Never Gave*, a role he reprised back home at the St. John's Arts and Cultural Centre for a Resource Centre for the Arts (and Country 99 FM) production directed by Janis Spence. In St. John's he was backed by Bryan Hennessey, Adrian Doyle, Roger Howse, and the always familiar Kelly Russell as Williams's famous Driftin' Cowboys. In the show's poster, Ron looks every bit the part of the lanky American icon. Williams died in his Cadillac in Oak Hill, West Virginia, while on the way to a scheduled performance on New Year's Day, 1953, in Canton, Ohio. The same year Williams died, MGM released *Luke the Drifter* in a 78 RPM box set. The lyrics of these songs are cherished among the great minimalist Country and Western troubadours. They are considered recitative morality fables incorporating a sort of drawling blues done on the spur of the moment.

Early in his career, Williams developed the habit of singing preaching type songs under the name of Luke the Drifter, a nom de plume for an idealized character who went across the country preaching the gospel, and doing good deeds while Hank Williams, the drunkard, cheated on women and was cheated on by them in return.

The Williams grave site in Montgomery, Alabama, famous also for its association with black civil rights icon Rosa Parks, pays homage to both Hank Williams and, oddly, to Luke the Drifter.

In 1950, Williams began recording as Luke the Drifter for his religious-themed recordings, many of which are recitations rather than singing. Fearful that disc jockeys and jukebox operators would hesitate to accept these unusual recordings, Williams used this alias to avoid hurting the marketability of his name. Although the real identity of Luke the Drifter was supposed to be anonymous, Williams often performed parts of the material on stage. Most of the material was written by Williams, in some cases with the help of Fred Rose and his son, Wesley. The songs depicted Luke the Drifter travelling around from place to place, narrating stories from different characters and philosophizing about life. Some of the compositions were accompanied, unusually, by a pipe organ. An example would be the song "Men with Broken Hearts" sung in the persona of Luke the Drifter.

> Some lose faith in love and life
> When sorrow shoots her darts
> And with hope all gone, they walk alone
> These men with broken hearts

Ron loves this whole idea of Luke the Drifter and the very notion of being able to have an alter ego—or perhaps several. There are parts of him that build toward the alter ego: the hats, the scarves, the boots. Like Williams's Luke the Drifter, Ron's would be a nice fit as a personality who belongs in old western movies.

"Ron likes the great story, the great art, like the poetry of the westerns," says Greg Malone. "The heroic character, you know, how they overcome the difficulty. He's always looking for the line of poetry in it. He's always looking for that. The great story of survival and finding home."

Ron talks about this, including, for example, the old Sergio Leone-directed 1968 classic spaghetti western *Once Upon a Time in the West*, which starred Jason Robards, Charles Bronson, Henry Fonda, and Claudia Cardinale. The film features long, slow scenes in which there is very little dialogue and very little seems to happen, that is until the scene is broken by brief and sudden violence. Leone was far more interested in the rituals preceding violence than in the violence itself. The tone of the film is consistent with the desperate-seeming, arid, semi-desert landscape in which the story unfolds, and imbues it with a feeling of realism that contrasts with the elaborately choreographed gunplay.

In one famous scene, the three bad guys are waiting at a train station for Bronson. The train is several hours late. In the long slow wait for action to prevail, there is the slow turning of a creaking old windmill, one of the gunslinger's knuckles cracking, and one of the figures shooing a buzzing fly off his face. It seems so real, it's surreal.

This movie and this scene inspired Ron's song "Someday," from the *Get Back Change* album. In "Someday," the protagonist in the song is longing for the day when the lost lover will be filled with regret, but eventually realizes that there is nothing left in the eyes, the embrace, or the heart.

Someday

Someday you'll want me to want you
Someday you'll want me to care
Sometime when time's not much older
You'll glance to your shoulder
And someone won't be there
Someday you'll wish you could hold me
Like I wish I could hold you dear
Someday you'll want me to want you
Darlin' don't I wish someday was here

All the warmth has gone out of your arms, dear
And the colour is gone from your smile
And the dreams that we shared
In some dim yesteryear
Have faded I fear
They're like shadows, my dear
And the promise I saw in your eyes love
Was illusion from the start
All the warmth has gone out of your arms, love
And the love has gone out of your heart

Seems that I have been love's tragic player
I played the part of a fool
And as the curtain draws near
It's ever so clear
That love's been unfair
To the players, my dear
For a fool and his love soon are parted
As the petals of roses decay
My love appears brokenhearted

Now that your love has faded away

Ron talks about another old western angle that clings to him. Having just watched the Cohen brothers' film *The Big Lebowski* around the time we spent driving together, he was excited that the film features a song called "Tumbling Tumbleweeds," written by Bob Nolan, of Sons of the Pioneers fame, who also wrote the tunes "Cool Water," "Ghost Riders in the Sky," and a host of other famous western songs that only people of a certain lineage would know or recognize.

"I had to google Nolan to find out more. I was always under the impression he was from New Brunswick, but he was actually born Clarence Robert Nobles in Winnipeg, Manitoba. It's just trivia, I know, but he wrote some of my favourite songs from that period."

Ron talks about the night he was inducted into the Canadian Songwriters Hall of Fame. He performed one of Canada's most famous folk tunes and Newfoundland fisher's anthem "I'se de B'y" together with fiddler Jamie Snider. But on that same night, he was enthralled as Ian Tyson sang some of his songs with the vocal group Quartette (Cindy Church, Caitlin Hanford, Gwen Swick, and Sylvia Tyson); some of Ian Tyson's repertoire echoes that Bob Nolan western cowboy genre.

He was also enthralled that Gordon Lightfoot was front and centre, giving Ron a thumbs up for his performance and over his induction.

"Well, in all the westerns, everything was really over-simplified, right?" says Greg Malone.

He refers, in part, to the highly formulaic approach to television and silver-screen westerns in the early days and the whole bad-guy-in-the-black-hat, good-guy-in-the-white-hat routine, with the good guys always winning out.

"You had the good ones like John Wayne of course. We used to watch the late 1950s, early 1960s TV western show *Have Gun—Will Travel*, which starred Richard Boone. He was a guy of honour, integrity."

Malone says Boone's character, Paladin, tended to respect minority rights even back then, referring to Paladin's and the show's treatment of Native Americans. He says that you could watch a show like Paladin and get real human value out of it.

"The stories were incredible. Like really well thought out stories about morals. It's not just an entertainment shootout. It's very well thought out. So, Ron liked that kind of stuff, like the noble, the one who overcomes. Because he had a lot to overcome. He came into town an insecure bay boy. He had to prove himself in town," which Malone says in Ron's case would have been at about the age of sixteen or seventeen.

"It's always that with the townies and the bay boys; you had to prove that you're not ignorant.

"And everyone did. It was a rite of passage. You came in and you tried your time in town. Because, I mean, where was he going to go? He's an artist. He's not going to stay [in Ferryland]. He's Sonny. He's like Sonny. He's going to leave."

" He seemed at the time,
and he still does and continues to be,
a real luminary in our musical sky. "

PAUL KINSMAN
(keyboardist)

—————
PART V
—————

THE LEGACY

A PICASSO OF SONG

"AT STANFEST," SAYS BROADCASTER ERIC MACEWAN, "I have heard other songwriters refer to Ron as the Picasso of songwriters. Such is the esteem he is held in by his peers."

MacEwan and his Stanfest friends are not the only people who see Ron in a Picasso light.

An American journeyman guitarist, singer, and songwriter named Jason Wilber caught Ron playing one night at The Ship, an experience which compelled him to write the song "Watching Picasso."

It wasn't the first time someone has attempted to pay tribute to Ron, but this is one Ron said he really liked.

"Something that did occur and might lend some perspective is the number of tribute songs written about me," said Ron. "I don't know if that's important to you. Never has been for me except on one occasion when I genuinely liked the composer/artist and really liked the song. Jason Wilber came to a show at The Ship some time back with John Prine and later that night wrote a really nice song called 'Watching Picasso.'

"There are also other tributes," he said, "some pretty good, some passable, and some just terrible. These are always difficult to respond to as you don't want to be hurting someone's feelings or denigrating their intent and sometimes they won't go away. They need your word of thanks and appreciation. That can be a dubious road."

Wilber, though, has some cred. He has travelled the world as lead guitar player for artists like John Prine, Greg Brown, Iris DeMent, Todd Snider, and Hal Ketchum. Beyond even Carnegie Hall to Red Rocks to Massey Hall and the London Palladium, Wilber has performed in all fifty United States, and all over Canada, Europe, and the UK. Wilber's work with John Prine includes the Grammy Award winning CD *Fair & Square*, and the Grammy nominated CDs *Live on Tour* and *In Spite of Ourselves* (which spent thirty-two weeks on the Billboard Country Charts). John Prine's penchant for duets has put Wilber in the enviable position of accompanying him on recordings with Emmylou Harris, Lucinda Williams, Josh Ritter, Patty Loveless, Iris Dement, Trisha Yearwood, and Sara Watkins.

So what is it that possessed this American visiting The Rock to write about Ron Hynes?

"I was on tour with John Prine, and Jimmy Rankin was opening for us," says Wilber. "We arrived in St. John's the day prior to our concert and went to dinner somewhere in town."

Over dinner, Cape Breton singer/songwriter Jimmy Rankin suggested they go see and listen to a friend of his who was playing at a pub.

"But he didn't say anything about who Ron was or his music or anything," says Wilber. "So I just kind of assumed his friend was in some local bar band or something."

The boys went to The Ship and saw Ron perform.

"Based on the noisy bar environment and the fact that Jimmy hadn't told us anything about this guy, I wasn't really expecting much."

But after a few songs, Wilber realized his mouth had been hanging open.

"I wasn't prepared to hear something so great in this little out-of-the-way bar. I always have an amazing expansive feeling when I discover something totally new to me that is totally great," says Wilber. "So I was really in a great creative frame of mind after that show."

When he returned to his hotel room that night, he started penning the song about the artist he had just seen and heard. It was a tune that came to him right away; it was just a matter of reliving or recalling his experience from earlier that evening. He started telling the story in what he calls "song language." Wilber was so wrapped in Ron that he went out the next morning and bought all of the Ron Hynes recordings available at O'Brien's Music.

"When I was trying to find a way to describe how I felt seeing Ron sing his songs, I was reminded of the feeling I have when I'm standing in a museum looking at paintings I really love. It's that expansive, creative kind of high I was talking about after seeing his show. It occurred to me that the difference in this situation was that I was watching the performance as it happened, which is different than looking at a painting that has already been completed."

So that is why Wilber lyricized, "Sketching out his world with a voice and guitar."

"I chose Picasso, Monet, and Renoir, because I like their paintings and they seemed to have something in common with Ron's songs. That was just a feeling, I didn't try to analyze why I thought that. It was just something that bubbled up from my subconscious or wherever songs come from. I think I may have had Gauguin and some other painters in the song at first, but their names didn't sing as well in terms of phrasing. Of the three painters that I kept in the song, Picasso seemed best for the title."

Chris LeDrew connects Ron's songwriting to the place where he was born and comes back to. He says that some places, like Newfoundland, can be partly defined by their artists, and particularly musicians.

"Ron's mood, or the tone of Ron's material, definitely reflects the tone of Newfoundland," says LeDrew. "It is the tone of the Newfoundland weather. The thing about Ron is Ron has some heartfelt ballad material and sort of sad, emotional material. Ron's got some funny stuff too. "A Good Dog is Lost" [in which Ron yelps], and in these types of songs Ron can really make you laugh with some lines. So, Ron's got that sort of self-deprecating humour in there.

"We [Newfoundlanders] can go, as you probably can tell, we can go weeks with just fog. Ron's lived that life there year after year looking out a window. Yeah, I think a lot of what he does musically touches the overall mood, or tone, or atmosphere of his music. Listening to something like 'Leaving on the Evening Tide,' 'Away,' any of those ones that deal with like topical, I guess, or locational sort of songs, have that feel. You can almost feel the fog, or cold, or wind, stuff like that.

"I think as far as Ron is concerned, you could put his songs in several sub-categories as far as topics go. He's got love songs. He's got leaving songs. He's got Newfoundland-type—'On the Evening Tide' and 'Away'—and then he's got the 'Godspeed' type tunes about people or events, songs about the McLellan suicide or the Ocean Ranger going down. His love songs are great. Very imaginative, very emotional, very creative."

Just as Wilber would say, they can be as emotional, or more so, than a great painting.

Music producer Paul Mills first met Ron in 1973 shortly after Mills had started working as a producer for CBC Radio.

"Back then," says Mills, "CBC used to produce what were called broadcast recordings which were four-song EPs distributed to CBC stations across the country for airplay."

These were all fully produced studio recordings of Canadian artists and bands.

"One of my producer colleagues in the department at the time was Ian Thomas. Ian had just released his first hit single, 'Painted Ladies,' and he was leaving his job there to pursue his music performing career fulltime. He had one broadcast recording project lined up which he would be unable to complete and he asked if I would take it over for him. It was a young singer-songwriter from Newfoundland named Ron Hynes."

"I took it on," recalls Mills. "Ron came with his own guitar player, Sandy Morris, and I hired studio musicians to complete the band: drums, bass, keyboards, pedal steel. We had a great time doing the record and it turned out well."

Time passed and Mills didn't see much of Ron, although Ron guested a couple of times on the folk-music program, *Touch the Earth*, which Mills was producing and which was hosted by Sylvia Tyson. Then in 2002, Mills suddenly got a call from Ron asking if he was interested in working with him on his next album project.

"Well that was one of the easiest decisions I've ever had to make. It took less than a nanosecond for me to say yes!" The album was called *Get Back Change*.

As Mills wrote for Ron's website:

> Ron arrived at my home studio in Toronto (the Millstream) with 13 songs complete and ready to go. I often work with songwriters on what we call "song polishing"—making little improvements here and there. I asked Ron if he wanted that kind of input from me, but he said, "Nope these songs are finished."

While some producers might have considered that answer to be a sign of artistic arrogance, Mills refers to Ron's response as "the confidence of a master craftsman."

The two worked on the arrangements together and they brought in drummer Al Cross and bassist David Woodhead to lay down the basic bed tracks. Once they were completed,

Ron headed back to Newfoundland, telling Mills that he trusted him to complete the production.

"This was most unusual for me because I always work with artists in a collaborative fashion, making sure that they are happy with each thing we add."

Not having Ron there for the overdub sessions made Mills nervous but Ron had insisted on leaving the final production elements in Mills's hands. So during December of 2002 and January of 2003, Mills overdubbed electric guitar, banjo, keyboards, steel, dobro and strings, with backup vocals by Jenny Whiteley and Sylvia Tyson.

Mills sent the rough mixes of everything off to Ron in Newfoundland and uneasily awaited Ron's reaction. A few days later the phone rang. It was Ron.

"I nervously awaited an angry voice screaming, 'What have you done to my songs!'" recalls Mills, "but instead I got three words: 'I love everything!'"

After Mills's huge sigh of relief, Ron said there was actually just one guitar lick he wanted changed, but that was it. Released in the summer of 2003, *Get Back Change* went on to win Record of the Year and Country Record of the Year at the 2004 East Coast Music Awards (ECMA).

Sandy Morris isn't overly surprised that Ron would trust Mills in that manner with his music.

"I think he has his own way of inserting his will, if you know what I mean," says Morris. "I don't think he's gonna do anything that is not comfortable to him. But I don't know, he has taken a lot of direction as far as vocals. He'll listen if he respects you. There is a certain thing about sitting in a studio, and playing or singing something, and not having the perspective of listening to it from the outside. You're always worried that if you're actually trying to accomplish something, it's great to have that input—like somebody saying you're speeding up a little on that last phrase, or you've got to give it more on this part or whatever."

With that sweet start as collaborators, Ron and Mills went on to work on two other album projects. The self-titled *Ron Hynes* was also an ECMA winner and, among other things, chronicled Ron's at least temporary victory over drug addiction, and *Stealing Genius*, the cleverly titled album which featured a collection of new songs inspired by or written with the best of Newfoundland's authors and poets.

A PICASSO OF SONG

"With each project, Ron and I have become even better collaborators and closer as friends," claims Mills. "He is a total pro in the studio and unswerving in his commitment to the songs and delivering the best possible performance."

With three records in hand, Mills considered it a privilege to have worked with a singer and songwriter of Ron's caliber: "He's simply one of the best songwriters this or any other country has ever produced."

Mills is not alone in his assessment.

Keyboardist Paul Kinsman believes Ron is in the very upper echelon of song writing in Canada.

"He's like a thoroughbred of song writing, and not just because he's a Newfoundlander, but I think he is in a rare club in the country, you know? Probably only five or six guys like him."

And he talks about the music scene in St. John's and how Ron stands out amongst the crowd.

"We all knew each other. It was very incestuous. But with him in particular, he seemed at the time, and he still does and continues to be, a real luminary in our musical sky."

Kinsman's father was a church choir conductor and organist for fifty years and it was inescapable therefore that Paul would have classical training on piano. As he says, "Trinity College and Royal Conservatory kind of stuff." So ending up backing an artist like Ron Hynes was not a very predictable musical outcome.

Even though he is a St. John's East guy, Kinsman first met Ron while he was playing music at a radio station in Cornerbrook, on Newfoundland's west coast.

"I was always kind of aware of him, right, because he looms large in the consciousness of anybody over twenty-five years old. But the first time I actually met him was about 1980. It was right after the *Living in a Fog* album came out

"I remember speaking to Ron there during a break. I got my courage together— *this is Ron fucking Hynes*—and I would have been twenty-one, maybe twenty-two. He had 'Sonny's Dream' and he was perceived to be the king, he was the grandest of the grand, right? He was the Elvis of the Grand Band.

"And I spoke to him, and I said 'Hey Ron,' and he turned to me and, honest to God, it took this long." Kinsman mimics Ron's response, turning his back and performing a long, slow turning of his head. "It was like his head was on a lazy Susan and it's like his body stayed and his head just turned around. I don't know if he was bothered or maybe, you know, we all get into this to feed some part of our soul, some part of our ego. And I don't think Ron is used to anything but adulation.

"So that was the first time I met him. He would probably never remember that. And I'm really good friends with Stamp because we were playing together in Barry Canning's band, and so at some point—'94 maybe?—Boom called me, and I play Hammond organ as well, so I'd drag my Hammond organ down for the "Primitive Thunder" sessions then. That's what we called it, but he demoed a lot of songs.

"Sandy Morris is an awesome guy and I knew Boom and I knew a couple of other guys of the Grand Band. So, Boomer got me in on these demos. He said, 'So why don't you come and do some demos with Ron.' Ron says, 'Great, we'd like you to add some keyboards.' I was only starting to get to know some of those Grand Band guys who were kind of, you know, excuse the hyperbole, but they were like the fucking Beatles in Newfoundland. At that time, man, they were, and they still are to that generation. They were a pinnacle of Newfoundland music at the time. There hadn't been a lot of keyboards around his music up to that point. It's pretty guitar-driven stuff.

"On these sessions, on these demos, was when I got to know him a little bit. I was feeling really good because I kind of felt like I was becoming some sort of musical peer to these guys who meant so much to me and I thought so highly of, right? Like if Sandy was talking to me and treating me like one of his own, I was feeling, like, pretty chuffed, man. Chuffed. It's an English saying. And that gave me a lot of confidence knowing that Sandy and Boomer felt that I could cut it, right? Kinsman said Ron liked what they were hearing.

"That really stuck with me, besides playing with all these dudes, you know, who were like ten years older than me, and it was kind of like playing with my heroes.

"Ron wasn't remote at the time. He would stay out in the control room and talk to me through headphones. 'Try this, try this, try this.' And he came into the studio with me, and kind of leaned over the organ, like he was at a shooter bar."

Kinsman says the degree to which Ron stayed with him and coached and encouraged him throughout the recordings boosted his confidence tremendously and has always lingered with him.

"At one point," Kinsman says, "Ron said he wanted me to bring it on a bit more. If it's my part, I own it. You know, if you're going to do a part, own the fucking thing."

Ron told Kinsman as much and he pulled it off.

"And I did so, and three years later, when we did the *Standing in Line* album, the song was slated for that album. It was a very small little thing but I still remember it to this day as it was musically meaningful to me, right? I had done a lot of things over the years. At that point, that was a real pinnacle for me to just feel that kind of acceptance."

By 1997, keyboards had made their way into Ron's music and Kinsman was performing with Ron and the other guys regularly.

Kinsman went on to twenty years of session work because working with Ron gave him street cred. Great Big Sea's Bob Hallet says, as others have, that a rising tide raises all boats.

"And it kind of did, so it made me feel better about my own playing, my own musicality, and that was just at the time, and a few years later, I got together to play on that *Standing in Line* album. I've been playing with Ron pretty much ever since, except for the real dark drug days when he wouldn't be able to make eye contact with me."

Since initially working with Ron, Kinsman has gone on to record nearly 500 tracks on various albums.

Frank Watt has had the good fortune to work as both musician and recording engineer with some of Canada's best songwriters and artists over the past forty years. Watt oversaw the production in 2015 of Ron's latest recording, *Later That Same Life*, at his Studio By The River in Lindsay, Ontario. What astonished Watt about Ron was his ability to recall songs without referring to any lyric sheets or music, something which he says very few artists are capable of.

"Ron Hynes impressed me more than any writer I've worked with," says Watt. "Some songs are easy to remember usually due to their repetitive nature, but Ron's songs are stories with very interesting lyrical content."

Nothing could be truer about Ron's material. It's not full of repetitive, easy-to-remember hooks, the type that nearly always make top-forty songs popular. On his CBC radio show, *Randy's Vinyl Tap*, singer/songwriter Randy Bachman explained this phenomenon using the example of the six repeated key notes in The Archies song "Sugar, Sugar" which made the song memorable in its entirety. The same is the case for the unforgettable opening guitar line and the following emphatic vocal grunt in Bachman's own "American Woman." Ron's songs are not top-forty pop songs that leave an ear-worm in your head all day. His material is more ponderous. He is more Leonard Cohen-like, with rich, layered, emotional, and more complex lyrics.

From another perspective, Chris LeDrew thinks that although he's not writing songs like "Sugar, Sugar," Ron is creative in a similar manner to artists who have written popular music.

"Yeah, Ron is very creative like that. He is almost like a pop writer in that he understands how important it is for the audience to be brought in by the rhyme, by the structure of the song. He understands structure; he's, you know, he's a Beatles fan, and I'm sure Ron is a fan of pop music as well in that way."

"When Ron arrived at my studio, he still wasn't quite sure of which songs he was going to record," says Watt. "After all, he is the man of a thousand songs and I think that may have past 2,000 by now. As Ron started to work on the bed tracks with Dennis Pendrith, I noticed no lyrics of any kind on paper and that's the way the whole album went. I don't think I saw Ron pick up a pen once."

Pendrith is one of those connections Ron has made musically over the years which demonstrate the plateau he has reached on the Canadian scene, top-drawer musicians and the finest vocalists. Pendrith, for example, is a veteran bass player from the Toronto area, currently a regular on CBC Radio's *Vinyl Café* with host Stuart MacLean, but who was the main touring and studio bassist with artists such as Murray McLauchlan, Bruce Cockburn, and Raffi. Pendrith has also recorded sessions with Stan Rogers, Dan Hill, Sharon, Lois & Bram, Gordon Lightfoot, Fred Penner, Tom Paxton, Sylvia Tyson, and Rita Chiarelli. And of course, Ron Hynes.

GREAT BIG FAN

ALAN DOYLE HAS MADE HIS MARK as singer, songwriter, and actor alongside his Australian friend Russell Crowe. Best known as the frontman for the perennially popular Great Big Sea, Doyle is a Newfoundland entertainment originator in his own right. But among his greatest motivators and inspirations is Ron Hynes.

"He's a songwriter's songwriter," says Doyle. "He's the one that all the songwriters love the most. I think primarily because he hasn't really been a hit machine, right? And I don't know if he ever had any interest in doing that.

"Ron Hynes is my favourite songwriter, always has been," says Doyle. "I think Ron is the best songwriter in Canada because I can't think of anybody else who speaks of the most regional things and makes them seem so global."

Doyle says Hynes can write seven songs a week, from start to finish, because he's learned his craft so well. "Starting songs is easy," Doyle says of Hynes, "finishing them is tough."

"He's ours. I mean, I'm kind of partial, and who's the best, who knows? But I always think about Stan Rogers and Ron Hynes as the two most underestimated songwriters in Canadian history. I look at the catalogues of some of the greats, and I look at the catalogues of Ron and Stan Rogers, and I go, hmmm…"

And he remained prolific; although no one, probably including Ron himself, really knows how many melodies and lines of lyrics he wrote.

"Oh my God, who knows?" says guitarist Sandy Morris. "He calls himself The Man of a Thousand songs, but I keep telling him he must be up to 2,000 by now. 'The Man of a Thousand Songs' was on *Crier's Paradise* which was back in the '90s, a couple of decades on." And there have been boatloads of new material created since then.

Doyle refers to Ron as a poet.

"I'm not sure Ron has ever tried to write a song that could rock a stadium as much as Bon Jovi, but I do every time.

"Ron doesn't think about how his songs will make an amazing hockey-rink concert. I don't know if it ever occurs to him or not, but you know, for me, I find I'm a performer at heart and not a wordsmith at heart, and I still consider myself a performer first, a musician second, and then a songwriter."

It's Doyle's trigger to want to bring the house down. That is his job. Ron, on the other hand, was the reverse, writing songs about situations and people which, as Donna Morrissey says, takes him deeper inside than most songwriters, what she coined as "the grand voyeur" in Ron.

"I don't really have a big personal relationship with him," says Doyle. "Ron and I have known each other kicking around the scene for twenty years. He probably has an affection for me and a bunch of the younger guys that are still doing it, and he knows we are all massive fans of his."

Although he is inspired on many levels by Ron, he never tried to imitate Ron musically or to mimic him in any way. Many artists, he says, begin that way, with mimicry or impersonation.

"I didn't even try to impersonate Ron because I couldn't. I couldn't write those kinds of words. I couldn't write that kind of poetry. I probably still can't but my eye turned to what I was doing. I don't need to write a song about a girl on a beach in California. I'll write a song about a girl on a beach in Petty Harbour."

And that instinct, he says, really came from Ron's approach to songs, especially with the release of *Cryer's Paradise*, which truly opened Doyle's eyes at about the age of ten.

"The biggest thing was the topic. The topic. He wrote songs that sounded cool about stuff around me. Around everyone in the southern shore of Newfoundland. He wrote songs about people you saw.

"'Sonny's Dream' was a song about a kid looking up at guys around his town talking about their dads, uncles, grandfathers, who leave constantly. It's not about Boston. Yeah, really starting to think about writing songs for myself, and *Cryer's Paradise* came out and all the songs and all the story songs about people from St. John's, and the greater surrounding area. The character songs, and all that stuff."

Doyle says Ron revealed that the most interesting people are less often known or heroic figures than they are the ordinary people from anywhere.

GREAT BIG FAN

Even though *Cryer's Paradise* opened Doyle's mind to topical songs and song writing, it wasn't as though he wasn't already wrapped up completely in music.

"I was in bands my whole life. My dad and my uncles, and the history of the Doyles. Ron will tell you. It's like the history of the Doyles in Petty Harbour. They are the entertainers, they are the band or whatever. My father and all his brothers are all musicians and my mom was a musician from another town. My grandfather and his brothers were all singers.

"My father and all of the guys played, but none of them ever had a record. So when our first record showed up, it felt like an exclamation point for the whole lineage. Not just for me."

Conversely, with Ron, Doyle believes there was no musical lineage. There was only one household musician and that was Ron's Uncle Sonny O'Neill. "People think Sonny is just a guy in the song," says Doyle. "He's a guy that taught Ron how to play the guitar. Ron still has the guitar. He still has the accordion. He bought it off Sonny, so really most of what Ron got or brought was really all from him. He didn't have that generational father to look up to, to teach him all that stuff. It was just guitar playing from Sonny. That's about it."

Doyle has never left behind his infatuation with Ron and his music and lyrics.

"I could probably sing, I think, I could sing every Ron Hynes song the way people know all The Beatles' songs."

There've been times when Doyle's repertoire as a performer needed to call upon every Ron Hynes and every Stan Rogers song out there. It was a repertoire Doyle developed while standing on street corners singing and playing and then later in small bars and pubs, as he honed his craft and an audience of his own, well before Great Big Sea came into play: "Before Great Big Sea started, I spent two years going up and down these various streets."

And Doyle says he's not the only Atlantic Canadian performer who knows Ron's songs inside out. "We did a gig when Ron got sick. We put together a band of local players that played on the show down there. I didn't see a music stand anywhere. I'm serious. It was like, 'Do you do 'No Kathleen'? What key do you do it in? D. Ugh. Go!'

"'No Kathleen,'" Doyle pauses. "It's a perfect example of why Ron Hynes is awesome. There are no winners in that song. Yet, it is beautiful."

No Kathleen

She laid her head on the bar,
Watching tiny little stars dance
around in front of her eyes;
He cried on her shoulder,
Sat there and told her sad stories
and pretty white lies.

And if not for that one indiscretion,
It would have been an uneventful day;
If not for that single obsession,
Things would never have gone that way.

But she had one last drink and
she didn't think twice,
In fact, she didn't think at all;
My, my, how far can a little girl fall?

Oh, they walked out of the bar,
she climbed into his car,
And they drove to somewhere
deep in the night;
Where she slipped off her ring a
nd the rest of her things,
And he switched off the
tiny dome light.

She fell back in his arms
without the slightest alarm,
Forgetting everything her
mama once said;
And just for a moment
in the back of her mind,
The tiny picture came and
went in her head.

Oh, she remembered a man
who was waiting at home,
And a baby barely learning to crawl;
My, my, how far can a little girl fall?

At six fifteen the baby woke up at home,
And the crying shook her daddy awake;
At a quarter to seven
he made the decision,
He thought he'd never have to make.

Then at eight forty-five that girl
came back to life,
In the back seat of a fancy car;
To a world of disgrace and
a smile on the face,
Of some stranger from a downtown bar.

At nine o'clock she put
the key in the lock,
Just a little too late to explain;
She took one minute more before she
opened the door,
She went over her story again.

Well, the child and the man
were both long, long gone,
And the note said, Goodbye,
and that's all;
My, my, how far can a little girl fall?
Oh-oh-oh-oh, my, my,
how far can a little girl fall?

"There's about a hundred words in it. You know everything about every person. If you read carefully enough, and you listen carefully enough, you don't need to ask a single question when the song is over. You know what I mean? The tiniest stories are the biggest stories, and I envy the way he can do that, because it's a skill I've not yet developed, if I'll ever be able to develop it. Paint a picture of a person." Doyle likens "No Kathleen" to another Ron Hynes song, "How Far Can a Little Girl Fall," recorded by Terry Kelly. Sitting in a coffee shop in downtown St. John's, he looked at me and spontaneously sang every syllable of the song.

"I was never particularly fond of 'How Far Can A Little Girl Fall,'" said Ron. "I wrote it in St. John's shortly after separating from my first wife. I was babysitting for her while she was downtown one night with someone she'd started seeing. It was reactionary and unrealistic."

Ron talked about the song as though it was a distant relative he liked but was never close to.

"I always did like the melody though, and Terry Kelly does a nice version."

Keyboardist Paul Kinsman recalls that Ron played the song a few times at gigs, but it's astonishing to him that Ron can have created such an amazing, stirring song, and did not need to draw on it more than he has. "It's an unbelievable lyric and he does this all the time," says Kinsman. "And he'd just throw that out like it was a piece of tissue he just blew his nose in, and he'll never think of it again."

One reason might have been that he simply had so much material he could afford to turn away from some compositions.

"He does," says Kinsman. "He has a large body of work. There's probably plenty of songs like 'How Far Can a Little Girl Fall,' that would blow people's minds, that he's never recorded. It makes you wonder if they mean that much to him as they do to other people. Because he has so many of them. Like having fifty kids, you know?

"The songs have a weight to them. And, when you put down that load at the end of the night, you realize what you've just done. You've played three hours of some of the heaviest songs written here."

Many marvel at Ron's sound, at how he could move beyond the world of three chords, which musical history is simply full of, and make something sound so distinctive. Those who know music attribute it to Ron's uncanny ability to create amazing arrangements, an attribute which transcended even great song writing. This is a quality he would have seen in one of his earliest musical heroes, Gordon Lightfoot. Over time, Ron definitely developed a signature sound.

Ron said he discovered at one point "that it actually takes you twenty years before your songs sound like you."

THE GRAND VOYEUR

FREQUENT RON HYNES ACCOMPANIST BRIAN BOURNE talks about how Ron not only lived with a guitar slung around his neck 24/7 but also about his song writing capability: his ability to get inside a story and tell it like it really is.

He relates the anecdote that a northerner starts a story with "Once upon a time in a land far, far away," but a southerner starts a story with "Ya'll ain't going to believe this shit." There is no question in Bourne's mind that Ron is the southerner.

"Well, he's the great philosopher, is he not?" says Bourne. "We all become one when we have kids," he jokes, but when it comes to Ron, he means it. "I mean, couple that with guitar playing, the melodic structure, the construction of the song, the poetry behind it…it's a many faceted thing."

Chris LeDrew believes Ron's strength rested neither in his singing, nor in his musicianship. Rather it emanated from his ability to create melodies with meaningful, penetrative lyrics—to tell great stories. And telling stories is really what Ron was all about, whether through his music or ramblings on a drive in the car or in an e-mail. The thing is, you never knew where the line was between truth and fiction. But at least he came by this trait honestly.

"The line between truth and legend for my whole life is really, really thin," Ron admitted. "Sometimes my stories will be actual fact, and sometimes I'll go back and I'll tell them again and I blur into fantasy, into a legend. And I think I get that from my father because when my father was home in the summertime, and he would be home at Christmastime, he would always have these great stories. But I remember Mom says, 'Tom, that's a lie, that's a lie. That's not the same way you told that story last year.' And he'd say, 'Well, yeah I know, I know. I know,' you know? It may not be exactly the truth, but it's a good story."

In addition to thinking of Ron as a philosopher, Halifax-based, Newfoundland-born author Donna Morrissey, widely acknowledged as one of Canada's leading novelists, has a special place in her heart for Ron's songwriting and a wonderful way of characterizing him.

"We all live in story," she says. "Most of us can never pen our stories for varied reasons. And so we hunger for the writer who captures a bit of us. Pens us in words that sing of our love, our sorrow, our yearnings. Ron Hynes is such a poet, songwriter. He is a grand voyeur in this rough, sweet life, a melody writer of the first order, a story teller, a philosopher, a poet, and a kick-ass performer. And we sit, enthralled, voyeurs to our own stories."

Morrissey's attraction to Ron is no doubt, like other lovers of his art, partly due to her love of his melodies, but perhaps also because Ron has acted as a voyeur, peeking inside her mind by probing her writing, as was the case when he composed "My Father's Ghost."

No wonder she says then that his lyrics and melodies can make her hair stand on end.

"'My Father's Ghost' was written in Woody Point in September of 2008," says Ron, "as were most of the songs for the *Stealing Genius* album."

Woody Point is a small community at Gros Morne National Park in southwestern Newfoundland where journalist, broadcaster, and author Stephen Brunt, Susan Brunt's brother, established the Woody Point Writers' Festival.

"My Father's Ghost" is based on the book *What They Wanted* by Morrissey, which explores both new and familiar terrain for her: the wild shores of a Newfoundland outport and the equally wild environment of an Alberta oil rig.

Ron described the inspiration for the song: "As the community is being resettled and the family is crossing over to mainland Newfoundland, her grandmother looks back at her house fading into the dark distance and, knowing she'll never see it or set foot inside it again, remarks that 'At least now I won't have to get up early every morning and mop up the salt water round the rocking chair.'

"That was the entire song right there in those few words," said Ron.

> He was sitting on the stairway and my heart filled up with dread
> His hands were clenched, his clothes were drenched, I knew that he was dead
> The dawn was fairly breaking as she headed down the path
> Where the water crashed across the rocks with all its rage and wrath
> But her heart had gone to ashes and the ice chewed through her bones

And her footsteps fell like granite as she came back home
She stood inside the doorway and she turned towards the cove
She took down the blessed crucifix and she burned it in the stove
And we all stood in the kitchen like travellers in the rain
Waiting on the platform to board some lonely train
All that was sixty years ago, my mother's in the ground
Brother, sister moved away and left me the house and land
And I sell my socks and sweaters to the tourists from away
There's a monthly old age pension and it keeps the wolf at bay
And I count the days…

"Words like that should make Leonard Cohen stand up and take notice," wrote Lee Mellor in 2012 for *The Scene* music industry magazine, whose review and analysis covered the entire *Stealing Genius* output, including this excerpt about "My Father's Ghost":

> The standout ballad on the first half of *Stealing Genius* is the Donna Morrissey inspired "My Father's Ghost." The production is sparer here, with Hynes's acoustic guitar comfortably carrying the first verse, Tom Leighton's accordion and Burke Carroll's pedal steel slowly bleeding in to create a hair-raising backdrop to a tale of death, apparitions and aging.

Mellor goes on to write that he'd been told Ron was a "Newfoundland song writing legend."

> Having heard *Stealing Genius*, I can see why. This is not about the man. It's about his stories. Over the years, they have collectively formed a patchwork tapestry which has become his legend. Is that not the path where all the great ones have tread?

Mellor says Hynes's lyrics are "ingenious on many levels: description, substance, and (when he puts the effort in) the Newfoundlander's adroit rhymes are capable of making the most gifted rapper bow his head and shuffle home, pants hanging down." He went on to write that the production is, for the most part, solid, and at times reminiscent of an east coast Willie Nelson or Waylon Jennings, with horn and string sections that wisely do not overstep their boundaries.

"Hynes's voice," wrote Mellor, "though probably not considered classically good, is convincing and laden with wonderful idiosyncrasies—the kind of uniqueness we might encounter in a Bob Dylan, Neil Young, or again, Willie."

"*Stealing Genius* was the most disciplined effort I'd ever done in that I wrote every day and kept regular hours for sleep, food, exercise, and creative time," said Ron. "It was literally like forced creativity."

He'd moved into a house belonging to friends after the Woody Point Writers Festival was done. He was with his Maltese puppy named Iris and a couple of guitars. It was an unusual thing for Ron to hunker down and write so determinedly, as though he'd become a one-month song writing factory.

"In August, 2008," said Ron, "I was somewhat overdue for the next CD release and had nothing except a song inspired by a Stan Dragland short story about the breakup of a relationship, a song called 'House.'"

Unashamedly, as biographer, I get to say here that "House" is without question one of Ron's most beautiful songs.

"I'd also begun to feel that it might be a good change to go do something else for a while, even more to go be someone who lived somewhere else and was something else, like if I was Joseph O'Neill and was a carpenter and lived in Portugal."

This hypothetical Joseph O'Neill is a composite of Ron's middle name (Joseph), his mother's maiden name (O'Neill), the fact that Ron has always had an interest in carpentry and auto mechanics, and as he puts it, "I'm curious about Portugal because of its historical Newfoundland connection and because of women with dark hair and darker eyes."

"On one hot summer afternoon while attending the Woody Point Writers' Festival, I purchased a book by Randall Maggs called *Night Work: The Sawchuk Poems*.

"I wandered around Woody Point all day reading aloud and in the midst of the read I saw what could be the next CD."

Ron went right back to the writers' festival theatre where the festival was being held and bought books by Des Walsh, Stan Dragland, Joel Hynes, Donna Morrissey, Al Pittman, and any other authors' or poets' books from Newfoundland whose work he liked.

"I then spent the entire month of September reading, writing, sleeping regularly, doing daily walks with Iris, some trout fishing. I was awake by 6 a.m. every day, had breakfast, worked till twelve, made lunch, walked with Iris, wrote till six, made dinner, wrote till midnight and slept. The same regimen every day for a full month.

"I had lyrics all over the house: by the bed, on tables, on chairs, above the fireplace. I read a whole bunch of work by Des Walsh, Randall Maggs, Al Pittman, Joel Hynes, Donna Morrissey and whatever else was in the house and whatever I'd brought to the space. It took about thirty days to write the whole project."

Ron was particularly fond of two pieces inspired by Des Walsh's work (whom Ron's partner, Susan, refers to as the Johnny Cash of Newfoundland poets), those being "I Love You More Than God," which he considers to be his best love song, and "Love and Hunger."

When September came to a close, Ron had about twenty songs, all inspired by the work of all of the artists he'd read while residing at Woody Point. Those songs formed *Stealing Genius*, his third recording for Borealis. Those songs, and of course his earlier material, formed the repertoire for a tour, until he was diagnosed with throat cancer, which sidelined him until 2013.

Ron and Susan Brunt initially met that August of 2008 at the Woody Point Writers' Festival, an event founded by her brother Stephen which has built a stellar reputation, attracting a wealth of phenomenal writers and media people like CBC radio host Shelagh Rogers. When they met, Susan really had no idea who he was and introduced herself by saying, "Apparently you're famous, but I'm sorry I've never heard of you. My brother sent me over with a drink for you."

"He loved that I had no idea of his fame or infamy," says Brunt, who only emerged to be interviewed following Ron's death. She had initially declined to be interviewed.

"I was charmed by him and as I became familiar with his work, I was so impressed by his talent. At the same time I had no interest in his fame, nor did I want a piece of it and I think this set me apart from a lot of people he encountered. I think Ron felt safe with me."

The two saw one another a couple more times over the following year, says Brunt, "and then connected again at the festival in August of 2009. At this point, we decided to try out a long distance relationship."

According to Chris LeDrew, there was a lot to learn from Ron in terms of playing and songwriting.

"I can't remember when we were introduced as such. I don't know if there was someone that introduced us, but I was starting to write songs. Ron was usually pretty good with emerging songwriters. Usually very friendly. You didn't quite know what you were going to get when you said hello to Ron, but in those days around '91/'92 he was fairly friendly. So we just met that way, and I went to Ron's house one night for a party, and that's when I got to know him a bit better.

"We talked a little bit at that party, and it's funny, earlier that night I had sprained my ankle, and I was down to LSPU [The Longshoremen's Protective Union performance hall] to see a show, and I sprained my ankle and Dermot O'Reilly had some sort of painkillers, so he said, 'Oh, you got something wrong with your ankle. Here, take a few of these.' So I took a few of them, yeah, I took whatever, and I was drinking beer too or whatever. I was talking to Ron in his kitchen, and he was talking to me about the business and whatnot. I was talking away with him and all of a sudden, I fell, right? I just passed out while I was just talking to him in the kitchen

"I went straight passed him right onto the kitchen floor. He probably won't even remember. I guess I came to about a minute or two later and Mary Walsh had me by the legs, and Ron had me by the arms, and they were carrying me out of the kitchen.

"At the time it was wild. Wild times. One time Ron held a songwriter's thing at the LSPU Hall, like a weekend summer's retreat. Myself and a couple of my buddies were involved in that. So it was early '90s before I got to know Ron a bit.

"We were sucking up every minute of it because, for me, it was a way to be inspired to write, to hang out with Ron, and Ron is like, 'Play me your latest song.' You play it, and he would say, 'It's a piece of shit.' He'd say you should do this or that with it."

Later though, LeDrew had the opportunity to write together with Ron, but nothing that could pass muster enough to get recorded.

"He was very assertive," says LeDrew. "He was definitely the alpha writer when you were writing with Ron. You know what I mean? I guess it depends on who he was writing with, but for me, the couple of times I wrote with him, he was very assertive about his ideas, and very engaged in the process."

In terms of co-writing, there were only a few which Ron talked about favourably. "It's not natural," he said, "I'm just good at it." Among those co-writing efforts he has enjoyed, there are those with his ex-wife, Connie, on the *11/11* album, "Hard Workin' Hands" with Nova Scotia's Dave Gunning, "A Good Dog Is Lost" and "Tiger Lily," both co-written with his youngest child, Lily, and "Sorry Lori," about his eldest daughter Lori. Her version of that song is apparently different from Ron's, hers being more accurate. "Mine's legend, which is *an exaggeration of the truth*," says Ron.

One artist Ron has written extensively and successfully with is singer/songwriter Newfoundland native Terry Kelly. Now based in Halifax, Kelly still performs, but is also an accomplished athlete (he distinguished himself as the third blind person in the world to run the mile in under five minutes), a professional speaker, and as he frames it, a lover of life. He has released seven full-length recordings, resulting in seven East Coast Music Awards and nominations for four Canadian Country Music Awards, and a JUNO. He has received the King Clancy Award, and honourary doctorates in Civil Laws and in Fine Arts, the Canadian Country Music Association's Humanitarian Award and is a member of the Order of Canada. He has shared the stage with symphony orchestras, and has performed his original music in Europe, Australia, New Zealand, and for the troops in Afghanistan.

Ron and Kelly met through several musical friends, including Declan O'Doherty, producer of the WGB album, *Living in a Fog*. Kelly made appearances on the WGB television show and the two hit it off. Kelly has gone on to record several Ron Hynes songs including "Sonny's Dream" and "How Far Can a Little Girl Fall."

Collaborations involving Ron and Kelly typically began with Kelly starting a piece, with Ron weighing in to add or finish the idea. It was never really the same twice. For the song "Safe Home," for example, Kelly had worked out the chorus and the bridge. After

Ron weighed in, he came to a point where he simply said, "You go ahead and finish," which at first left Kelly frustrated, thinking perhaps Ron just couldn't be bothered to complete what Kelly thought was a pretty good tune. Unbeknownst to Kelly at the time, it was a gift, because it proved to Kelly that he could write songs. It was Ron who Kelly credits with helping him find his musical *voice*, his *signature*.

In a vein similar to being left to finish "Safe Home," Kelly reiterated the previously mentioned story about recording engineer Paul Mills being left by Ron to finish the post production on the *Get Back Change* album, which was an outcome Mills had never experienced with an artist before. He was terrified Ron would think he frigged up his songs. But Ron put his trust in Mills and he was thrilled with the results.

Fully acknowledging that Ron has a profound gift for songwriting, Kelly says Ron had told him that any songwriter worth their salt should never experience writer's block because, as he put it, "Every lyric, every word, if we wait, is there for us to have" or the thought that "Whatever lyrics and words you choose to come to you, then they do." Sounds easier than it is, of course, but what Ron was talking about was being patient. Kelly compares this with his personal life, in finding and accessing the right lyrics and phrases.

"That's the way I look at life, but had never thought about music that way," until Ron described the process. Kelly reinforces the approach using the words "recognizing, believing, and knowing."

There have been a couple of twists and turns in Ron's and Kelly's songwriting and recording exploits. For the song "River of No Return," which they co-wrote, there are actually two slightly different versions of the song. Neither likes the other's version according to Kelly, but they were good enough about it that it doesn't matter, mostly because they'd been long-term friends since the early 1980s.

In the early 1990s, the two were invited to co-present an award at the ECMAs which were being staged that year in St. John's. Kelly thought it would be a funny lead up to the presentation to do a kind of Abbott and Costello back-and-forth routine about "River of No Return," each congratulating or complimenting the other on what a great contribution they had made to the composition of the song. The two worked out the dialogue backstage just before they went on and Ron fully agreed to play it out. Knowing

Ron's ability to be a straight man during his WGB days, Kelly thought it would be a no brainer for him. But when the two walked out and Kelly turned to Ron to say what a great job he had done with the song, instead of gushing back to Kelly with a similar compliment, Ron simply responded, "Thanks, man!" leaving Kelly dumbstruck. Kelly knows that in the walkout on stage, Ron simply forgot. Others who knew the plan were not quite so forgiving. Kelly today thinks it's hilarious.

Earlier on, Kelly had recorded the Ron Hynes song "There Goes the Fire," which outspoken Country 101 Halifax radio program director Paul Kennedy really liked. Shortly following, Ron released the song as well, according to Kelly, and Kennedy made no bones about telling Ron he thought his version was crap compared to Kelly's. Needless to say, Ron was not enamoured. Strangely, Kennedy was surprised that Ron was not happy with the remark.

Although he and Kelly and some others had satisfying co-writing outcomes, Ron generally viewed co-writing as some form of fabrication which comes from the business of being in the music industry.

"The best co-writers are the famous ones like Lennon/McCartney, Jagger/Richards, Bacharach/David. All those. But co-writing in Nashville or LA or wherever is bullshit, people writing specifically to get hits. That's not song writing. It's easy to explain co-writing. I hear hacks doing it all the time. They love doing it because it keeps them connected to media and the music biz. How many Gordon Lightfoot co-writes are there? How many Leonard Cohen co-writes? Those guys are songwriters, not hacks. You don't see co-painters, co-sculptors. You'll see the occasional co-novelist, but that's industry-based as well. Creative work should be solitary. One inspiration."

One song LeDrew did finish with Ron was called "Gone."

"It was like 'Gone is where I want to be, halfway between here and there' or whatever.

"The times we wrote it was usually always in his space. His house. We worked on a song one time. I think he was in bed. I think him and [ex-wife] Connie were in bed. I was sitting on the side of the bed. I actually stayed with Ron for a couple of weeks in between apartments. He had a loft in his house. It was up on Gower Street. He let me stay up there. So during that time I was staying there, we sort of interacted a bit. Not as much as you normally would with someone you were staying with. You know, at times we'd talk. It was actually an odd couple of weeks. Ron is a very private person so I kind of tried to stay out of the way while I was there as much as I could."

And there is a fair bit of age difference between Ron and LeDrew, twenty years in fact.

"He's a little younger than my dad."

According to Greg Malone, Ron has a history of being loosely collaborative with the people around him.

"He'd be writing down. He'd be telling you lines. What about this? What do you think of that? He'd tell you lines from the song, right? I've got a line that goes like this. What do you think? And you'd be driving along and Ron would be coming out with lines."

According to Malone, Ron would use the people around him as creative sounding boards.

"He would try lines on us. And he would try characters out on the boys too."

And this sounding-board approach was mutual as Malone and Tommy Sexton would try character and bit ideas out on Ron during the WGB days. Chances were if Ron liked something they were pitching, then that was a good sign the material would work.

"When we were doing the shows, you know, everybody was songwriters," says Stamp, "you know, not excluding myself and Sandy and stuff. We all contributed to a certain point, but like Jamie [Snider], he had his tunes, and when Ron came up with a song, like he'd write stuff for video. I think that's what shocked Dean Cameron when they came up. We did a video before videos. It was almost there. It was almost MTV. That was just about happening.

"There is one song that Ron wrote called 'Murder on your Heart.' It is still one of my favourite Ron songs," says Stamp, frustrated that Ron and the band hardly ever played it. He especially loves the middle, which has a gritty Peter Gunn television show theme sound produced on the guitar. It has that sinister type feel in the front, and you know, all about murder. And Ron just wrote it and it just worked so well. We played it live a few times. It was fantastic. It's not on one of Ron's albums. You'd only hear it on the Grand Band show."

Writing songs with Ron is one thing. Playing on stage with him is another.

From the days in Ottawa, frequent accompanist Brian Bourne and Ron would run into one another occasionally, crossing paths at one musical event or another. Around that time, Ron appeared in Halifax for some event and the two hooked up, putting Bourne in the position of providing accompaniment. Asked whether Ron is better as a solo performer or with an accompanist, Bourne isn't sure.

"Well, he is such a great songwriter that his songs are so strong," he says, but he dearly loves playing with Ron. "He is a dream to play with because it's such a high caliber where he has taken this songwriting thing," adding that he makes playing guitar look easy, with such a gentle approach, that in a strange sense, he is essentially self-accompanying.

According to keyboardist Paul Kinsman, Ron's is very satisfying music to play.

"It's just the way Ron gets around his chords, you know. Some leaves me a bit cold, like the real singer/songwriter stuff. It's kind of like, ugh, get to the bridge, man, get to the point. But it is, you know, stuff like 'Evening Tide,' geez, you know, these songs mean an awful lot to some people. Different songs mean a lot to different people. Stuff like 'Atlantic Blue,' it started off very intimate, but now when we do it live, it has keyboards. It's evolved a lot. These songs are really meaningful to people. I don't know how Ron would feel about this, but I kind of have, you know, you've been playing them for so long, you have some sort of amount of ownership with the way they are. All of us who played a lot with Ron feel that way about our parts, and about our things that we do in these songs that we brought."

So what would Ron say to that?

"What would he say? Fuck ya," says Kinsman.

More to the point, Kinsman feels Ron might not even think of musicians' relationships to his music that way, adding that it's generally hard to know or predict what Ron is aware of and what he's not.

"My relationship with Ron has been mostly musical, not very personable. Although, we know a lot about each other, but we're not close like him and Sandy, or Greg, you know. So to play his music makes people feel so happy. You're not playing songs for people who don't care if it is the man in the moon up there on stage. They're there to see Ron. The people are there to see Ron. They just don't happen to be there. They know these songs, they like these songs, and they keep coming back to hear it. So these songs mean a lot to people, and I feel the same thing that Ron does when we're up there together. I mean, I'm hearing the crowd. I'm getting the same feedback, and we are all kind of collectively feeling it."

Doing a Ron Hynes gig is not like a regular gig, says Kinsman.

"The songs are so world-class. They are not bullshit songs. And he throws stuff away that makes me angry that he can just write something and then never ever play it again. Just toss it out."

He's referring to songs like "How Far Can a Little Girl Fall," a number also mentioned by Great Big Sea frontman Alan Doyle, which Ron apparently never recorded.

Doing a Ron Hynes gig is such a turn-on that Kinsman actually put a stall on his wedding, back in 1999, in order to do a show.

"We played in Brampton. It was Pride of the Rock. I had told Boomer, 'So, we have a wedding date. We are going to get married on the 19th of June.' He said, 'No you're not. You're going to be in Brampton with Ron playing for a few thousand drunk Newfoundlanders out in a field.' And I told my wife, Phyllis, and, honest to God, we moved the date to the following week. She knows what Ron is all about. She knew it wasn't just any old *I'm going on the road for a weekend*, right? She knew it was something special. Thankfully, it was within a couple of days of setting the date that we found this out. We were able to change things, you know."

The gig apparently was fantastic.

More recently, in the summer of 2015, Kinsman backed Ron for his final time at the George Street Festival in downtown St. John's.

"That's the biggest music festival in St. John's. We played the headline slot on the Saturday night before a crowd of 5,000-plus people and we rocked it. Ron, me, and Boomer, Chris LeDrew on bass and Chad Murphy electric guitar. He did all the hits, 'Sonny,' 'St. John's Waltz,' 'River,' etc. and the crowd had a great time. So did Ron, actually. Youngest daughter, Lily, sang 'No Kathleen.' Ron's daughter Rebecca was there. Colleen Power did 'Mary Got a Baby,' and a huge singalong with the crowd for 'Sonny's Dream.' It was good for people to see him. And he deserved to have a cool, triumphant show with a big crowd that was happy to see him."

In hindsight now, Kinsman is particularly happy he got to see and spend time with Ron at that point.

"That night he and I actually reconciled a slight disagreement we had been having for a few weeks," says Kinsman. "I felt good about everything after, though, our relationship and the gig. Ron was happy after a triumphant show. All good."

Chris LeDrew is probably more enthusiastic about playing with Ron than about the experience of writing songs with him.

"Oh, I love playing with Ron," says LeDrew. "Yeah. I'd love to play with Ron all the time because his songs are so frigging good. And the band, whoever he got, was always really good. Boomer and Kinsman. Everyone loves playing with Ron. That is a gig anyone would jump at, you know? Because he's just so good; the music is so good. And he is demanding and it is intense playing with him.

"It's because he is so surly. You just don't know where he is going to go. You are just hoping for the best. And he's got a lot of passion when he sings. You know, the songs are great. It is so fun. It is such a great feeling to contribute musically to one of those songs, even if it is just in a fleeting moment of a live performance. You feel like you've added your little bit or something or you've expressed yourself within his songs."

THE BARD OF GEORGE ST.

EVERYONE REFERS TO RON AS THE Man of a Thousand Songs. But when you listen more closely to peoples' views about his art, it's much deeper than that. If Johnny Burke was the Bard of Prescott Street, then Ron may be The Bard of George Street—at the foot of that famous street stands his statue. For it is his words, his poetry, which most people agree is at the heart of his art.

What did he set out to do? Did he want to just play guitar and write pop songs like some of his falsetto and other early musical heroes? Or did he, as writer Lee Mellor penned in *The Scene* magazine in 2012 while reviewing Ron's *Stealing Genius* album, dare to force his audience, his listeners, "to confront: poverty, heartbreak and loss" with words which easily "transforms this 'ugliness' into beauty."

"Ron sang the songs of our generation," says Greg Malone. "He sang our life basically. We were the people in his songs all across Newfoundland. That's who he is writing about. The crowd downtown in 'St. John's Waltz,' all the people, some dead, some still living. He is the songwriter of our generation. So, in a way, his songs are background music to our lives and our cultural scene and everything. They are all punctuated by Ron's songs for about twenty years over time. It's a Newfoundland thing, and a St. John's thing. He's like the poet laureate or the troubadour of our generation. It's true. It's true. Ron loves words and writing. I do a lot of writing, so Ron loves how the lines go and the comedy too. He is just fascinated how all that goes. The right word with the right melody."

And Malone is right. The more you watched and listened to Ron, the more you felt the overwhelming sense that every single word, every syllable he wrote counted.

Oddly, there has never been a Ron Hynes poetry book.

"The lyrics are easy once the idea is there or some semblance of chorus or storyline," said Ron.

"Ninety-nine per cent of the time the lyrics come first. Mostly I'm hearing a groove or a tempo or musical attitude in my head as I'm writing the lyric. Either the melody comes full blown with the lyric or I'll wait for the lyric to dictate its own melody. Melody has always been hard for me. I have to be patient and wait and eventually it comes, sometimes along with the lyric, sometimes an hour, a day, or a week later, sometimes a year. I know that may be hard to grasp or understand but it's the way I've always done it. It's the only way I know how. This stuff is hard to explain.

"I don't like sounding generic or repetitive...and it has to sound like me, like a Ron Hynes song. I can't really explain that, no more than I can explain how to write a song. All I know is I've got a handle on it when I'm doing it."

U.S. musician Jason Wilbur was so impressed with Ron's song writing from the first few minutes of the show he caught at The Ship, that he wrote the song "Watching Picasso" about him.

"Ron sings and writes from his own unique perspective, with his own unique musical and lyrical style, as opposed to writing in someone else's style or within the generally recognized parameters of a genre, with clichés, etc."

Keyboardist Paul Kinsman tries, like Wilbur and others, to pin down what it is about Ron's songs that grip people.

"I'm not exactly sure what it is that resonates with people with all of Ron's songs. You know, other than the songs that are, you know, they seem Newfoundlandy, like 'Lighthouse,' like 'Sonny' and like 'Evening Tide,' but there's other songs that have nothing at all to do with the Newfoundland experience that people love too. 'A Picture of Dorian Gray,' and 'Last Chance' is about a guy in a hotel meets a young woman, sold his money, and a Roman god came and took away a couple of bad guys. A car and all this. It's like a Dylan-esque kind of narrative. I mean, that has nothing to do with Newfoundland at all, but it's still up there."

Wilbur emphasizes the adage *write what you know* as it applies to Ron.

"He is a perfect example of someone who writes what they know and he does it in a way that allows the listener to relate to the underlying themes and archetypes. The songs are easy to relate to even if you don't have the same cultural or geographic reference points. In fact having those be different makes it more interesting, I think."

Wilbur referred to Ron as the Bob Dylan of Eastern Canada.

ONE MAN GRAND BAND

"He stands on his own, but I say that partly because everyone knows who Bob Dylan is, so he's a good reference point. Ron's songs have that kind of searching-for-something quality that a lot of Dylan's songs have too." Wilbur clarifies that he's talking about Ron's writing style, not Dylan's singing style.

WATCHING PICASSO by Jason Wilber

The crowd crashed like waves over shots over pints
While we sat struck dumb with surprise
To quote my hero Old Joe, a radiance did show
But the din didn't ever subside

It was like watching Picasso, Monet, or Renoir
Sketching out his world with a voice and guitar
My God how good must you be said the man next to me
Before folks might just listen a while

He played and he sang simple and plain
And out poured a quiet masterpiece
By the cigarette machine on a dim corner stage
That creaked like a tired ship at sea

I don't even mean to judge or indict
It's not like this was Carnegie Hall
I guess no one expects to witness genius
Unless it hangs on a museum wall

If you're ever up that way near old St. John's Bay
Where the shadow of the Signal Hill lies
Climb up Solomon's Lane to the door marked Ship Inn
And sit down and listen to Ron Hynes

Ron's *angel*, oncology nurse Suzy Power, has had his songs rolling around in her head for thirty-five years. There is perhaps no more eloquent or poignant way to look at him than through her angel eyes.

"I have trouble putting my finger on exactly why he is felt to have such a remarkable gift and why he is so well loved," she says. "I believe that the reasons are the same for both. As well, it's also why some musicians and singer/songwriters are known as true artists and why others ought not to be referred to as such."

Power talks about how a painting or a book or a dance piece can be very moving and create a feeling of connection to an audience, a viewer, a reader, or a listener.

"So can Ron's lyrics," she feels. "Maybe, on a basic level, that's what we all want. To feel like someone *gets* us and to know that realization that we are simply not really that different from all the other souls who are moved by the same work of art. Ron uses our simple language with common and comfortable references to nail exactly how we feel as the little dramas in our lives play out. We feel a connection to Ron, like an old best friend or brother, because how else would he know exactly how that felt unless he knew, understood, and loved us? That's the magic of Ron. One line stands out and then there's that connection.

"There's a simple sweetness and humility and faith in Ron's lyrics that simply warms my heart."

Power believes that Ron had a self-awareness and openness about it that could rarely be appreciated or seen in others. In his composition "The Mother Who Bore You in Pain," she senses an incredible depth of empathy and compassion for those who love him, for his friends and family who have worried about him.

As borne out by numerous interviews, but especially by Power, Ron had a group who are fiercely devoted to him. These are not the typical or even more fanatical fans, but his real and true friends and family members, people like Sandy Morris.

"Ron is hugely loved and admired here because we are all about music in Newfoundland," says Morris. "We are all about song writing. I mean, we've got a huge tradition of songwriters, aside from all the traditional stuff, you know, handed out by word of mouth, all that stuff that came from Ireland and England and all these things."

On top of the traditional music, Morris says Newfoundland and Labrador has tons of famous songwriters and some not so famous, like guys out around the bay who'd worked and lived ordinary lives but they just happened to write very clever songs.

"There was a guy from down in Placentia, one of the islands of Placentia, called Peter Leonard. Peter the Poet they used to call him, and he was just brilliant: catchy tunes and catchy lyrics. He knows how to craft, right? So there is a whole tradition of that here."

"So then Ron comes along and writes stuff that everybody relates to," says Power. "Ron knew the world's secrets. That's his art. In a song, Ron tells me that he knows my secrets—even the ones I haven't told to anyone. The things I was afraid to even think, like in the line from 'Dry'—'morning came with the same sad surprise.' I never told anyone that I felt that sometimes, but he knew."

And finally, for Power, Ron was a love poet, whose company might include the likes of Elizabeth Barrett Browning.

If one takes Suzy Power as any form of measure, it is the poetry of Ron Hynes which has the most impact on people.

Ron himself considers "Sonny's Dream" to be the most important gift sent from God one day four decades ago, but the wonder of "Sonny's Dream," as it is with many great and memorable tunes, is that it is the combined phenomenon of penetrative lyric and melody which listeners cannot erase. As a poet, Ron has written dozens of great melodies to go with great stanzas, but none had the universal appeal of his signature piece.

THE RON SWAGGER

RON HAD A WAY OF PRESENTING and carrying himself that people could not overlook.

While some people are loud and need to narcissistically draw attention to themselves, Ron was much more subtle.

His nephew, Joel Thomas Hynes, captured the essence of Ron's swagger perfectly in a scene from the MacGillivray feature film, *The Man of a Thousand Songs*. He said that if Ron walked onto an airplane and walked down the aisle, people would have no idea who he was, everyone would stop reading what they were reading, listening to what they were listening to and talking to who they were talking to, to pause and wonder, *Who is that man and what does he do?*

Oncology nurse Suzy Power talked about how Ron's swagger, even when entering the cancer clinic, drew attention to him instantly. It was a combination of his hat, his boots, his gait—an entire package that was very distinctive.

Susan Brunt loved the fact that Ron had a swagger.

"I first saw this in Woody Point. I was at a party and Ron had been off somewhere else doing a show. He arrived late when the party was in full swing and it was like everyone paused as he literally swaggered in carrying a guitar, wearing his hat, dressed beautifully in a rock and roll way and looking like, as my friend described him, a cross between Matthew McConaughey and Keith Richards."

Brunt says that his swagger was always there to varying degrees, whether Ron was on stage or strolling on the Danforth.

"I'd be walking along the Danforth thinking Ron was beside me talking away and then realize he was not there. I'd turn around and he'd be at least half a block behind me, walking with the Ron Swagger, taking his time and taking it all in."

The two went to the Munich Film festival the year *The Man of a Thousand Songs* documentary was shown and where Brunt says she had a great time.

While there, they had a keeper there named Frank.

"Ron and I were waiting for him one afternoon sitting in a café outside the film fest headquarters and the paparazzi were there waiting for some A-list actor to arrive. I can't remember who it was, but they obviously got bored. They saw Ron, didn't know who he was, but thought he was someone and came rushing over and swarmed us."

There were at least twenty-five photographers yelling at us and snapping endless pictures.

"Ron loved that moment," says Brunt. "I thought it was hilarious and couldn't stop laughing the whole time."

It was definitely the Ron swagger, Brunt says, that intangible quality, that drew the photogs.

And apparently drew her in the very beginning of their connection at Woody Point.

RIDING OFF INTO THE SUNSET

RON WOULD HAVE LOVED THE OLD western analogy of him riding off into the sunset. Sadly, however, his departure wasn't quite so romantic. His exit was just plain sad, although dignified.

In the analogy of old westerns, the hero always leaves a teary-eyed, broken-hearted damsel behind as he leaves and sets out to do whatever it is he must do; there is that lingering sense of independence and heroism. In Ron's case, he left a teary-eyed, broken-hearted fan base behind when he died at the St. John's Health Sciences Centre at around 6 p.m. on Thursday, November 19, 2015.

He'd known it was coming for some weeks. He wrote me an e-mail on October 25, 2015: "Will keep you posted on this regularly, but there's a small chance I'm not as long as I was hoping for this world. Better get this book out soon lol."

Two of the women still close to Ron in their own unique ways were Connie Hynes and Susan Brunt. Both declined interviews for this book while Ron was still alive. After his death, Connie was in contact but was understandably just too overwhelmed by grief to talk about the man who she saw as the love of her life. She stayed in Newfoundland for a period to help her and Ron's daughter, Lily, through her own grieving.

But Brunt decided to open up.

In the final months of his life, Brunt was in contact with Ron a fair amount. She saw him in August of 2015 in Toronto and he was in great spirits. When she commented on that, he said, "Yes I am happy." Then he paused for a moment and added, "I think I've finally forgiven my mother."

"I think that was true and he had found some peace on that front," says Brunt. "He remained optimistic really until he became very ill at the end and went to hospital."

Brunt is not unaware that she mostly saw Ron in his *golden time*, as White called it, meaning that she wasn't experiencing some of his darker moments during their times together or that when he was, he knew enough to shield her from it. That was possible only

Ron Hynes and Susan Brunt in Cornerbrook, NL, summer 2011.

because they were living thousands of kilometres apart and because, when he was in Toronto, the lowlifes selling drugs to him weren't in the mix.

The time they did spend together was mostly simple, every day stuff. There was some exposure to the music subculture but little if any exposure to the drug subculture.

"We hung around, drank coffee, went to movies, ate out occasionally, went to see someone perform, saw his daughters in Toronto. It was a quiet life really."

To the degree that Brunt did get drawn into Ron's alluring music lifestyle, touring with Ron twice in the summer of 2010, from Ontario to Newfoundland and back, joining him for the CBC *Vinyl Café* and Grand Band shows whenever they reunited, she had a blast.

"I attended a lot of industry events with him which he hated going to. I met the people he respected, trusted, and loved as a result, and made friends with many of them. But he would have been happier watching *The Godfather* on my couch and having a cup of tea. He had an encyclopedic knowledge of films and knew every word of *The Godfather* script."

Their time in Toronto was precious. Ron, she says, loved to look after people, especially her. He'd be up early making coffee and bringing it to her, warming up the car, shovelling snow, and driving her to work and picking her up.

After an initial period of unease about this new person in her life, Brunt's daughter finally made one hundred percent peace on the day Brunt was called to the girl's school as she wasn't feeling well. Ron was so clearly worried about her that he won her over.

Ron's diagnosis and bout with cancer was extremely difficult on both of them. She travelled back and forth from Toronto to St. John's to accompany him periodically to his chemo sessions. The whole while she was quite aware of just how ill he was, while he was "really quite blithely optimistic. Or at least he kept up that façade with me, and for me.

"He was fun and funny and loved me sincerely and deeply.

"The day before he went to bed and didn't get up again, he was texting me because he was worried about me shovelling snow this winter. I know he thought that he would be here in Toronto, metastatic cancer be damned, shovelling my snow for me. Really all Ron wanted where I was concerned was to be allowed to take care of me. Finally I would say that when I was with Ron, I felt loved completely and unconditionally. He was proud to love me and proud that I loved him."

At that same time, White and Lily were constants at his side along with other family members. He had constant loving wishes from loved ones and true friends who were all on their way to be with him. It's been described that he was peaceful and fearless and died surrounded by love.

According to Ron's friend Susan Cotton, the pathway to the end began when he'd returned back from a provincial Newfoundland trip at the beginning of October with a limp that he hadn't had before.

"It got bad enough that I finally convinced him to go back to the cancer centre for a checkup. He had been concerned for several months that the throat cancer had returned."

Ron's intuition was not completely misguided. While he found out his throat cancer had not returned, he was instead informed that he had cancer spots on his right lung and on his right hip. It was suddenly clear why he'd been limping over recent weeks. He was immediately given five radiation treatments on his hip, but the limp did not improve as had been predicted and hoped. He lived with Susan during those weeks as being out in Ferryland in his condition was not even a remote possibility. So she probably saw him more in those final weeks than any other individual.

"He was very much looking forward to his new CD coming out, and had lots of plans for the future," says Cotton. "After his diagnosis in October, he was busy writing new songs. And he was always watching movies. He loved movies more than anyone I've ever known." Especially those old westerns.

In addition to his staying at Cotton's house, she went to nearly every show of his in Newfoundland from May through November, 2015.

"I drove him to Twillingate for his first ever show there, and we went to the museum there and visited [Twillingate-born opera singer] Georgina Sterling's gravesite. He has a song on his new CD about her. We also went to Swift Current, Lewisport, Placentia, Portugal Cove South, and Brigus. His best shows were the smaller venues which suited his new voice. These shows were always magical."

"We had started a house concert series so he could make some money to pay bills while he was sick. We only had two in the end, but they were both wonderful. These took place on November 1 and 8 at our home in Torbay."

Another source says Ron knew exactly how sick he was and chose to do those last two house concerts.

Between the two concerts, on November 6, he wrote me an e-mail. It was just thirteen days before he died:

> Not feeling the best Harvey but soldiering on just the same…
> managing to stay medicated enough to get thru live performances and
> am doing in-house concerts at home, bringing the audience to me
> so to speak. They all sell out and there have been some great and
> memorable evenings in the house I occupy in Torbay with friends.
> Who knew.

Wayfaring Stranger

I am a poor wayfaring stranger,
Travelling through this world of woe;
And there's no sickness, toil or danger,
In that bright land to which I go.
I'm going there to see my father,
I'm going there no more to roam;
I'm only going over Jordan,
I'm only going over home.

I know bright clouds will gather around me,
I know my road is rough and steep;
But glorious fields lie out before me,
Where God's redeemed no longer weep.
I'm going there to see my mother,
I'm going there no more to roam;
I'm only going over Jordan,
I'm only going over home.

I long to sing *Salvation's Story*,
In concert with that angel band;
And I long to wear that crown of glory,
When I sail home to that soothing land.
I'm going there to see my Saviour,
I'm going there no more to roam;
I'm only going over Jordan,
I'm only going over home.

I am a poor wayfaring stranger,
Travelling through this world of woe;
But there's no heartache, toil or danger,
In that bright land to which I go.
I'm going there to see my father,
I'm going there no more to roam;
I'm only going over Jordan,
I'm only going over home.
I'm only going over home.

"For the first concert he was golden, charming, real, kind, humbled, and *on*," according to a source. "He was dressed in a beautiful suit and said he felt nervous for the first time in years. He played for a couple of hours and hung around after chatting with the guests."

The November 8 house concert would be similar, but would turn out to be his last. He went to bed a few days later and declined very quickly. The last song he sang for his audience that final performance was "Wayfaring Stranger," which is noted to be a variant of a well-known early nineteenth century spiritual/folk song.

Fellow musician and lifelong friend Sandy Morris says that he and Ron hadn't been too close over the past decade or so. It didn't help that Ron was typically hard to track down. If Morris or others wanted to get hold of him, the custom was to leave a message at O'Brien's Music or at the Rose and Thistle pub in St. John's.

Then suddenly, out of the blue, he received a text from Ron about two months before he died. It was followed by a scattering of random, follow-up texts. When the first one arrived, Morris was touring with Chris LeDrew, who also received one from Ron the same night. They would later learn from The Ship manager and concert and event production specialist Tony Murray that Ron had begun texting people prolifically.

Shortly after the texts began arriving, Morris ran into Ron at the Rocket Bakery on Water Street in St. John's and was struck by how frail he looked and awful he sounded. In typical Ron fashion, however, Morris says he was dressed to the nines. The two engaged and hugged one another, talked about the cancer having returned and about what kind of day Ron had had. He'd spent part of it driving around downtown St. John's with a long-time Newfoundland guitar player named Lew Skinner.

"Skinner had taken Ron to lunch that day and then they went driving around town in Lew's big Lincoln Town Car. I think Ron kind of felt like Hank Williams in a way when he was in that car."

Coincidentally, the last time Joel Hynes saw Ron play was at The Ship about a month before he died; it was the same place he'd seen his uncle perform live for the first time when Joel was just sixteen. He was driving that evening around 6:30 when he saw Ron standing outside Tim Horton's on the corner of Prescott and Duckworth streets.

"He was just sort of standing there, a very solitary figure, staring up over the skyline with his mouth open like he was witnessing some catastrophic event. I pulled up next to him and shouted out to him and he looked at my truck and turned away. I jumped out of the truck and shouted again and he looked right through me. It was eerie. I said Ron! It's me, Joel! He was so gaunt. He looked tired, malnourished even. He asked me if I had smokes and when I offered him one of the flavoured cigars I was smoking he asked me for a ride to Caines's [store]. He had to lift his right leg into the truck and couldn't remember whether he'd hurt it or not. He went into Caines's to buy cigarettes and his bank card was declined, so I bought him some smokes. We barely spoke between Caines's and The Ship. He got out on Duckworth and slammed the door without saying goodbye or thanks or anything. Such a rock and roller."

Joel says he did not feel hurt over the incident, although he was a little rattled. He had long ago learned how to take "that side" of Ron. But this time there was something different.

"He was a ghost," says Joel. "Some part of me knew beyond a doubt that he was dying but I couldn't look at it. I guess I'd started to believe he'd cash in on that longevity gene the Hynes boys seem to possess. I just would not allow the possibility of his death to enter my mind, of his not being here on this earth. That night I went to see his show at The Ship and he was amazing. He had the crowd in the palm of his hand. I cried to 'A Good Dog is Lost.' He was brilliant, true to his own lyric in 'The Man of a Thousand Songs': 'When I hit that naked spotlight, I got everything in tune.'"

Joel says he had a fabulous chat with Ron on the steps outside after the show.

"I remember feeling like I was going to smash anyone who looked at him the wrong way. Then I went in and helped him break down his stage and I carried his guitar up to the street and loaded it into a car. I can't remember if I hugged him. I can't remember if I told him I loved him. I never saw him alive again."

Joel says he feels haunted by the bookends that he first and last saw Ron perform at the same location, The Ship, nearly twenty years apart.

Two months after running into Ron at the Rocket Bakery, on Thursday, November 19, Morris was on his way out the door of his house, heading to the Masonic Temple for opening night of the Spirit of Newfoundland dinner theatre Christmas production. The phone rang and it was White telling him Ron was gone.

Once at the hall, he and Boomer Stamp, who also knew and who was also backing the show, couldn't look at one another for fear of giving away to others in the performance company that Ron had passed away. They were fearful of dampening down what was supposed to be a joyous Christmas show. Keeping it strictly to themselves, they wondered how the cast could possibly get through the show if they knew what had happened.

But remarkably, or weirdly, just five minutes before the opening curtain, the lights in the theatre went out and the emergency lights came on. Those lights were programmed to provide about twenty minutes worth of power. Only when the show went on hold did cast members open up and start talking about Ron; it suddenly became clear to Morris and Stamp and everyone else in the production that everyone had already heard the news and everyone was also trying to keep it a secret until after the show. The performance ended up being postponed.

Greg Malone, meanwhile, was over at the LSPU Hall, now also known as the Resource Centre for the Arts, preparing to go on stage for another holiday production when that hall also went dark. The news was certain to reach him because his wife, White, was with Ron when he passed. That show too was postponed.

Morris and Stamp would soon learn that whole downtown blocks had gone black when the city was hit with a significant power outage. Street lights were out, testing drivers' patience at busy downtown corners, pubs and restaurants went black, and the Ron Hynes statue at the foot of George Street was shrouded in darkness. Morris talks about it, and no doubt others share his view, as though the blackout was a phenomenon associated with Ron's passing. Others felt the same way, including people in far-flung places, like the blogger who goes by the handle The Townie Bastard, who, even though he lives in Iqaluit, is a huge Ron Hynes fan. Even though he was far away, when he heard of Ron's death, he blogged about the widespread power outage coinciding with the event and about his love for Ron, the artist.

"If that's not proof that the man was magic," he wrote, "I'm not sure what is."

"A part of Newfoundland's heart and soul went away this evening," he blogged. "We were thrilled when we heard Ron was coming to Iqaluit and bought tickets as soon as they went on sale. This was after his surgery for throat cancer, so his voice wasn't what it once was. But he was still a performer and a professional. His sets were great, he told good stories and he was unfailingly polite and kind to everyone who came up to him. He made an impact in town. There's a lot of sad people in Iqaluit this evening as well if my Facebook and Twitter streams are any indication. There needs to be a day of mourning and some kind of state funeral for Ron. I wasn't kidding when I said that in my lifetime, the only Newfoundlander I can think of whose passing will have had an equal or greater impact was Joey Smallwood. This needs to be a life celebrated and remembered."

He wasn't alone in his social-media commentary. Twitter and Facebook were completely awash with people, both average folks and Newfoundland celebrities, expressing their love, their sorrow, and paying their virtual respects to Ron.

There was a pall over the city, according to Morris, who says people were more than aware due to local news coverage that Ron was sick again with cancer, but that there seemed little expectation that he was about to die. It came as a shock. The only thing Morris could liken the wave of emotion to was the Ocean Ranger oil-rig disaster which took eighty-four lives off the coast of Newfoundland on February 15, 1982, the public's sentiment for which was so beautifully captured in Ron's song "Atlantic Blue." Morris swears he can't recall any political or business figure or artist whose death drew such a strong response and such adulation from the public.

Newfoundland favourite son and host of CBC's *Rick Mercer Report*, Rick Mercer, posted online: "RIP and Godspeed Ron Hynes. The Poet Laureate of Newfoundland and Labrador, the man of a thousand songs has died."

Even places and institutions had something they needed to say. The staff at The Rooms, Newfoundland and Labrador's official provincial museum in St. John's, wrote this posting online: "Rest In Peace, Ron Hynes. His life's work is the soundtrack of the history of our people."

The staff at Bridie Molloy's, one of the most popular pubs on George Street, chimed in with, "We've had our share of history…thankful for Ron Hynes' rich musical history here in Newfoundland."

Journalist Rob Antle tweeted, "In a world of romance, don't miss out on the chance, to be dancing the St. John's Waltz."

Come-from-away St. John's CBC morning radio host Anthony German wrote, "Fellow mainlanders, when I moved here a great friend of mine told me, think of Ron Hynes as Newfoundland's Bob Dylan."

National CBC Radio 2 host Tom Power wrote, "Ron Hynes was our poet. He wrote songs that told the story of who Newfoundlanders were, are, and are becoming. This is such a loss. RIP."

Great Big Sea frontman Alan Doyle was, like so many others, deeply affected by Ron's death.

"I think the void for us is that we don't have that guy leading the charge about what the coolest thing is anymore. We're gonna have to do it ourselves," he said.

Doyle added that the work Hynes left behind will be hard to live up to.

"The body of work that he has left with us is such an enormous treasure for our province and for our people because it is us, it's our stories and our songs," he said. "We had somebody who could record our history in songs that he could sing at a concert and it's just a beautiful testament."

Doyle said Hynes was "the biggest rock star in the world" to him, and he felt lucky he had the chance to write music when he and Hynes wrote for Doyle's *Boy on Bridge* album.

Another former Great Big Sea band member, Bob Hallett, tweeted, "More than any other artist I know, Ron Hynes was always true to himself and his music. We are less for his passing."

St. John's musician Colleen Power first sang with Hynes when she was just twenty-four years of age. Referring to him as a "musical heavyweight," she says Ron took her "under his wing."

"Probably the main reason why I became a songwriter is because of Ron," said an emotional Power in a CBC radio interview. She added that, as a friend, Hynes was good for a laugh, but even then was still a strong mentor for her and other local musicians.

"It was kind of hard to separate the mentor from the friend, because as a friend he was very encouraging to me as a songwriter and gave me all kinds of advice over the years," said Power.

"We didn't have a lot of money, and he never, ever did either, but he was very generous as a friend. If you showed up at his gig he'd be like, 'Do you want $50? How you doing? Do you have any groceries?' That's the kind of friend he was."

Ron's girlfriend, Susan Brunt, reaffirmed that he was terrible with money, but extremely generous. "If you needed nine cents and he had ten, he'd give you ten," said Brunt. "Of course this was all to his own financial detriment. He told me he never worried about money and was always confident that there would be more around the corner."

His death, Colleen Power said, has created a hole in the music and culture of Newfoundland and Labrador: "There will never be another Ron Hynes and I don't know what we're gonna do without him."

Well known, former St. John's city councilor Sheilagh O'Leary said she grew up listening to Ron's music and watched over the years as he grew into a legend. "I was one of many who grew up on Ron and WGB and *CODCO*. I mean that was the generation for me. That was our staple. There was a cultural renaissance happening in Newfoundland," said O'Leary. "He sang who we were as Newfoundlanders and who we are, the beauty but also the pain and some of the ugly stuff too. There was no brushing it over."

But no one was more outward in their reaction to Ron's death than his nephew Joel Thomas Hynes, who took to Facebook with a lengthy, heart-wrenching post which focused hard and frankly on the dark side of Ron's life. An actor and writer himself, Hynes wrote that his uncle was destitute when he died, going so far as to sell his treasured guitars "for a pittance to feed his demons and line the pockets of drug dealers." "A note to say thank you for all the messages and emails and phone calls and handshakes and hugs and tears and laughs and stories," wrote Joel.

> It's been rough, hard to know where to put all this. Personally, I've never experienced such bottomless grief and my heart goes out to all his many loved ones—family, friends and admirers of his music and

enigmatic character. Ron was a fiercely ambitious, prolific artist, a wondrous man with a brilliant gift, no contest. But while his passing is still fresh in everyone's hearts and minds, I'm feeling a sense of duty to offer up a hard truth that's being downplayed or overlooked in all this—the reality of what his battle has been these past years. Yes he died of cancer, but cancer was a seemingly inevitable symptom of the much darker, much more aggressive, hungrier "disease" of addiction. Ron died with next to nothing left, emotionally estranged from those who tried their best to reach him, materially destitute, spiritually adrift, physically shattered. It was beyond shocking how much he resembled his father on his deathbed. Except my grandfather was 92 years old, and for all that, grandfather had a bit more light in his eyes.

Joel wrote that Ron had no property to call his own.

There was a time, when he moved to Ferryland after my grandmother died, when those of us close to him thought, wow, he just might make it. He just might let himself grow old with his guitar out on the deck with a cup of tea, watching the grass grow and counting his blessings. But that obviously wasn't to be the case. Despite what you may have heard, or thought, or hoped, he remained a hard-core addict right to his final days. And it killed him. That's what killed him. He passed the point where he was strong enough to save himself. And he was surrounded by so much love, so much worry and heartache and concern, so many loyal hearts who were desperate to offer him help that he just couldn't or wouldn't accept. And in the end he choose drugs over everything and everyone he ever loved. And he let himself die. And that's the hard truth.

The biggest shame of it all, Joel wrote, was that Ron was such a brilliant musician who could have had the world in the palm of his hands, "but instead choose to hide in the back alleys and bathroom stalls of grungy bars, who sold his life's blood chasing a darkness that deceived him right to his final breath…I can attest to Ron's being destitute. When he was on something and feeling down, he raved on about all his spent energy and ideas and having nothing left to show for it, always blaming his agents and the music business instead of himself."

Joel admitted to being a lifelong addict himself, going on to hammer away at the plight of Newfoundland as a place where drugs and alcohol have and continue to take a heavy toll on the province, especially men and especially the young, all of whose immediate and extended families are impacted and suffer. He cried out in his post for someone in a position of influence and leadership to face the problem head on in a new and effective way.

Hynes's outpouring caused quite a stir with individuals on Facebook and with the media. Some applauded him for having the courage to say what he said. Others were not so flattering in their reaction.

Sandy Morris wasn't far from where Joel was, acknowledging that in the end, the draw of crack and cocaine was too strong for Ron. He talked about people in St. John's and elsewhere who were heartbroken as they watched Ron "waste away" from drug use over the years, many of whom tried to help by encouraging him to go to rehab centres.

"We did a fundraiser for him two years ago and we raised a pile of money and the emotion he got from people who were rooting for him, knowing he had cancer, meant nothing to him," said Morris. "I mean, I'm sure it meant something to him somewhere, but the addiction had such control over him."

Mary White told the CBC she tried dozens of times to get Hynes to seek help but without much success. She said he did get clean for a time and spent weeks in a rehab facility, but started using again after he was diagnosed with throat cancer in 2012. She said the drugs that helped him get through cancer treatments left him fatigued and sick. "People did everything they could and Ron knew that and he did everything he could to avoid the people who were most trying to help him," she told the CBC. "He tried a lot to shake it, but there was not much he could do in the end."

White, Morris, and Joel Hynes all say there should be more help and treatment services for drug addicts in the province, which they say has seen a spike in crime and drug use in recent years.

ONE MAN GRAND BAND

With their initial emotional private and public cleansings behind them, people began to gather together and come from near and from afar.

Keyboardist Paul Kinsman, for example, was on a Canadian tour playing with Alan Doyle. He was out at a dinner party at the home of one of The Bare Naked Ladies on a night off in Toronto when he received a text from Boomer Stamp informing him that Ron had just passed away.

"It was a rough night," says Kinsman. "We were away from all our friends but in a town that knew him well."

Still in shock from the news, Kinsman, fellow Newfoundland musicians Cory Tetford (formerly of the Newfoundland band Crush) and Barry Canning, followed the dinner party with a trek to a pub next to the Danforth Music Hall (Doyle had a previous interview commitment and only joined them later). There they raised a few toasts to *our brother in arms.*

"Someone at the pub must have gotten on the phone because within a couple hours we were joined by the rest of Alan's band, many of our Toronto friends, and other Newfoundlanders, all friends and admirers of Ron. It was good to have each other's company that night. Details after this point are foggy but many stories were told, laughter and tears flowed and, inevitably, a guitar appeared. The Ron Hynes songs rang out until the wee hours.

"The Barenaked Ladies are a great bunch of guys. They didn't know Ron but certainly knew his reputation. They realized we were in mourning for our friend and showed their support and respect by learning 'Sonny' and coming out on stage and singing with us the next night in Peterborough. Alan and Cory sang the verses, and they harmonized on the chorus. It was certainly a moment I'll never forget."

Kinsman, Doyle, and the others arrived home from Toronto Sunday evening in time to attend Ron's memorial service.

On Monday morning, November 23, Ron's friends and family gathered in downtown St. John's to put him to rest.

As a boy, Morris sang in the choir from the back of the Basilica of St. John the Baptist on the city's Military Road. But, oddly, he had never been on the altar; never that is until Ron Hynes's funeral mass. It was a grand place for a send-off. It was standing room only.

"You couldn't fit a pack of cigarettes in that church," says Morris.

He and others performed songs as people clung together, cried and danced just below the altar and in the aisles. It was an unusual sight for any church, let alone the sanctified Basilica. Highlights of the service included Cory Tetford singing "Amazing Grace," accompanied by keyboardist Paul Kinsman. The folk trio, The Once (Geraldine Hollett, Phil Churchill, and Andrew Dale) joined Morris and Amelia Curran in performing Ron's "Leaving on the Evening Tide." Alan Doyle led the whole gang on "St. John's Waltz." Ron's daughters Elena and Rebecca sang "30 for 60" and his other daughters, Lori and Lily, sang "I Love You More Than God." Rick Mercer read "When I Think of Death" by Maya Angelou, and Des Walsh and Cathy Jones both delivered readings.

It had to have been special, no doubt, for everyone to see Ron's four girls singing at his service. If he'd had any inkling of that possibility, it might have been one of the most overwhelming moments of his life. According to Susan Brunt, Ron loved his children: "Any regrets he had in his life were related to them and given that he had grown up with a largely absent father, I think he did the best he could."

At the end, all hands sang "Sonny's Dream." According to Morris, it was sad and serene in some moments and then joyous at other moments. "You could feel the love in the room," he says. "There was a universal spirit."

You could feel it in Greg Malone's eulogy. You could see it in Rick Mercer's teary face as he wheeled Ron's ex-wife, Connie, up the aisle in her wheelchair, necessitated by debilitating, degenerative disc problems in her back.

"Well, he got a full house. He'd like that," Malone began his tribute. "Who else would we weep for if not for Ron? Who more deserves our tears than he? All those lovely songs are now the ties that bind our hearts to his and to each other."

Paul Kinsman said the service was like a state funeral, including the fact that it was broadcast live province-wide.

"In my opinion, only two people could fill the place like that, and that's Ron Hynes and Jesus Christ himself," said Kinsman. "With a Buddhist prayer and dancing in the aisles, it was probably one of the more unique memorial services at the Basilica of St. John the Baptist."

Immediately after the service, Kinsman, Tetford, and Doyle walked down over the hill to the sculpture of Ron on George Street to pay their respects and try to sort out everything that had happened.

"Personally speaking, I still haven't," says Kinsman two months later. "I can't believe he's gone, and Boomer and I agree that we'll never play those songs the same way again without Ron singing them."

Sandy Morris joined Ron's other contemporaries for a musical celebration of his life at The Ship on the following Thursday, November 26. Everyone took a turn on Ron's prized J200 Gibson, the very one that he is depicted holding in the George Street statue.

But perhaps the loneliest guy at the end of the day was Ron's manager, Charles MacPhail. For a guy who was confronted on a daily basis with Ron's constant complaining, and conflicted with his obsession over Ron's music and with trying to find him work, MacPhail was very hard hit when he heard the news. MacPhail and I had talked several times in the days leading up to Ron's death and it was clear what was coming down.

"Ten minutes after Ron's death, I received a call from White in St John's," says MacPhail. "I answered and said, 'Hello White. I am sure this is a call I don't want to receive.' And she replied, 'I am sorry, Charles, but he is gone.' I couldn't believe the sadness and loss I felt, not wanting to accept the end. It was terribly hard to get my head around, thinking the phone will ring after so many times of him being MIA in the past to hear, 'Whaaaaaa?' when I answered it or 'Whassup, bro?' I knew that I would never receive that call again."

MacPhail spoke with Chuck Brodsky on the phone shortly after he got the news. Brodsky is a noted storyteller, songwriter, troubadour, and a modern-day bard, sort of in the ilk of Ron himself. Brodsky told MacPhail he had lost many friends, yet nothing seemed to have hit him as hard as Ron's passing.

"I understood completely. It's hard to live 24/7 with a portion of each day dedicated to something 'Ron' and then having that tap turned off so abruptly. The map became blank."

MacPhail is sorry that Ron didn't get to see his biography completed or to hold his last CD, *Later That Same Life*, in his hands.

"It's just a brilliant piece of work and nothing like any of his previous recordings," says MacPhail. "As Ron put it, 'The songs are presented as stark and raw as the skin and bones that held me together all those dark days and nights.'"

MacPhail says he is incredibly happy that both the book and the CD did happen, even though there were times when he wanted to give Ron a piece of his mind.

Within days following Ron's funeral, MacPhail busied himself by planning a February 2016 celebration of Ron's life at Hugh's Room in Toronto, with similar events to be planned for Ottawa, Halifax, and Prince Edward Island to follow. Funds from those celebrations will be channelled toward clearing up finances related to Ron's estate.

"I loved him and he knew that and he knew I would never colour things for him," says MacPhail, meaning he always told it as it was, which was really the only way to manage Ron.

I too found myself in this situation, of having to be direct with Ron, just a few weeks before he died. Out of nowhere, he suddenly attempted to intervene with controlling demands regarding the publishing of this book. I stood my ground and was relieved when he backed down very quickly, writing me in an email on October 27:

> Harvey my man, this baby is all yours. Just run with it and I'll run
> with you. Here's hoping you tour well, cause Charles has plans for us.

Ron was fully intent on participating in a book-signing tour in Newfoundland and Labrador and on the mainland, which would have been fascinating to say the least.

Ron was not one of those people to map out a retirement plan, no more likely than he was going to live to be a hundred. But before Ron died, Boomer Stamp had expressed a few ideas to him. It was predicated on a bit of a fantasy tour you might say, which he shared with his friend.

"I said, Ron, here's my retirement plan. I've got plans for a month and a tour back and forth the country."

Stamp imagined the tour as featuring Ron with a "nice little band," including piano, bass and drums, a couple of backup singers, and maybe the luxury of a multi-instrumentalist who could pick up a horn and an accordion.

"We'd do soft-seater concerts, and then mix those with some pubs so we could have a bit of fun. He'd fucking rock the room. He'd be screaming his head off."

That might have been Stamp's dream for how to wind it all up, but it probably wasn't Ron's. Ron was more attuned to being in a quiet, thoughtful place like Woody Point, or at the family house in Ferryland and writing songs. Or maybe stretching out on Susan Brunt's couch in Toronto watching *The Godfather* series yet again.

He'd performed so many small-venue gigs that he was more or less burned out on that routine. The exception, of course, would have been Toronto's Massey Hall, the one remaining place that Ron fantasized about playing. He still held dear that dream to perform there, seeing it as a pinnacle of Canadian performance venues. Charles MacPhail dearly wishes he could have made Massey Hall happen.

Ron never got to have his dream Massey Hall gig, but that fantasy would only have been a single evening event experienced by a smidgeon of people compared with the countless number who've seen him perform live, and who've been impacted by his impressive body of television work, live stage performances as a singer and actor, and, of course, his numerous recordings. But it seemed Ron was never truly satisfied with the body of work he had created, songs which have traversed the world both with and without him, as they will continue to do over the years.

There is no more apropos way to sum up Ron than Mr. Budgell himself, Greg Malone, linking Ron's life to those penetrative lyrics of "Sonny's Dream": *It's a hundred miles to town, Sonny's never been there, and he goes to the highway and he stands there and stares, and the mail comes at four and the mailman is old, but he still dreams his dreams full of silver and gold.*

"He travelled that hundred miles and he found the dream at the end," says Malone. "Yes, and he longed to go to town to travel that hundred miles, and he got there. He had his guitar; he had a few songs and he got there."

And his songs, Malone concludes, "were full of silver and gold."

DISCOGRAPHY

SOLO ALBUMS

1972
Discovery (World Records/Audat)

1987
Small Fry: The Ron Hynes Album for Children (Independent)

1993
Cryer's Paradise (EMI)

1997
Face to the Gale (EMI)

1998
Standing in Line in the Rain (Independent)

2001
The Sandcastle Sessions (Independent)

2003
Get Back Change (Borealis)

2006
Ron Hynes (Borealis)

2006
Stealing Genius (Borealis)

2015
Later That Same Life (Independent)

ALBUMS WITH
THE WONDERFUL GRAND BAND

1978
The Wonderful Grand Band (Grand East Records)

1981
Living in a Fog (Grand East Records)

ACKNOWLEDGEMENTS

Over time, Ron and I developed a warm rapport which involved joking over e-mail and my attending any concerts of his I could get to. Although he was hesitant or skeptical (or both) about this book at first, in the end, he went all the way. I can only hope he knew fully how important I believe his story is and that I would only treat that story with the utmost regard and dignity. The book never would have occurred without the enthusiasm and dedication of Charles MacPhail. Although there were numerous other people who helped greatly in researching and understanding Ron and his life, four played a particularly crucial role and I cannot thank them enough: Sandy Morris, Paul Boomer Stamp, Greg Malone, and Eric MacEwan. I would also like to extend great thanks to Mary White, Paul Kinsman, Alan Doyle, Brian Bourne, Chris LeDrew, Suzy Power, Susan Cotton, Susan Brunt, Bill MacGillivray, Lee Mellor, Mike O'Brien, Gordon O'Brien, Edwina Campbell, Thomas 'Sonny' O'Neil, Terry Kelly, Jason Wilber, Jeanne Beker, Erick Vickerdike, Al Rosen, Christy Moore, Paul Mills, Frank Watt, Derek Chafe, Joel Thomas Hynes, and Donna Morrissey. Thank you to Breakwater Books publisher Rebecca Rose and James Langer for their insights, patience, and wisdom in seeing the value of this project. Finally I wish to thank my partner, Charlotte Stewart, who repeatedly reviewed the text, and having gotten to understand Ron through numerous discussions, made an invaluable contribution toward getting the story right. She endures much during the writing of my books, this being no exception.

Photographs on pages 3, 4, 6, 13, 27, 73, 125, 143, 176, 181, 184, 236, and 240 are used by permission of Bud Gaulton ©2015.

Photographs on pages 38-39, 40, 52, 82-83, and 159 are used courtesy of Sandy Morris.

Photograph on page 219 used courtesy of Susan Brunt.

HARVEY SAWLER was born and grew up in Hamilton, Ontario, but has lived most of his life in Atlantic Canada. He began writing as an eighteen-year-old newspaper reporter covering stories as diverse as the 1974 Pierre Trudeau campaign trail and the murders of two Moncton police officers. He has written more than a dozen fiction and non-fiction books. He is also a leading Canadian tourism consultant. He lives in Bellevue Cove, Prince Edward Island, with his partner, Charlotte Stewart. You can visit him at www.harveysawler.com.